The Folkloresque

The Folkloresque

Reframing Folklore in a Popular Culture World

Edited by
Michael Dylan Foster
Jeffrey A. Tolbert

Utah State University Press
Logan

© 2016 by the University Press of Colorado

Published by Utah State University Press
An imprint of University Press of Colorado
5589 Arapahoe Avenue, Suite 206C
Boulder, Colorado 80303

The University Press of Colorado is a proud member of
The Association of American University Presses.

The University Press of Colorado is a cooperative publishing enterprise supported, in part, by Adams State University, Colorado State University, Fort Lewis College, Metropolitan State University of Denver, Regis University, University of Colorado, University of Northern Colorado, Utah State University, and Western State Colorado University.

The paper used in this publication meets the minimum requirements of the American National Standard for Information Sciences—Permanence of Paper for Printed Library Materials. ANSI Z39.48-1992

ISBN: 978-1-60732-417-1 (paperback)
ISBN: 978-1-60732-418-8 (ebook)
Cover art by Faryn Hughes

Library of Congress Cataloging-in-Publication Data

Names: Foster, Michael Dylan, 1965– | Tolbert, Jeffrey A.
Title: The folkloresque : reframing folklore in a popular culture world / edited by Michael Dylan Foster, Jeffrey A. Tolbert.
Description: Logan : Utah State University Press, 2016. | Includes bibliographical references.
Identifiers: LCCN 2015011321| ISBN 9781607324171 (paperback : alk. paper) | ISBN 9781607324188 (ebook)
Subjects: LCSH: Folklore in popular culture. | BISAC: SOCIAL SCIENCE / Folklore & Mythology.
Classification: LCC GR41.7 .F65 2016 | DDC 398.09—dc23
LC record available at http://lccn.loc.gov/2015011321

Contents

Acknowledgments

This volume was born through collaboration and conversation. In 2010, during a graduate seminar at Indiana University, the two of us (Tolbert a student in the course, Foster the professor) discovered we had both been exploring a similar set of ideas—what we are calling the folkloresque. We were approaching issues from different directions and with radically different examples in mind, but both of us felt that a great deal could be learned from studying the ways in which popular culture uses, understands, and interprets folklore. In the ensuing years, independently and together, we mentioned our developing ideas to others, many of whom found them as exciting and potentially fruitful as we did. Finally we decided to put our thoughts—and those of others—together in an edited volume.

Most of the contributors to this text are trained in folkloristics but embrace an interdisciplinary approach, employing theory from related disciplines to explore how creators and audiences of popular culture understand concepts such as "folklore" and "tradition." Working with different contributors as we put the volume together drove home to us the relevance and resonance of what we were doing, but also reminded us how disparate our understandings of the relationship between folklore and popular culture can be; the book is a collaborative effort, but its chapters and ideas are by no means in lockstep with each other. We present them rather as part of a conversation that we hope others will continue. We also hope that the folkloresque will penetrate beyond folklore's disciplinary boundaries to engage all readers interested in the contact zone of "popular" and "folk" cultures and to encourage genuine collaboration between scholars who have been working on the same issues but not necessarily talking to each other about them.

We are deeply indebted to Michael Spooner of Utah State University Press, whose enthusiasm for the project inspired us every step of the way and whose sensible advice kept us on track. Two anonymous readers of the manuscript provided invaluable feedback on the book as a whole and on individual chapters. The final product is much improved because of their insightful comments.

Earlier versions of several chapters (those by Blank, Evans, Buterbaugh, Foster) were presented at the 2014 annual meeting of the American Folklore

Society in Santa Fe, New Mexico. The audience at our session was extremely encouraging, reminding us once more that many other scholars are exploring similar issues in complementary ways. We thank the audience members for their insightful questions and comments, and for their enthusiasm. We also want to extend our sincere gratitude to colleagues and friends in the Department of Folklore and Ethnomusicology at Indiana University, particularly Diane Goldstein. In addition to all of our collaborators, many others supported our work throughout, both individually and collectively; we especially thank Mitsuko Kawabata, Dylar Kumax, and Michiko Suzuki. We are also grateful to Laura Furney of University Press of Colorado for shepherding us painlessly through the production process, and to Robin DuBlanc for her precise and thoughtful copyediting.

MICHAEL DYLAN FOSTER
JEFFREY A. TOLBERT

The Folkloresque

Introduction
The Challenge of the Folkloresque

Michael Dylan Foster

In 2005, I was invited to give a lecture about the exceedingly popular Japanese animated film *Spirited Away* (2001).[1] Specifically, I was asked
to explain the Japanese folklore in the movie. Chock-full of deities and
demons, physical transformations, ritual purifications, and magic spells,
the story feels as if it has been told before, as if the events and characters
are adapted from age-old narratives and beliefs. But when I sat down to
prepare my lecture, I was at a loss. Where *was* the folklore in the movie?
The filmmakers were clearly influenced by Japanese (and European) folklore, and it was a pleasure to puzzle out some of the allusions. But these
allusions were fuzzy: characters and actions on the screen pointed only
vaguely, if at all, to actual referents outside the film. Similarly, although the
narrative structure itself felt resonant, it too did not directly reference any
specific tales but seemed a skillful cobbling together of many. In short,
the film was infused with a folklore-like familiarity and seemed weighty
because of folkloric roots, but at the same time it was not beholden to
any single tradition.

Of course, the movie itself is not folklore. As a commercially created
product, it exists in a fixed form that neither exhibits variation through time
and space nor changes with each performance. Like most commercial films,
it was shared with people through formal, institutional channels rather than
the informal, person-to-person modes most commonly associated with
folklore. And although the narrative and imagery of *Spirited Away* may be
influenced by myths, legends, folktales, and beliefs, the film is by no means
a retelling of traditional narratives. At the same time, however, neither is it
wholly "fictional" or invented from scratch. Indeed, when I finally gave my
lecture, I found myself struggling for appropriate language to describe this
subtle but compelling phenomenon in which folklore is vaguely referenced
for its power to connect to something beyond the product itself. How
can we characterize the hazily allusive quality that infuses certain popular

DOI: 10.7330/9781607324188.c000

creations, this *sense of folklore*? As I prepared my lecture, the word that struck me as most appropriate was *folkloresque*.

In the years since that lecture, the folkloresque has haunted me. Conspicuous uses of folklore within popular culture are pervasive, perhaps even more so (or at least more noticeable) with the recent proliferation of new media platforms and other technological advances. In discussing the folkloresque with colleagues and students, I discovered that the idea resonated with others in ways I had not conceived of myself, and that it might provide a meaningful heuristic for broadening our understandings of both folklore and popular culture and the symbiotic relationship between the two. In the pages that follow, I attempt to delineate this emerging concept and also try to plant some theoretical seeds with the hope that they will flourish or mutate in the work of others.

The chapters that follow this introduction further take up the exploration of the folkloresque through specific studies. In some cases, the ideas presented in those chapters do not dovetail with what I set out here, or with each other, but that is one of the objectives of this project: the folkloresque is a concept in progress, ripe for dialogue and dialectic. The goal of this book is not to create monolithic understandings or definitions; rather, we hope to stimulate a conversation that will challenge us all to rethink categories that perhaps have begun to outlive their value but that we still hold onto for convenience because they are part of our academic tradition and our shared vocabulary. And that is why I hope this new word, *folkloresque*, will become part of the lexicon. Particularly now, as expressive culture is increasingly influenced by Internet-driven communication, digital media, and global commercial forces, the questions raised here are all the more urgent—and the folkloresque is all the more relevant. While I write this from the perspective of a folklorist, I hope the ideas set forth here will resonate with scholars of popular culture, the media, and cultural studies as well.

IN A WORD

We propose the folkloresque as a heuristic tool, a kind of conceptual crowbar, to pry open the black box of how folklore functions in a world of cultural and artistic expression increasingly dominated by forms of commercial and mass production labeled "popular culture." It is a tool that encourages us to reenvision categories such as *folklore* and *popular culture*, to explore how they mutually influence each other, and to productively problematize distinctions between them. While the term *folkloresque* has been used on occasion with various meanings in previous scholarship, as far as I know nobody has ever systematically delineated it or attempted to develop it for its interpretive potential—but that is what we would like to do here and in the rest of this book.[2]

Simply put, the folkloresque is popular culture's own (emic) perception and performance of folklore. That is, it refers to creative, often commercial products or texts (e.g., films, graphic novels, video games) that give the impression to the consumer (viewer, reader, listener, player) that they derive directly from existing folkloric traditions. In fact, however, a folkloresque product is rarely based on any single vernacular item or tradition; usually it has been consciously cobbled together from a range of folkloric elements, often mixed with newly created elements, to appear as if it emerged organically from a specific source. In some cases the *form* rather than the *contents* provides this veneer of folklore; the folkloresque can reference folklore in either *langue* or *parole* or both. In addition, the folkloresque concept includes products that, while clearly born through commercial processes, explicitly or self-consciously showcase their relationship with folklore by alluding to folk knowledge or jargon or including characters labeled as folklorists. In short, the folkloresque signals popular culture's recognition that folklore is a valuable brand.

A common aspect of a folkloresque item of popular culture is that it is imbued with a sense of "authenticity" (as perceived by the consumer and/or creator) derived from association with "real" folklore. This capacity to connect an item to an established body of tradition has the effect of validating the work in which it appears, increasing its appeal to popular audiences. Because the folkloresque is often part of mass-mediated popular culture, in many cases it leads to greater exposure to a wider audience for local and culture-specific traditions; in some cases this inspires a feedback loop in which the folkloresque version of the item is (re)incorporated into the folk cultural milieu that it references.

The *Oxford English Dictionary* explains that the suffix "-esque" is used to express a sense of something "resembling the style" or "partaking of the characteristics of" (*Oxford English Dictionary*, 2nd ed., s.v. "-esque"). It articulates a connection with the root word to which it is affixed but at the same time keeps this connection indistinct. It also has the related function, as in "picturesque," of implying that something is *worthy* of the root word to which the suffix is attached: worthy of being a picture, for example, or worthy of being folklore.[3] So the term *folkloresque* articulates three related meanings: (1) that an item (or element of an item) is in the "style" of folklore; (2) that it is connected to something beyond/before itself, to some tradition or folkloric source existing outside the popular culture context;

and (3) that the product itself is potentially of folkloric value, connected in some way with processes of folklore creation and transmission.

Folk Culture: *See* Popular Culture

Let this suffice for the moment as a (relatively) concise description of the folkloresque. It will, of course, get more complex. But before proceeding I want to set out what I mean by *popular culture*, which, like so many other key terms, is a moving target. Building on the work of theorists such as, but certainly not limited to, Raymond Williams, the Frankfurt School, Louis Althusser, Antonio Gramsci, E. P. Thomson, Pierre Bourdieu, Stuart Hall, and the Birmingham School, the discourse on popular culture today is wide ranging and all the more significant within the context of globalization and rapid technological change. Popular culture scholarship is often located under wider academic rubrics—of cultural studies, media studies, and communication—but it also bleeds into economics, political science, sociology, anthropology, comparative literature, film studies and, of course, folkloristics. Popular culture, as Chris Rojek explains, "is a field dealing with a) relations of power; b) social transformations, expressed at economic, social, political, aesthetic and subcultural levels; and c) the system of coding and representation of popular and cultural data" (Rojek 2012, 1).

Rojek is describing the discipline of popular culture studies here, but *popular culture* also signifies the subject of study: a "culture" of production and consumption in which discourses, practices, and things (narratives, games, images, toys, and the like) are created and shared (or, more likely, sold). Like *folklore*, the term itself is often taken for granted, bandied about with ease and an assumption of collective understanding, and yet it is almost impossible to pin down. It is a floating signifier, open to varied interpretations and infused with different meanings by different actors in different contexts.

We can, however, find some common threads that tie together many of these meanings. Often, for example, popular culture is associated with entertainment and frivolity, posited as escapism in distinction to more serious forms of cultural expression.[4] It can be interpreted in opposition to so-called high culture or Culture with a capital C, as the culture of the nonelite classes, of people in the "mainstream"—that is, the culture (and sometimes subculture) of the common folk. Similarly, popular culture may be associated with mass culture, which tends to imply a dependence on facilities for mass production and mass distribution and less reliance on personal or intracommunity interaction. Mass cultural content is often transmitted through the conduits of *mass* media, including television, movies, the Internet, comics, popular literature, and so on. Finally, popular culture also overlaps with notions of consumer culture, forcing us to think in terms of commodification and to explore questions of production, consumption, market forces, and consumer choice.

Of course, many of these categories are blurry to start with, and all the more vexing within the current maelstrom of technological innovation. The boundaries, for example, between mass media and personal expression are so commonly permeated as to be all but meaningless (where, for example, does Twitter, YouTube, or Instagram fit in?). So for the purposes of this essay, let me suggest an open-ended understanding of popular culture that takes all of these factors into consideration—but only as general orientations. Within this tentative characterization, I would emphasize most significantly the commercial factor, the orientation toward commodification and monetary exchange value; perhaps we can think of popular culture as a set of processes and products that exists within a commercial-industrial structure and are oriented toward financial remuneration—to making money.

By stressing this last point—the profit motive—we also establish a meaningful counter-distinction to similar forms of cultural expression usually labeled *folklore*. Defining folklore, of course, opens up a whole other (related) can of worms, something I would assiduously like to avoid in this limited space. But I do want to suggest that the processes and products of folklore tend to be oriented toward *informal, unofficial, noncommercial, noninstitutional* modes of production, transmission, and consumption. Even in contexts in which traditionality, aesthetics, and the dynamics of "small-group" or face-to-face communication are questionable, we can usually still maintain that the processes and products of folklore are rarely created with official, institutional, or commercial sanction and mass sales or major profit in mind.[5]

I propose these distinctions and orientations with deliberate tentativeness, because in fact studying the folkloresque is intended to peel back the layers that have gone into establishing such orientations in the first place. Another reason for setting out to blur the boundaries between folklore and popular culture is because, realistically speaking, they are already blurred. In the opening paragraph of a recent monograph on "pop culture," for example, anthropologist Shirley A. Fedorak (2009, 1) declares that "popular culture is the culture of our everyday lives. Human groups have always created music, folktales, festivals and artwork in an attempt to make sense of and celebrate their world." Of course, these examples—to say nothing of the reference to "everyday lives"—are precisely what folklorists have long studied. In the index of Fedorak's book there is no entry for "folklore" itself, but under the heading "folk culture" are the words "*See* popular culture"

(155). It is imperative for folklorists to engage with popular culture discourse because, it seems, folklore is already seen as popular culture.

And this brings me back to the folkloresque as a bridge concept that links these not-so-disparate fields of inquiry. To be sure, folklorists have historically been concerned with popular culture, mass media, and commercialism, but often only to stake territorial claims or discuss questions of distinction or origins. It is time now to revisit these issues with a neutral tone that accepts the processes of popular and commercial culture as contingent on and indeed continuous with the processes of folklore. While the folkloresque is conceptually related to older theoretical conceptions of folklorism (*folklorismus*) and even fakelore, I want to stress from the outset that it is by no means a pejorative term; rather, it is an inclusive concept for productive analysis of the ways motifs, folk ideas, and images operate within the production of commercial products.

FAKELORE AND FOLKLORISM

In 1950, when Richard Dorson first introduced the term *fakelore*, he set off a firestorm of controversy and inspired questions about authenticity and authority, literary and commercial production, the role of academic folklorists and, ultimately, the *selling* of folklore. I quote from his original article in the *American Mercury*:

> In recent years folklore has boomed mightily, and reached a wide audience through best-selling books, concert and cabaret folksingers, even Walt Disney cartoons. But far from fulfilling its high promise, the study has been falsified, abused and exploited, and the public deluded with Paul Bunyan nonsense and claptrap collections. Without stirring from the library, money-writers have successfully peddled synthetic hero-books and saccharine folk tales as the stories of the people. Americans may be insufficiently posted on their history and culture, as the famous New York *Times* survey indicated, but their knowledge of these subjects is erudition, compared with what they know about their own folklore. (Dorson 1950, 335)

From a contemporary perspective, Dorson's polemic reeks of an elitist academic-centric view of folklore, and certainly must be understood within the specific context and period of its production.[6] At the same time, however, his allusions to "best-selling books" and "Walt Disney cartoons" still resonate with the uses of folklore in popular culture today. Such appropriation fits neatly within the rubric of the folkloresque, but the questions of interest are not whether something is spurious or genuine, fake or real, but rather, what is it that Disney and these "money-writers" do so "successfully"? Or, for that matter, how and why is the "public deluded"? By exploring these questions, we reveal the workings of cultural production, both commercial and otherwise, and, more important, get a sense of the motivations and everyday lives of the people doing the consuming.

If folklorists study people (= folk), then it is critical to explore what people think of *as* folklore—regardless of how a folklorist might categorize it. Even if Disney, Paul Bunyan, or Dorson's "claptrap collections" are not classifiable as folklore (by a folklorist), they are certainly a form of popular culture that people identify with folklore—exactly what we are calling the folkloresque. Whether or not the product in question can be traced back to an oral tradition or to some other "genuine" source is less important than the fact that people *feel* it is folkloric.

My aim here is not to disparage Dorson or dredge up an old debate, but simply to note that the folkloresque allows us to boldly study Paul Bunyan narratives, for example, without having to make disclaimers about their provenance. Certainly one of the more fascinating aspects of their study is exactly what Dorson was wary of: that they were fabricated and promulgated for commercial purposes but somehow found their way into the popular imagination. Dorson was critical of people deceptively passing off invented items as real folklore, but he himself did not necessarily dismiss such texts as meaningless—his point seems to be that they are just not a subject of study for academic folklorists. In contrast, my own point (and I suspect Dorson might concur) is that these very products, the folkloresque, should now be a subject of serious study. One might argue, then, that the folkloresque is nothing more than a contemporary relabeling of "fakelore," but the very act of relabeling asserts that these products, and the processes associated with them, are as culturally revealing and valuable as "genuine" folklore.

The folkloresque similarly dovetails with the discourses on folklorism and folklorismus that began emerging in the 1960s (most notably in Europe) and inspired critical thinking about commercial and political (re)contextualizations of folklore. In 1984, Hermann Bausinger characterized folklorismus as "the use of material or stylistic elements of folklore in a context which is foreign to the original tradition" (translated and quoted by Šmidchens 1999, 52). Today we are immediately struck with the impossibility of determining when a context is "foreign" or a tradition "original" and, as Guntis Šmidchens points out, "the distinction 'primary tradition vs. folklorism' is based more on the beliefs of folklorists than the European folklore traditions to which it is usually applied. The processes and conduits of transmission, reception, and variation in so-called folklore and folklorism are in fact too similar to warrant separate terminology on this basis" (Šmidchens 1999, 53).

Of course, instances of folklorism include narrative and performance as well as material culture. When discussing folklorism with my students, for example, I show them an object I purchased at a souvenir stand in Arizona: a handmade refrigerator magnet in the shape of a tiny Hopi ceramic pot. Does it matter, I ask them, that refrigerators (or magnets) were not part of "traditional" Hopi culture? Or would it make a difference if the product were not handmade in Arizona but rather mass produced in China? Bausinger (1986) significantly noted that dismissing cultural phenomena because they do not fit a narrow definition of folklore "avoided accurate description of the real world" (Šmidchens 1999, 57). Indeed, Hans Moser, the scholar credited with introducing folklorismus into German folkloristic discourse, "urged his colleagues to study the seemingly fake in addition to 'real' folklore and folk cultures" (Bendix 1997a, 337). In a sense, the folkloresque represents a simultaneous broadening and refinement—and continuation—of the discourses created by these early pioneers.[7]

Folklorism also made an appearance in early twentieth-century Soviet scholarship; Mark Azadovsky invoked the word to imply "an awareness on the part of authors or folklore performers that they are dealing with people called the 'folk' and a thing called 'folklore'" (Šmidchens 1999, 56). To be sure, folklorism is a slippery concept and has been defined in numerous ways. Gulnar Kendirbaeva, for example, describes it broadly as "the professional artistic creation of folklore in all its forms: in science and in pedagogy, on the stage, at festivals and during holidays (including ceremonies), in the mass media, in recordings and advertisements, in tourism, in crafts, and in everyday life" (Kendirbaeva 1994, 98). Šmidchens redefines folklorism through its function, as "denoting the conscious use of folklore as a symbol of ethnic, regional, or national culture" (Šmidchens 1999, 64). In my own work I have emphasized, like Azadovsky and Šmidchens, the critical role of *awareness* or *consciousness* in the production of folklorism (Foster 1998). And Dina Roginsky (2007) notes that folklore and folklorism are not mutually exclusive—that there can by "synchronization" between the two, with the same individuals participating in both modes of cultural production.

THE ODOR OF FOLKLORE

The discourse of folklorism productively broadens the field of inquiry, but at the same time cannot completely escape the binary trap of language in which something called *folklore* is the source, the organic material, out of which something secondary (or artificial) is created. Inevitably, the quicksand of authenticity discourse sucks us back into a "preoccupation with the relationship of what is given to something that is posited as prior" (Bruner and Kirshenblatt-Gimblett 1994, 459). Regina Bendix (1997b) and others (e.g., Bauman and Briggs 2003) have carefully demonstrated how the quest for authenticity has shaped the discipline of folklore studies, and there is no need to rehearse this history here. I simply note that the concept of the folkloresque, while it may not allow us to completely escape this binary, provides a new mechanism for exploring its structure. When people buy a folkloresque product, they often see in it a reference to something *they* consider folklore; unpacking the dynamics of the folkloresque, both with regard to its production and its perception, reveals the quality that makes something *seem* folkloric.

In a discussion of the way in which certain products are indelibly associated with their country of origin, cultural critic Koichi Iwabuchi introduces an idea he calls *cultural odor*: "the way in which cultural features of a country of origin and images or ideas of its national, in most cases stereotyped, way of life are associated *positively* with a particular product in the consumption process." His point is not that all products reek of their country of origin, but that certain aspects of some products resonate symbolically with the consumer's image of the country or culture in question. Borrowing this idea, we can describe certain popular culture products—those we are calling folkloresque—as emitting an odor of folklore, as it were, which "is strongly and affirmatively called to mind as the very appeal of the product" (Iwabuchi 2002, 27). Iwabuchi's olfactory metaphor is helpful for thinking of the intangible properties of a product that can conjure up the symbolism and imagery associated, in this case, with folklore (an attractive foreign "country" in the world of popular culture). At the same time, however, it leaves us still struggling to isolate these properties.

And here is the crux of the problem. How do we know something is folklore, or that a popular culture product is folkloresque? "I shall not today attempt further to define the kinds of material I understand to be embraced within that shorthand description; and perhaps I could never succeed in intelligibly doing so. But I know it when I see it."[8] These are the notorious words of U.S. Supreme Court Justice Potter Stewart, and the "material" in question is "hard-core pornography." But the statement could also apply to folklore—difficult, if not impossible, to define, but still somehow recognizable. In a popular culture product, the folkloresque is the retention of this character—an odor, an accent, a know-it-when-you-see-it quality—of folklore.

Assertions of recognizability without clear definition, like Justice Stewart's, are of course mired in subjectivity. But in many cases such subjective assessments are "popular," that is, shared by a large number of individuals, whether we call them a folk group or an "interpretive community" (Fish 1980), suggesting a consensus about the folkloric quality of a product. The study of the folkloresque allows us to examine the invisible philosophies and implicit ideologies that come together to create such a consensus within a given community. We are not interested in authenticity or origins but in the perception (and interpretation) of authenticity and origins. Etic analysis may highlight the inventedness of tradition and allow us to see that the very objectification of folklore is a product of modernity, but the folkloresque provides insight into the emic world of contemporary producers and consumers in which "folklore" itself is an "ethnic genre" (Ben-Amos 1976). Whereas both fakelore and folklorism tend to approach phenomena from a folkloric perspective, the folkloresque allows us to inhabit the other side of the problem and see the same phenomena from a popular culture perspective.

LITERATURE, FILM, NEW MEDIA

The conception of the folkloresque proposed here does not come out of the blue. If anything, we are simply labeling a phenomenon, and accompanying process of inquiry, that has long been brewing in folklore scholarship. As noted above, the ideas here clearly resonate with discussions of fakelore and folklorism. Others have already flagged the dynamics we want to highlight here: regarding contemporary "urban legends," for example, Jan Harold Brunvand notes that they have "migrated from *folklore* into *popular* culture where they became stereotyped, standardized, exploited, commodified, and repackaged in a number of ways" (Brunvand 2001, xxvii).[9] Media scholars are also becoming interested in the dynamics of what Henry Jenkins has called "convergence culture": "where grassroots and corporate media intersect, where the power of the media producer and the power of the media consumer interact in unpredictable ways" (Jenkins 2006, 2). If we include literature and film in the popular culture mix, the folkloresque has already informed the development of contemporary folkloristics; we are merely identifying it as a particular type of cultural product well worth the attention of folklorists as well as popular culture scholars.

The relationship of folklore to literature, for example, has long been discussed in terms of remediation, allusion, borrowing, and intertextuality—concepts all relevant to the folkloresque. Frank de Caro and Rosan

Augusta Jordan describe what they term "re-situation" as "simply the process by which folklore is somehow taken from its position in a sociocultural context (de-situation) and placed into a literary or artistic context, whether by description, textual quotation, or some other means (such as the adaptation of a plot structure)" (de Caro and Jordan 2004, 6). Much of the scholarship on folklore in literature has focused on the use of proverbs and fairy tales, perhaps because such genres are most easily understood in terms of recontextualization.[10]

In distinguishing between folklore and literature, there can be a default tendency in some discussions to treat narrative folklore as oral, or at least as derived from oral sources. As Cristina Bacchilega (2012, 450) points out, however, "Not all oral traditions are folk, not all folk literature is oral, not all verbal art is literary or oral." Moreover, such distinctions are all the more problematic in an age of technology in which forms of first-hand immediate performance may be entirely textual (text messages, chat rooms, Twitter) and oral "face-to-face" communication may be mediated (Second Life, Skype), edited, or transmitted through time lags (YouTube, Vimeo). Clearly, divisions between oral and written, mass and personal, mediated and face-to-face have to be rethought. Bacchilega (2012, 450) notes that "interpreting uses of the folklore in contemporary literature and culture is now a well-established scholarly practice," but at the same time, "the association of folklore with old-fashioned rather than postmodern ways or subaltern knowledge persists." Probing the dynamics of the folkloresque, in contemporary culture as well as in the past, helps push folklore into postmodern scholarship.

In film and other forms of visual and mass media, connections with folklore have also been well rehearsed. In 1994, Linda Dégh stressed that "it is not enough to recognize that mass media play a role in folklore transmission. It is closer to the truth to admit that the media have become part of folklore" (Dégh 1994, 25). More recently Mikel Koven (2008) has argued stridently for the importance of analyzing the role of folklore in films in a way that goes beyond what he aptly and disparagingly calls "motif spotting" (3). And Pauline Greenhill notes, "Folkloristic scholarship concerning intersections of folklore and film has greatly expanded since the beginning of the twenty-first-century" (Greenhill 2012, 484).[11] Furthermore, as emerging technologies and fresh (often unimagined) apps and forms of entertainment increasingly dominate popular culture production, folkloristics has also begun to explore video games (e.g., Miller 2008), the Internet (de Vos 2012; Foster 2012; Frank 2011), and all manifestations of digital culture (Blank 2009, 2012).

One approach to popular culture has been to use folklore method-ologies to examine processes on the Internet and elsewhere that exhibit traditionality, variation, artistic communication, and other familiar orienta-tions. Accordingly, it is not surprising that folklorists have been particularly interested in fan culture and audience studies.[12] But the tools of folklore have much more to offer in the emerging media environment; as Kiri Miller notes with regard to digital gaming, "Folklorists' approaches to the nature of storytelling and play are quite different from those of most digital game theorists; their ethnographic orientation, their experience with variable texts and performance practices, and their disciplinary emphasis on representa-tions of the past in the present could bring new perspectives to this mate-rial" (Miller 2008, 258). Moreover, as S. Elizabeth Bird points out: "Certain popular cultural forms succeed because they act like folklore" (Bird 2006, 346). And as others have stated simply, "Commodified culture is multifac-eted, complex, and as likely to be a site for social meaning as any other" (Goldstein et al. 2007, 173).

My aim here is not to offer a survey of folkloric engagement with popular culture but simply to note that it has been happening for a very long time. The study of the folkloresque emerges out of, and builds on, this engagement. But it also suggests a specific type of engagement; my own characterization of the folkloresque does not refer to *all* interactions between folklore and popular culture, nor does it conflate popular culture with folklore (although this is a valuable experiment). For example, I am not (or at least not explicitly) talking about fan studies or the folkloric pro-cesses by which popular culture and mass media are used by communities and individuals—such as Robert Glenn Howard's (2008) powerful concept of the "vernacular web." We accept that social media, and all the other interactive experiences of the Internet, are nothing if not folkloric. But the folkloresque, in a sense, refers to just the opposite: popular and commer-cial processes in which folklore is used by companies and individuals. That is, we are concerned with how producers/consumers of popular culture interpret folklore and consciously draw on it for the sense of authenticity and authority it offers. In this sense, the folkloresque can be thought of as a specific genre of popular culture.

INTEGRATION, PORTRAYAL, PARODY

At least, this is a starting point. Again, we offer this book as an initial foray, but also as a challenge to others to more fully explore some of the direc-tions we embark upon. With that in mind, I would like to suggest three major categories of the folkloresque: *integration, portrayal,* and *parody.* These three types of folkloresque expression provide entrance into broader and deeper discussions; accordingly, this is the way we have organized the book itself—in three sections, each drawing on one of these broad concepts as a governing theme for the chapters it contains. Most important, however, I want to qualify these categories from the start by saying that they are not necessarily the only possible categories. Moreover, there is no question that they overlap with each other. But they do serve, I hope, as convenient conversation starters—because the goal is to start a conversation.

Integration

This line of inquiry considers how popular cultural producers *integrate* or stitch together folkloric motifs and forms to make a product that appears to be inspired directly by one or more specific traditions. The folkloresque of this mode works through the mechanisms of allusion and pastiche, a hodgepodge suturing of bits and pieces of other things to create a coherent new whole. Here we may start with "motif spotting," tale-type labeling, or sifting out tradition from invention, but the point is not simply to identify sources. Rather, it is imperative to look carefully at the diverse, complex, and creative ways that authors, screenwriters, video game creators, and other artists infuse their works with specific elements from diverse traditions, and also to explore the reasons for and effects of this borrowing.

One good example of integration is the film *Spirited Away*, mentioned above. But the dynamics of integration inform all sorts of popular culture phenomena, such as the ongoing American obsession with zombies and vampires, or contemporary fiction and films such as *The Lord of the Rings*, *Harry Potter*, and the *Twilight* series. But this form of the folkloresque also characterizes more classic examples—the "fairy tales" of Hans Christian Andersen, for instance, or, for that matter, Paul Bunyan lore. What value is added through this process of borrowing and cobbling together, and what does it reveal about the cultural context and values of a given moment? Within this form of the folkloresque, older folkloric and newly created elements are exposed to mutual contamination; the folkloresque may not be folklore but it is also not completely invented.

The use of folklore in this way, in terms of both form and content, can be unconscious (part of the folklore-creative process itself) or it can be very much an intentional act. An example of the purposeful way in which folklore can be appreciated, manipulated, and reinvented is the classic text of *The Wonderful Wizard of Oz*, complete with its witches and wizards and magical spells. It is no coincidence that L. Frank Baum introduces his work by invoking the influence of "folk lore, legends, myths and fairy tales," and then asserting that his own book "aspires to being a modernized fairy tale, in which the wonderment and joy are retained and the heart-aches and nightmares are left out" (Baum 1900, 5).

With the proliferation of digital technology, folkloric elements and references increasingly animate video games and Internet sites; indeed, it seems as if explicitly folkloric characters and motifs are often the driving force behind many of the most popular video games and role-playing games (RPGs), which in turn are at the heart of a multibillion-dollar global industry. In these contexts, folklore is frequently identified as such, by the word *folklore* or a related generic term (i.e., *myth*, *legend*, *fairy tale*), and explicitly and strategically deployed to imbue products with meaning through association. The notion of the folkloresque, then, opens up a new way to consider the contact zone between the traditional and the commercial and between the culturally specific and the transnational metaculture of the global popular arena.

In a sense, we can think of folkloresque of the integration type as a process of *bricolage* by which commercial interests cannibalize folklore, extracting component parts and reassembling them in a product that retains a *connection* to folklore, or *seems* folkloric, or has the *style* of folklore—and, most important, *sells* because of this perceived relationship. This relationship works through a metonymic process, whereby the folkloric element generates meaning by its connection to a broader tradition.[13] And this connection with folklore in turn serves as the "value added" aspect of the product. The way consumers receive a folkloresque product depends on the particular interpretive community or folk group of which they are a part. Although they may recognize an item as a commercial construct, perhaps created by a single author or producer, they might assume that the product is based on or representative of ("real") folklore. This assumption is particularly significant when a popular culture item crosses cultural or national borders. To older Japanese consumers, for example, the "monsters" of the Pokémon franchise are invented within a commercial context; for consumers from America and Europe, these same products often become associated with "Japanese folklore." Thinking of such commercial products as folkloresque inspires a fresh, nonpejorative approach that treats them not as derivative or corrupt but as part of an ongoing creative process.

Portrayal

This category of the folkloresque is an expression of the "commonsense" image of folklore within popular culture. Through this optic, we examine the ways in which folklorists as people and folkloristics as a discipline are portrayed. In many popular cultural products, for example, folklorists are depicted as experts on esoteric traditions, adventurer figures with special knowledge or insight into mysterious worlds. Sometimes they are portrayed as armchair ethnologists surrounded by piles of thick, old, obscure books. In one common narrative type, the arcane knowledge of the folklorist—usually of no use to anybody—suddenly becomes the key to solving a mystery or crime. This folkloresque image of the folklorist can be found, for example, in the film *Candyman* (1992) or more recently in *Fatal Frame*, a horror video game series in which folklorists are portrayed as collectors of dangerous supernatural lore whose presence can unleash ghostly horror but whose knowledge is also needed to save the day.

Folklore as a discipline is also often portrayed in a similarly ambivalent light, as an archaic and esoteric field of study, at once irrelevant to modern life and at the same time spiritually potent. Generally speaking, the popular culture image of folkloristics (and folklorists) is one or two generations behind the reality of what contemporary folklorists actually do. As Robert Glenn Howard put it in a recent interview, "I wish it weren't true, but a lot of people imagine 'folklore' as 'old stuff.' But that just isn't the case" (Owens 2013). Many folklorists today, like Howard, are deeply engaged in the study of emerging technology, social networking, and other cutting-edge phenomena, but such research does not easily mesh with popular culture images of the discipline. There is a time lag between the professional world and the popular culture world, between academic inception and vernacular reception. This sort of disconnect between the reality of an academic (or perhaps any) profession and its vernacular image may be common, but it is particularly meaningful in the case of folkloristics, which after all takes as its subject the study of the vernacular.

The folkloresque of the portrayal genre, then, reminds us not of what folklore is but of the popular culture *image* of what folklore is. Not surprisingly, for example, there is a popular action role-playing video game called simply *Folklore*, that begins in a clichéd folkloric setting in a small Irish village and includes all sorts of supernatural creatures and mysteries.[14] Television, too, is chock-full of portrayals of folkloristics, folklorists, and folkloric concepts—everything from *MythBusters* to *Supernatural* to a series on NewTV simply called *The Folklorist*, described as "exploring the iconic and lesser-known historical occurrences in our world's history."[15] Such portrayals reveal a great deal about the values, worldviews, and assumptions of producers and consumers, and also about the particular culture(s) in which the producing and consuming is performed. Folkloresque portrayals also have "real-world" consequences: many students come to the academic study of folklore, or at least take an introductory class in the subject, because of their early exposure to folkloresque images of the field and its subject matter.

Parody

The third broad category of the folkloresque, which I am calling *parody*, is particularly complex. By parody, I do not necessarily mean a comical or humorous product, but rather one that seems self-consciously and often self-referentially imitative of folklore. Folkloresque parody reflects a seemingly intentional appropriation of folkloric motifs and structures for the purpose of caricature or similar modes of critical commentary. The Greek *para* can mean both "against" and "alongside of," and literary theorists suggest that parody is simultaneously a form of ridicule and of homage (Chatman 2001, 33). Whether it is mocking or celebratory, a common characteristic of folkloresque parody is its evident awareness of its own derivativeness. Indeed, the parodic folkloresque is often characterized by an explicit self-referential quality, a kind of insider/outsider knowledge into which the audience is invited to enter; although I call this category "parody," it could just as easily be glossed as "metacommentary."

Parody of this sort may express a critique of the source material (that is, folklore); it may comment on itself as a popular culture product; or it may self-reflexively offer a send-up of popular cultural uses of folklore (that is, the folkloresque). It is no coincidence that parody has often been considered a postmodern form (e.g., Rose 1993), and certainly the parodic folkloresque presumes a readership/audience with a sophisticated awareness of the popular culture product being critiqued in addition to familiarity with the folkloric elements invoked to enact the parody. An example of this approach is *Enchanted*, Disney's 2007 movie in which already-clichéd Disney appropriations of traditional fairy tales are imaginatively combined to create a romantic comedy that plays with both popular culture and folkloric conventions. Similarly, the classic *Princess Bride* (1987) and the entire *Shrek* franchise—from the children's books to the DreamWorks films—operate in a parodic folkloresque fashion.

I would add that the recent spate of filmic reworkings of traditional folktales, including *Red Riding Hood* (2011), *Mirror Mirror* (2012), *Jack the Giant Slayer* (2013), and *Maleficent* (2014) might all be analyzed productively through the lens of the parodic folkloresque as commentaries on contemporary American culture that work their critique not only through reference to a known folkloric precedent but through highlighting their difference to this earlier "text." In one sense, such film productions might simply be considered "updated" versions of existing folklore. If, however, as Seymour Chatman has asserted, "it is only by imitating another text, an original which the reader can recognize or consult, that stylistic parody arises" (Chatman 2001, 35), then such folkloresque products also problematize the stability of the "original" folkloric source. In addition, they provide entertainment on a number of levels. Just like so-called post-tourists, who "almost delight in the inauthenticity of the normal tourist experience" because "they know that there is no authentic tourist experience, that there are merely a series of games or texts that can be played" (Urry 2002, 11), there are certainly "post-consumers" who take great pleasure in the multileveled irony of the parodic folkloresque.

The parodic folkloresque is simultaneously a form of metafolklore and also a popular culture appropriation of the power of folklore and its assumed association with "authentic" tradition. The Internet is a vital—and vexingly complex—hive of such folkloresque activity: popular culture products not only constantly reference folklore, but new forms of folklore (e.g., Photoshop folklore and image macros) make reference to themselves and to other popular culture products in an endless cycle of parody and commentary that is often aware of its own cyclicality. Perhaps it is no coincidence that the phrase "I am aware of all Internet traditions" has itself become a well-circulating meme.

I should add a critical caveat to the suggestion that parody is self-aware and conscious of its appropriation of folkloric elements and structure. Ultimately, parody is in the eye of the beholder. In some cases a producer may be completely unaware of the derivative nature of the product and it is left to the savvy consumer to discern the folkloric borrowing that went into its creation. As a close reader of texts within the context of their production, such a consumer can find critical commentary in the particular choices made by the producer, despite (or because of) a lack of intention on the producer's part. That is, the parodic folkloresque emerges not only in the act of creation but also through practices of consumption and interpretation (e.g., see Schrempp's chapter 11 in this volume).

APPROACHING THE FOLKLORESQUE

To reiterate, the three forms of the folkloresque suggested here are overlapping, intersecting, and by no means mutually exclusive; I offer them only as very provisional categories within which to consider certain phenomena. I wish I could suggest a grand theory that could be applied to these three different types and also to diverse case studies. But as is perhaps already evident, the folkloresque is as varied as folklore and popular culture, and any attempt at a grand theory would be meaninglessly reductive. So in the next few pages I simply gesture to a number of possible directions or foci that could be pursued within, or complementary to, any of the three categories mentioned above.

Motifs

As outlined above, integration, portrayal, and parody are modes by which popular cultural products purposefully articulate a relationship with folklore: either through direct reference to a single existing tradition or through a creative amalgam of elements from multiple traditions. One way to understand the dynamics of this *referencing* is through returning to the old folkloric study of motifs. Certain popular culture texts, such as *The Lord of the Rings* or *Game of Thrones*, seem to evoke entirely "believable" worlds. Such examples are successful not because they are fabricated from scratch, but precisely because they are informed by tried-and-true motifs; indeed they achieve "truthiness," as Stephen Colbert might put it, because of the creator's skillful (conscious or unconscious) cobbling together and/or embedding of familiar motifs into the fictional realms of Middle Earth or Westeros and Essos. As Sharon R. Sherman points out about J.R.R. Tolkien's work, for example, "Precisely because the tales are so closely based on myth, folktale, and epic, and populated with ogres, witches, and elves, they have struck a familiar chord with readers and viewers" (Sherman 2004, 292). Their "authenticity" comes from their connection to "authentic" folklore, by which I mean their use of motifs and narratives found in earlier storytelling traditions and often (though by no means exclusively) oral forms of transmission.

Some of the elements that go into such popular cultural works are actually recorded in the tale-type indexes or Stith Thompson's encyclopedic motif index. This latter work in particular represents a massive experiment in deconstruction, breaking narratives down to, as it were, a molecular level: "If an attempt is made to reduce the traditional narrative material of the whole earth to order (as, for example, the scientists have done with the worldwide phenomena of biology) it must be by means of a classification of single motifs—those details out of which full-fledged narratives are composed. It is these simple elements which can form a common basis for a systematic arrangement of the whole body of traditional literature" (Thompson 1955, 9).

Thompson explains that "sometimes the interest of a student of traditional narrative may be centered on a certain type of character in a tale, sometimes on an action, sometimes on attendant circumstances of the action" (Thompson 1955, 10). If the index extracts these motifs from the folkloric texts in which they are embedded, the folkloresque within popular culture then reassembles them in different configurations or in conjunction with motifs from other fields (science fiction, for example) into new and, if successful, saleable commercial products. In crude but accurate terms, we might call this a kind of "chop-shop" operation, by which still-useful parts are removed from old vehicles and repackaged for sale in a competitive market. Approaching the folkloresque through the study of motifs, therefore, should not stop at simply identifying their usage; it should push toward redefining what a motif is in the first place, and also understanding the processes by which popular culture producers draw on their cultural meanings. The goal is to understand how the chop shop works.

Indexical

It is no coincidence that Thompson calls his opus an "index." On one level, an index is simply an ordered list for the purpose of keeping records and providing access to materials. But the notion of indexicality suggests a significant referential connection between two "things" and is of theoretic importance in philosophical, semiotic, and linguistic discourse. Most famously, perhaps, the semiotic of Charles Peirce posits a tripartite structure of signs made up of what he calls *icon*, *index*, and *symbol*. Peirce stresses that an indexical sign, particularly the kind he classifies as *deictic* or *referential*, is characterized by "the sense that there is a direct continuity between the sign and its object; for example, as the way a pointing finger draws an imaginary line to the object it refers to" (Liszka 1996, 38).

Within a popular culture text or product, then, the perceived folkloric motif (whether literally indexed by Thompson or not) can be thought of as an indexical sign that points directly to a particular tradition and therefore stimulates the consumer to mentally or emotionally access all that he or she knows about that tradition. It is the contiguity here, the "real relation" (Colapietro 1989, 16) between the motif (sign) within the text and the tradition (object) outside the text, that draws the folkloric into the popular culture product. Although Peirce's system is thick with specific terminology, his notion of indexicality might be one productive way for further exploring the processes through which the folkloresque enacts an association with folklore and, even more abstractly, how it inspires a sense of that elusive quality we call "authenticity."[16]

The Database

Building on the notion of motifs and indexes, whether literal or semiotic, we can develop a more contemporarily relevant metaphor for understanding this indexing process: the database. Popular culture theorist Azuma Hiroki (2009) suggests that postmodern consumers of Japanese popular culture—specifically manga and anime—interact with products and information through what he calls "database consumption." He argues that in the 1990s consumers began to understand narratives in terms of their component parts rather than in terms of the stories that went with them. He suggests that they viewed products as drawing on a database containing "settings," by which he means characters, traits, physical attributes, superpowers—in a word (which he does not actually use): *motifs*.

While Azuma's argument is specific to the Japanese historical situation, his suggestion of the database as a model for a popular culture worldview is, I think, extremely relevant to the concept of the folkloresque. Metaphorically, if not literally, producers access a database of characteristics and elements proven to be loved by fans and assemble them to construct a new product that will, presumably, resonate with what consumers are already familiar with. In this view of the world, folklore—or in Thompson's words, "the traditional narrative material of the whole earth"—becomes nothing more than a massive database containing component parts for constructing or augmenting any number of commercially viable products—from comics to toys to video games.

One effect of constructing a popular culture product with folkloric components is that it instills the new product with durability. That is, a popular culture item or event is usually "popular" only for a short time: what is all the rage today may be completely forgotten tomorrow. In contrast, folklore is often characterized by traditionality, the notion that it retains (or appears to retain) a certain amount of stability over time and across space. By reaching into the massive database of folklore, popular culture producers draw on the presumed longevity of tradition and invest their products with staying power, the folkloric referent suggesting that the product transcends the fleeting moment of its present popularity. The folkloresque is a meaningful form of popular culture because popular culture dreams of being folklore.

Indeed, within certain popular culture products, tradition (however we define it) is evoked as an agent of authority.[17] By referencing folklore or folkloric elements, a popular culture product draws on "the empowering force of the discursive deployment of vernacular authority" (Howard 2013, 75). Robert Glenn Howard explains that "the concept of vernacular authority is based on the idea that any claim to be supported by tradition asserts power because it seeks to garner trust from an audience by appealing to the aggregate volition of other individuals across space and through time" (Howard 2013, 80). Although Howard is not speaking here of popular culture per se, "vernacular authority" is central to the selling power of the folkloresque because it invests the ephemeral commercial product with a more trustworthy, authorized, and "authentic" (as perceived by the consumer) raison d'être based on its (perceived) connection to tradition.

Plagiarism, Intellectual Property, Ownership

Certainly, then, the accessing of a motif database in order to assemble a new popular culture product inspires abstract questions about origins and originality, and touches on postmodern concepts of hyperreality and simulacra, in which reality and its representation may be seamlessly blended. It also raises more practical concerns about copyright and intellectual property laws. At one level, perhaps all processes of folklore are comparable to processes of plagiarism: both can entail imitation, borrowing, recontextualization, and the presenting of something old as if it were new. If folklore is characterized by versions and variants, "multiple existence in time and space" (Dundes and Pagter 1987, 268), then certainly—as with plagiarism—originality is always in question.

Of course, I am not indicting folkloric processes as criminal or immoral; rather, I want to point out just the opposite, that in the cultural imaginary folklore is in part defined as those very materials and processes that fall outside intellectual property law. This freedom inspires creativity and fluid transmission, but it also means that folklore resides in an open-access domain where it is subject to easy appropriation. One university website explaining plagiarism, for example, warns students to "document any words, ideas, or other productions that originate somewhere outside of you." It then explains that "there are, of course, certain things that do not need documentation or credit," and these include, "things like folklore, common sense observations, myths, urban legends, and historical events." (Purdue Online Writing Lab).[18] The fact that folklore is considered common property—nobody *owns* it—is the very thing that allows the proliferation of versions and variants, the repeating of proverbs, the retelling of jokes, the teaching of techniques, the borrowing of patterns—indeed, all the processes through which expressive culture is transmitted from person to person, from culture to culture, from one generation to the next.[19]

But this is also one place that the folkloresque, as a manifestation of popular culture, is distinctly different. Creators of popular culture products are free to "sample," as it were, to borrow at will from folklore, literally or metaphorically riffling through motif indexes and databases to take whatever they can sell. Folklore belongs to everybody and therefore to nobody. But once something is sold—and patented, copyrighted, or trademarked—it is legally transformed into property and enters an entirely different realm of discourse. If folklore is public common property, then the folkloresque is private commercial property. I am not offering a conclusion here, but just suggesting that the folkloresque gives us a lever with which to pry open some of the conceptual and legal differences in how expressive cultural is understood in the contemporary world—a situation made all the more complex by the ongoing globalization of the cultural arena.

This also brings us back to more abstract notions of tradition. Dorothy Noyes suggests that tradition entails mutual responsibility: "The receiver must respect, but the giver must let go." There must be "transmission of metaknowledge along with the practice itself: what it means, how it is to be used, everything that is shaven off when it is packaged as a product or an entry in a database" (Noyes 2009, 248). And therein lies one of the key distinctions between folklore and popular culture, for it is so often this metaknowledge, and the accompanying sense of responsibility on the part of the receiver (taker), that is shaved off in the packaging of a folkloresque product. Ultimately, the commercial producer's responsibility is to the bottom line, not to the people and cultures who have contributed to the database.

OTHER TIMES, OTHER GENRES

Throughout this introduction I have mostly drawn on examples from relatively recent popular culture. But I want to stress that as a concept, the folkloresque's heuristic value is not restricted to analysis of contemporary popular and commercial products but can be equally applied to older texts such as, for example, Victorian literature (see Manning's chapter 3 in this volume). That is, folkloresque processes are not new.

Moreover, although most examples in the chapters that follow are verbal or performative, folkloresque analysis could just as readily be applied to all sorts of material and customary genres of folklore and folklife. If one characteristic of popular culture is its commercial orientation, it is not surprising that video games, films, popular literature, and other narrative formats also generate physical objects—costumes, figurines, posters, and other material culture forms of cross-platform marketing. Moreover, the folkloresque as *style* can be found in all sorts of commercial production; mass-produced clothing, fabric patterns, ceramics, even architectural designs often not only borrow from folklore but make overt reference to specific traditions. Presumably, this connection attracts consumers not just aesthetically but also because it authenticates the product by linking it to something beyond the factories and industrial processes in which it was fabricated.

On a mundane level, the power of what I would call "the authenticity of the hand" is invoked throughout contemporary American (and other) society. How many products are marketed as "handmade," "hand crafted" or even, as in a coffee shop I once visited, "hand stirred"? From a folklor-esque perspective, what is important here is not whether there is truth in advertising, whether a human hand actually does the stirring, but why nos-talgia for the handmade, for the personal *touch*, has become such a powerful selling point for everything from furniture to beer. The notion of "home-made" similarly pervades popular and commercial culture, with restaurants such as the ubiquitous Cracker Barrel chain basing their business strategy on customers' desire for folksy decor and "homemade" comfort food.

It also goes without saying that the folkloresque might also be applied to all sorts of performance and arts, such as music and dance. Indeed, the so-called folk revival of the 1960s not only demonstrates the dynamic of the folkloresque but also indicates the real-world effects it can have. Contemporary notions of "folklorization" (see McDowell 2010) also fit within the framework proposed here. All this is to say that, by focusing pri-marily on verbal products, the essays in this collection represent only the tip of the iceberg. I hope, however, that they will provide models for approach-ing different genres, and that others will pursue these avenues.

A FOLKLORESQUE MANIFESTO

And this plea brings me to the penultimate section of this introduction, which I call, only somewhat facetiously, a *folkloresque manifesto*. The study of the folkloresque may open up a new set of inquiries but, more significant, it can help shape new attitudes toward these inquiries. Analyzing the folklor-esque requires that we assume different perspectives (multiple perspectives), not lingering on origins or even folklore per se, but exploring perception, social value, and function as well as the agency of creators and consumers of popular culture. In order to be "popular," popular culture must succeed: it must resonate in some meaningful way with its audiences, who are not merely receptors but active and highly critical participants. Consumers of a popular cultural product must "buy it"—literally and figuratively. Whatever shape it takes, the folkloresque suggests a metadiscursive dimension of popular culture through which producers and consumers together engage in thoughtful evaluations of cultural forms that are the building blocks of new material.

No matter how explicitly commercial, a folkloresque product can end up being (re)appropriated by the "folk" (often of a different tradition or culture from the product producer), who repurpose its component parts, introducing them—or the product as a whole—into a new folk cultural context. Particularly within the current global marketplace, such circularity may be cross-cultural, with one culture attracted to the seemingly folkloric aspects of another culture's commercial product. By conceiving of the relationship of folklore and the folkloresque as symbiotic or circular rather than oppositional, we can adjust our understanding of the relationship of the vernacular and the commercial, of the traditional and the innovative, and understand all of these manifestations as part of a complex and always shifting process of human creativity.

In essence, the relationship of folklore to the folkloresque is like a Möbius strip in which folk culture and popular culture are magically, paradoxically, two different sides of the same surface, never intersecting because they are always already intersecting. Intertextuality, transtextuality, mediation, remediation, and multiplatform functionality suggest that genres of expression are temporary and porous, and that transmission and transformation between them is the rule rather than the exception. The present moment is particularly volatile: the very question of what defines a text or product can no longer be answered with certainty, and new platforms and modes of communication emerge every day. We stand on the fault line of a paradigm shift brought about by, among other things, globalization and advances in information technologies that indelibly affect cultural expression around the world.

For folklorists this is a moment of great urgency and opportunity: a chance to employ a particularly relevant kind of expertise within a range of critical, timely conversations. To get in on the ground floor of the emerging paradigm, however, we should remember that, despite its bearing on so many discourses, folkloristic research is often overlooked by other disciplines. Media and cultural studies theses regularly posit "new" ideas regarding the circulation of motifs and images (and memes) that have long been at the very heart of the folkloric project. Even concepts as academically viral and vital as Benedict Anderson's "imagined communities" (Anderson 1991)—to say nothing of contemporary catch phrases such as "online communities" and "social networking"—are of course uncannily resonant with notions of "folk group" that folklorists have been working with for decades.[20]

But the argument cuts both ways, and ultimately the onus is on folklorists to be heard—to work across disciplinary boundaries or to work with others to establish entirely new disciplines. The folkloresque is one small gesture in this direction: a new word that will operate as a hypertextual link between different realms of discourse. You may find the chapters that follow offer views that radically conflict with the ideas suggested in this introduction. They may define the folkloresque differently, or approach it from different perspectives or with different objectives. They may rely on the very binaries the concept of the folkloresque is meant to problematize, or they may understand popular culture and folklore in contradictory ways. But if the essays assembled here leave you longing for more attention to these issues, then they will have succeeded—because a lack of conformity is one of the goals of this book.

Each chapter that follows may be read individually or in conjunction with the others. But if you find any of the ideas presented here insufficient—or, inversely, if you think they might apply meaningfully to other genres or other time periods—I hope you will continue the conversation with contributions that build on, contradict, and transcend the ones here. This book is also a call for scholars of popular culture, cultural studies, media, communications, literature, and film to take up the challenge of the folkloresque, to explore the symbiosis, and ultimately the inseparability, of commercial production and folk creativity—because the folkloresque is part of a critical discourse for the twenty-first century, and its interpretation sheds light not only on folklore and popular culture but on the dynamics of all cultural expression.

STRUCTURE OF THE BOOK

This book is divided into three sections based on the concepts outlined above—integration, portrayal, and parody. Each section opens with an introduction by my coeditor, Jeffrey A. Tolbert, explaining the specific chapters therein and indicating how they speak to each other and to the larger issues. Without duplicating that information, I briefly describe here the sections with the goal of showing how each provides insight into a specific form of the folkloresque and also suggests connections with the others.

The "Integration" section demonstrates how the folkloresque process of integration informs a variety of contemporary texts, from the Japanese animated films (Foster, chapter 1) that spurred my own interest in the subject to the contemporary work of popular writer Neil Gaiman (Evans, chapter 2). But this section also exemplifies the historical applicability of the concept through an exploration of eighteenth-century writings on fairy-lore (Manning, chapter 3) as well as the contingent relationship between popular culture and folkloric discourses in the constellation of texts, products, and events surrounding Superman (Peretti, chapter 4).

The "Portrayal" section similarly explores a range of materials and contexts, from contemporary video games (Tolbert, chapter 5) to Irish storytelling (Buterbaugh, chapter 6) to the complex ways folklore is used within the *Harry Potter* world (Holl-Jensen and Tolbert, chapter 7). As these particular analyses highlight, the image of folklore and folklorists is a vital—if somewhat anachronistic—element of the popular cultural imaginary.

The final section, "Parody," is perhaps the most challenging. It begins with two chapters on humor, one exploring the jokes circulating after a sexual abuse scandal (Blank, chapter 8) and the other analyzing sophisticated forms of metahumor and "joke metonyms" (Kelley, chapter 9). While humor seems a natural fit for a section on parody, these discussions also implicitly demonstrate that jokes, perhaps more than any other form of folklore, reveal the inherent porousness between folk and popular culture—clouding the very premises on which the concept of the folkloresque is built. But parody is not always about humor, and a chapter on a complex Japanese anime (Ellis, chapter 10) shows how the parodic folkloresque operates as a metacommentary on the processes of storytelling itself. And the final contribution, an analysis of popular science writing (Schrempp, chapter 11), takes the parodic folkloresque one step further, demonstrating not only that science and mythology are parallel in many ways but that, consciously or not, they may even parody each other. Ultimately, popular science itself is, in a sense, folkloresque.

The eleven chapters that follow take different, complementary, and sometimes contradictory approaches to the folkloresque. Although each one does not necessarily conform to all the ideas laid out in this introduction, they all participate in an increasingly meaningful and exciting conversation on the intersection, contrast, and fusion of folklore and popular culture. Of course, there are many other relevant texts, products, and genres we do not even touch upon here. But ultimately, we hope this book will be read in the spirit it is offered—with a decidedly forward-looking inconclusiveness.

NOTES

1. Directed by Miyazaki Hayao; Japanese title: *Sen to Chihiro no kamikakushi.*

2. For earlier usages, see Turner 1979; Chappell 2005. Both use the term differently from the delineation I am proposing here.

3. The *OED*'s first definition of "picturesque" is "like or having the elements of a picture" (*Oxford English Dictionary*, 2nd ed., s.v. "picturesque"). I also want to acknowledge different academic usages of the "-esque" suffix, most famously Bakhtin's "carnivalesque" and more recently folklorist Jack Santino's "ritualesque." See Bakhtin 1984; Santino 2011.

4. See, e.g., Smulyan's discussion of her inability to convince her students that popular cultural forms are not "empty of ideology" (Smulyan 2007, 1).

5. Folklore as a concept is, of course, notoriously difficult to define, and this is not the place to explore its discursive history. For the purposes of the present discussion, however, I characterize folkloric items and events as generally unofficial, noninstitutional forms of expressive culture. No author or designer or professional artist dictates what is correct or incorrect; often the item in question is of anonymous origins and/or the shared property of a particular group—from a family or village to an online community or nation. Of course, none of this is cut and dried: this is less a definition than it is a set of tendencies or orientations (see Oring 1986). For "textbook" introductions to the concept and its (possible) definitions, see, e.g., Georges and Jones 1995; McNeill 2013; Oring 1986; Sims and Stephens 2011; Toelken 1996.

6. Indeed, Dorson (1950, 336) is very clear that for him "word of mouth" is key and "folklore by any definition requires the proof of oral vitality." Moreover, he has carefully explained that his 1950 article (and its notorious neologism) "was intended as a rallying cry against the distortion of a serious subject" (Dorson 2005, 289) and emerged out of a desire to create a viable space for the study of folklore within American academia. See Dorson 1976, especially 1–29; 2005. For Dorson's take on Paul Bunyan, see Dorson 1976, 291–336.

7. I am wary of oversimplifying the discourses and definitions of folklorism and folklorismus here. For a more nuanced treatment of these concepts, see Bendix 1988, 1997b. For a fascinating conversation about the subject, see "Floor Discussion" 1984.

8. *Jacobellis v. Ohio*, 378 U.S. 184 (1964) http://caselaw.findlaw.com/us-supreme-court/378/184.html.

9. See also, e.g., the essays in Narvaez and Laba 1986; also Bluestein 1994; Brunvand 2004.

10. Early discussions about the relationship of folklore and literature include Hoffman et al. 1957, Dundes 1965. For the use of proverbs in literature, see Haas 2011 and especially the voluminous work of Wolfgang Mieder (e.g., Bryan and Mieder 1997; Mieder 2008). For recent work on fairy tales, literature, television, and film, see Bacchilega 1997, 2013, Bannon 2008; Greenhill and Matrix 2010; Greenhill and Rudy 2014; Short 2015; Smith 2007; Zipes 2009, 2010.

11. For an overview of the way in which folklorists have considered film in their work, see Koven 2008, especially 3–22; also Sherman 2004; Sherman and Koven 2007.

12. Indeed, connections between popular culture products and their assimilation into more informal folk cultural processes have received critical attention in so-called fanthropologies and other works on fan culture.

13. See Foley 1991 for discussion of this sort of metonymy within oral traditional epic performance.

14. The game is developed by Game Republic and published by Sony Entertainment for the PlayStation platform. The game was originally made in Japanese, in which it is titled *Folk Soul: Ushinawareta denshō*, which translates as *Folk Soul: Lost Traditions*.

15. http://folklorist.newtv.org (accessed June 16, 2015).

16. For an introduction to Peirce's semiotic and its specific relevance to folkloristics, see Chappell 1999.

17. For recent important discussions of tradition, see Blank and Howard 2013; Bronner 1998; Cashman, Mould, and Shukla 2011; Glassie 2003; Noyes 2009.

18. See https://owl.english.purdue.edu/owl/resource/589/2/ (accessed July 4, 2014).

19. I am simplifying here, and we have to remember that folklore's presumed position outside intellectual property and copyright laws can often be problematic. See, e.g., Brown

2003; also Handler 2003; Skrydstrup 2012. For a discussion of the correlation between folklore and plagiarism, see also Seeger 1962.

20. The lament of folkloristics as a minor, overlooked discipline is not confined to the United States; a very similar dynamic is found in my own area of research in Japan, where the scholarly relevance of folkloristics (*minzokugaku*) seems to be recognized only by folklorists.

REFERENCES

Anderson, Benedict. 1991. *Imagined Communities: Reflections on the Origins and Spread of Nationalism.* Rev. ed. London: Verso.

Azuma, Hiroki. 2009. *Otaku: Japan's Database Animals.* Translated by Jonathan Abel and Shion Kono. Minneapolis: University of Minnesota Press.

Bacchilega, Cristina. 1997. *Postmodern Fairy Tales: Gender and Narrative Strategies.* Philadelphia: University of Pennsylvania Press. http://dx.doi.org/10.9783/978081220 0638.

Bacchilega, Cristina. 2012. "Folklore and Literature." In *A Companion to Folklore*, edited by Regina F. Bendix and Galit Hasan-Rokem, 447–63. Hoboken, NJ: Blackwell. http://dx.doi.org/10.1002/9781118379936.ch23.

Bacchilega, Cristina. 2013. *Fairy Tales Transformed? Twenty-First Century Adaptations and the Politics of Wonder.* Detroit: Wayne State University Press.

Bakhtin, Mikhail M. (Original work published 1965) 1984. *Rabelais and His World.* Translated by Helene Iswolsky. Bloomington: Indiana University Press.

Baum, L. Frank. 1900. *The Wonderful Wizard of Oz.* Chicago: G. M. Hill.

Bauman, Richard, and Charles L. Briggs. 2003. *Voices of Modernity: Language Ideologies and the Politics of Inequality.* Cambridge: Cambridge University Press. http://dx.doi.org /10.1017/CBO9780511486647.

Bausinger, Hermann. 1986. "Toward a Critique of Folklorism Criticism." In *German Volkskunde*, edited and translated by James Dow and Hannjost Lixfeld, 113–23. Bloomington: Indiana University Press.

Ben-Amos, Dan. 1976. "Analytical Categories and Ethnic Genres." In *Folklore Genres*, edited by Dan Ben-Amos, 215–42. Austin: University of Texas Press.

Bendix, Regina. 1988. "Folklorism: The Challenge of a Concept." *International Folklore Review* 6:5–15.

Bendix, Regina. 1997a. "Folklorismus/Folklorism." In *Folklore: An Encyclopedia of Beliefs, Customs, Tales, Music, and Art*, vol. 1, edited by Thomas A. Green, 337–39. Santa Barbara: ABC-CLIO.

Bendix, Regina. 1997b. *In Search of Authenticity: The Formation of Folklore Studies.* Madison: University of Wisconsin Press.

Benson, Stephen, ed. 2008. *Contemporary Fiction and the Fairy Tale.* Detroit: Wayne State University Press.

Bird, S. Elizabeth. 2006. "Convergence Studies as Confluence: The Convergence of Folklore and Media Studies." In *Popular Culture Theory and Methodology: A Basic Introduction*, edited by Harold E. Hinds Jr., Marilyn F. Motz, and Angela M. S. Nelson, 344–55. Madison: University of Wisconsin Press.

Blank, Trevor, ed. 2009. *Folklore and the Internet: Vernacular Expression in a Digital World.* Logan: Utah State University Press.

Blank, Trevor, ed. 2012. *Folk Culture in the Digital Age: The Emergent Dynamics of Human Interaction.* Logan: Utah State University Press.

Blank, Trevor, and Robert Glenn Howard, eds. 2013. *Tradition in the 21st Century: Locating the Role of the Past in the Present.* Logan: Utah State University Press.

Bluestein, Gene. 1994. *Poplore: Folk and Pop in American Culture.* Amherst: University of Massachusetts Press.

Bronner, Simon J. 1998. *Following Traditions: Folklore in the Discourse of American Culture.* Logan: Utah State University Press.

Brown, Michael F. 2003. *Who Owns Native Culture?* Cambridge, MA: Harvard University Press.

Bruner, Edward M., and Barbara Kirshenblatt-Gimblett. 1994. "Maasai on the Lawn: Tourist Realism in East Africa." *Cultural Anthropology* 9(4): 435–70.

Brunvand, Jan Harold. 2001. *Encyclopedia of Urban Legends.* Santa Barbara: ABC-CLIO.

Brunvand, Jan Harold. 2004. "The Vanishing 'Urban Legend.'" *Midwestern Folklore* 30(2): 5–20.

Bryan, George B., and Wolfgang Mieder. 1997. *Proverbs in World Literature.* New York: Peter Lang.

Cashman, Ray, Tom Mould, and Pravina Shukla. 2011. "Introduction: The Individual and Tradition." In *The Individual and Tradition: Folkloristic Perspectives,* edited by Ray Cashman, Tom Mould, and Pravina Shukla, 1–26. Bloomington: Indiana University Press.

Chappell, Ben. 1999. "Folklore Semiotic: Charles Peirce and the Experience of Signs." *Folklore Forum* 30(112): 73–93.

Chappell, Ben. 2005. "Bakhtin's 'Barbershop': Film as Folklorist." *Western Folklore* 64(3–4), Film and Folklore: 209–29.

Chatman, Seymour. 2001. "Parody and Style." *Poetics Today* 22(1): 25–39. http://dx.doi .org/10.1215/03335372-22-1-25.

Colapietro, Vincent M. 1989. *Peirce's Approach to the Self: A Semiotic Perspective on Human Subjectivity.* Albany: SUNY Press.

de Caro, Frank, and Rosan Augusta Jordan. 2004. *Re-situating Folklore: Folk Contexts and Twentieth-Century Literature and Art.* Knoxville: University of Tennessee Press.

Dégh, Linda. 1994. *American Folklore and the Mass Media.* Bloomington: Indiana University Press.

de Vos, Gail. 2012. *What Happens Next? Contemporary Urban Legends and Popular Culture.* Santa Barbara, CA: Libraries Unlimited.

Dorson, Richard M. 1950. "Folklore and Fake Lore." *American Mercury,* March, 335–42.

Dorson, Richard M. 1976. *Folklore and Fakelore: Essays toward a Discipline of Folklore Studies.* Cambridge, MA: Harvard University Press. http://dx.doi.org/10.4159/harvard .9780674330207.

Dorson, Richard M. 2005. "Fakelore." In *Folklore: Critical Concepts in Literary and Cultural Studies,* vol. 1, *From Definition to Discipline,* edited by Alan Dundes, 281–89. London: Routledge.

Dundes, Alan. 1965. "The Study of Folklore in Literature and Culture: Identification and Interpretation." *Journal of American Folklore* 78(308): 136–42. http://dx.doi.org /10.2307/538280.

Dundes, Alan, and Carl Pagter. 1987. *When You're Up to Your Ass in Alligators: More Urban Folklore from the Paperwork Empire.* Detroit: Wayne State University Press.

Fedorak, Shirley A. 2009. *Pop Culture: The Culture of Everyday Life.* Toronto: University of Toronto Press.

Fish, Stanley. 1980. *Is There a Text in This Class? The Authority of Interpretive Communities.* Cambridge, MA: Harvard University Press.

"Floor Discussion." 1984. *Journal of Folklore Research* 21(2–3), Culture, Tradition, Identity Conference, March 26–28: 205–10.

Foley, John Miles. 1991. *Immanent Art: From Structure to Meaning in Traditional Oral Epic.* Bloomington: Indiana University Press.

Foster, Michael Dylan. 1998. "The Metamorphosis of the *Kappa*: Transformation of Folklore to Folklorism in Japan." *Asian Folklore Studies* 57(1): 1–24. http://dx.doi .org/10.2307/1178994.

Foster, Michael Dylan. 2012. "Photoshop Folklore and the 'Tourist Guy': Thoughts on the Diamond Format and the Possibilities of Mixed-Media Presentations." *New Directions in Folklore* 10(1): 85–91.

Frank, Russell. 2011. *Newslore: Contemporary Folklore on the Internet.* Jackson: University Press of Mississippi. http://dx.doi.org/10.14325/mississippi/9781604739282.0 01.0001.

Georges, Robert A., and Michael Owen Jones. 1995. *Folkloristics: An Introduction.* Bloomington: Indiana University Press.

Glassie, Henry. 2003. "Tradition." In *Eight Words for the Study of Expressive Culture*, edited by Burt Feintuch, 176–97. Urbana: University of Illinois Press.

Goldstein, Diane, Jeannie Thomas, and Sylvia Grider. 2007. *Haunting Experiences: Ghosts in Contemporary Folklore.* Logan: Utah State University Press.

Greenhill, Pauline. 2012. "Folklore and/on Film." In *A Companion to Folklore*, edited by Regina F. Bendix and Galit Hasan-Rokem, 483–99. Hoboken, NJ: Blackwell. http://dx.doi.org/10.1002/9781118379936.ch25.

Greenhill, Pauline, and Sidney Eve Matrix, eds. 2010. *Fairy Tale Films: Visions of Ambiguity.* Logan: Utah State University Press.

Greenhill, Pauline, and Jill Terry Rudy, eds. 2014. *Channeling Wonder: Fairy Tales on Television.* Detroit: Wayne State University Press.

Haas, Heather A. 2011. "The Wisdom of Wizards—and Muggles and Squibs: Proverb Use in the World of Harry Potter." *Journal of American Folklore* 124(492): 29–54.

Handler, Richard. 2003. "Cultural Property and Culture Theory." *Journal of Social Archaeology* 3(3): 353–65. http://dx.doi.org/10.1177/14696053030033004.

Hoffman, Daniel G., Richard M. Dorson, Carvel Collins, and John W. Ashton. 1957. "Folklore in Literature: A Symposium." *Journal of American Folklore* 70(275): 1–24. http://dx.doi.org/10.2307/536498.

Howard, Robert Glenn. 2008. "Electronic Hybridity: The Persistent Processes of the Vernacular Web." *Journal of American Folklore* 121(480): 192–218. http://dx.doi.org /10.1353/jaf.0.0012.

Howard, Robert Glenn. 2013. "Vernacular Authority: Critically Engaging 'Tradition.'" In *Tradition in the 21st Century: Locating the Role of the Past in the Present*, edited by Trevor Blank and Robert Glenn Howard, 72–99. Logan: Utah State University Press.

Iwabuchi, Koichi. 2002. *Recentering Globalization: Popular Culture and Japanese Transnationalism.* Durham: Duke University Press. http://dx.doi.org/10.1215/9780822384083.

Jenkins, Henry. 2006. *Convergence Culture: Where Old and New Media Collide.* New York: New York University Press.

Kendirbaeva, Gulnar. 1994. "Folklore and Folklorism in Kazakhstan." *Asian Folklore Studies* 53(1): 97–123.

Koven, Mikel J. 2008. *Film, Folklore and Urban Legends.* Lanham, MD: Scarecrow.

Liszka, James Jakób. 1996. *A General Introduction to the Semiotic of Charles Sanders Peirce.* Bloomington: Indiana University Press.

McDowell, John H. 2010. "Rethinking Folklorization in Ecuador: Multivocality in the Expressive Contact Zone." *Western Folklore* 69:181–209.

McNeill, Lynne S. 2013. *Folklore Rules: A Fun, Quick, and Useful Introduction to the Field of Academic Folklore Studies.* Logan: Utah State University Press.

Mieder, Wolfgang. 2008. *"Proverbs Speak Louder Than Words": Folk Wisdom in Art, Culture, Folklore, History, Literature, and Mass Media.* New York: Peter Lang.

Miller, Kiri. 2008. "Grove Street Grimm: *Grand Theft Auto* and Digital Folklore." *Journal of American Folklore* 121(481): 255–85. http://dx.doi.org/10.1353/jaf.0.0017.

Narvaez, Peter, and Martin Laba, eds. 1986. *Media Sense: The Folklore–Popular Culture Continuum.* Bowling Green, OH: Bowling Green State University Press.

Noyes, Dorothy. 2009. "Tradition: Three Traditions." *Journal of Folklore Research* 46(3): 233–68. http://dx.doi.org/10.2979/JFR.2009.46.3.233.

Oring, Elliott. 1986. "On the Concepts of Folklore." In *Folk Groups and Folklore Genres: An Introduction,* edited by Elliott Oring, 1–22. Logan: Utah State University Press.

Owens, Trevor. 2013. "Born Digital Folklore and the Vernacular Web: An Interview with Robert Glenn Howard." *Signal.* February 23, 2013. http://blogs.loc.gov/digitalpreser vation/2013/02/born-digital-folklore-and-the-vernacular-web-an-interview-with -robert-glenn-howard/.

Roginsky, Dina. 2007. "Folklore, Folklorism, and Synchronization: Preserved-Created Folklore in Israel." *Journal of Folklore Research* 44(1): 41–66. http://dx.doi.org/10.2979/JFR .2007.44.1.41.

Rojek, Chris. 2012. Introduction to *Popular Culture: Critical Concepts in Media and Cultural Studies,* vol. 1, *History and Theory,* edited by Chris Rojek, 1–19. London: Routledge.

Rose, Margaret A. 1993. *Parody: Ancient, Modern, and Post-modern.* Cambridge: Cambridge University Press.

Santino, Jack. 2011. "The Carnivalesque and the Ritualesque." *Journal of American Folklore* 124(491): 61–73. http://dx.doi.org/10.5406/jamerfolk.124.491.0061.

Seeger, Charles. 1962. "Who Owns Folklore?—A Rejoinder." *Western Folklore* 21(2): 93–101. http://dx.doi.org/10.2307/1520490.

Sherman, Sharon R. 2004. "The 2004 Archer Taylor Memorial Lecture—Focusing In: Film and the Survival of Folklore Studies in the 21st Century." *Western Folklore* 63(4): 291–318.

Sherman, Sharon R., and Mikel J. Koven, eds. 2007. *Folklore/Cinema: Popular Film as Vernacular Culture.* Logan: Utah State University Press.

Short, Sue. 2015. *Fairy Tale and Film: Old Tales with a New Spin.* New York: Palgrave Macmillan.

Sims, Martha, and Martine Stephens. 2011. *Living Folklore: An Introduction to the Study of People and Their Traditions.* 2nd ed. Logan: Utah State University Press.

Skrydstrup, Martin. 2012. "Cultural Property." In *A Companion to Folklore,* edited by Regina F. Bendix and Galit Hasan-Rokem, 520–36. Hoboken, NJ: Blackwell. http://dx.doi.org /10.1002/9781118379936.ch27.

Šmidchens, Guntis. 1999. "Folklorism Revisited." *Journal of Folklore Research* 36(1): 51–70.

Smith, Kevin Paul. 2007. *The Postmodern Fairy Tale.* New York: Palgrave Macmillan. http:// dx.doi.org/10.1057/9780230591707.

Smulyan, Susan. 2007. *Popular Ideologies: Mass Culture at Mid-Century.* Philadelphia: University of Pennsylvania Press.

Thompson, Stith. 1955. *Motif-Index of Folk-Literature: A Classification of Narrative Elements in Folktales, Ballads, Myths, Fables, Mediaeval Romances, Exempla, Fabliaux, Jest-Books, and Local Legends.* Vol. 1. Bloomington: Indiana University Press.

Toelken, Barre. 1996. *The Dynamics of Folklore.* Logan: Utah State University Press.

Turner, Victor. 1979. "Frame, Flow, and Reflection: Ritual and Drama as Public Liminality." *Japanese Journal of Religious Studies* 6(4): 465–99.

Urry, John. 2002. *The Tourist Gaze.* 2nd ed. London: Sage.

Zipes, Jack. 2009. *Relentless Progress: The Reconfiguration of Children's Literature, Fairy Tales, and Storytelling.* New York: Routledge.

Zipes, Jack. 2010. *The Enchanted Screen: A History of Fairy Tales on Film.* Clifton, NJ: Routledge.

Integration

Introduction

Jeffrey A. Tolbert

Heedless of disciplinary conventions, cultural theory, or academic claim staking, creators of popular culture have continually turned to folklore as subject matter. The abundance of folkloric themes and images within popular media and the tendency of scholars to focus their efforts on cataloguing these allusive uses of folkloric forms led folklorist Mikel Koven (2003, 181) to coin the term *motif-spotting*, by which he meant the study of specific, identifiable folkloric motifs as they appear in works of popular fiction.

The folkloresque mode of integration as an analytical category may begin with gestures toward motif-spotting, but it has the distinct advantage of privileging emic understandings over analytic ones. Our concern is not ultimately with whether a particular episode in popular media resembles an international tale type or exhibits a particular combination of motifs (although such correspondences clue us in to the presence of the folkloresque). Rather, the folkloresque enables us to move beyond identification to an integrated study of the thought processes, interests, and goals of creators as well as audiences of popular culture. In so doing we bypass what Koven (2008, 34) has elsewhere called the "folklore fallacy," the tendency of creators of popular culture to trust uncritically in the "authenticity" of their folkloric background material. The folkloresque locates authenticity within the minds of the participants in popular culture. This enables us to understand how authenticity, and thus market appeal, are constituted and performed through popular media. The first step in this process is to determine how popular audiences conceive of folklore, and why such a conception should matter at all. Studying the folkloresque allows us to interrogate popular cultural forms that either imitate or allude to "real" (that is, known, extradiegetic) folklore, moving past the easily digestible "folksy" layers to understand why this film or comic book or novel succeeds in conjuring a sense of the folklorically familiar.

We echo S. Elizabeth Bird's call to scholars to pay attention to what matters to popular audiences: "So we need to forget about whether or not

DOI: 10.7330/9781607324188.s01

popular culture 'transmits' folklore. Rather, we begin to consider that certain popular forms succeed because they act like folklore . . . Thus popular culture is popular because of its resonance, its appeal to an audience's existing set of story conventions" (Bird 2006, 346). This resemblance to existing forms of storytelling is the core of the integrative mode of the folkloresque and remains powerfully appealing to popular audiences, similar in effect to what Margaret Dean-Smith (1968) once called "folkery."

The contributors to this section explore the use of familiar (or seemingly familiar) folkloric material as a technique through which the creators of popular culture play with received notions of tradition and traditional forms, especially narratives. These creative individuals reassemble and redeploy disparate motifs and imageries, forming new, contemporary creations that nevertheless hearken back to "olden times," to fairy tales, legends, and myths long familiar to audiences.

This is the case with Miyazaki Hayao's film *Spirited Away*, which Michael Dylan Foster, in the first chapter of this section, examines in light of its strategic but "fuzzy allusion" to established folkloric motifs and characters (Miyazaki 2001). The film combines fragments of "real" folklore in such a way as to create an entirely new narrative, one that is independent of the real-world traditions on which it apparently draws. Foster shows that *seeming* to be folklore is as much a part of the folkloresque as is the straightforward recycling of actual motifs and tale types.

In the second chapter, Tim Evans explores the works of popular author Neil Gaiman, whose use of folklore is both complicated and complicating: it makes integrative use of countless folkloric motifs even as it challenges received notions about what folklore is and how it functions in an increasingly complex social world. For Gaiman, Evans argues, the issue is ultimately the elucidation of universal elements of human experience, which "must be pursued, and re-created from" all forms and periods of culture, folk and otherwise. Equally intriguing is Gaiman's explicit use of the work of real-world folklorists, including Richard Dorson and Benjamin Botkin. By relying on these scholars, Gaiman offers both implicit and explicit commentary on the nature of folklore itself and, by extension, on the value of folklore study.

Paul Manning describes, in the third chapter, how local folklore can be strategically assimilated into burgeoning popular literary movements. Through a close examination of the works of Anna Eliza Bray, Manning shows how the pixies, local supernatural creatures from Devonshire and Cornwall in England, were reframed as part of the larger fairy faith that was becoming a fashionable Victorian literary topic. Whereas the folkloresque can enable the recombination of folkloric elements into new popular forms, Manning shows how it can also highlight (or manufacture) compelling points of contact between new modes of thinking among the educated elite and preexisting localized expressions of folk belief. The political potential of the folkloresque is, in such instances, abundantly clear.

While the integrative aspect of the folkloresque is often self-evident within examples of popular culture, Daniel Peretti demonstrates in this section's final chapter how the folkloresque process can operate bidirectionally. Peretti considers the folkloresque framing conventions used by the creators of a popular comic book superhero, offering a valuable survey of the scholarly literature on comics and illustrating the many ways in which Superman comics in particular draw on established folkloric narratives. He goes on to describe compelling examples of the folkloresque Superman as the character moves from the pop cultural medium of comics into a more conventionally folkloric environment, adopted and redeployed by fans in the form of narratives, jokes, costumes, and more.

In every case explored in this section, the integrative aspect of the folkloresque serves to alert audiences to the presence of something they may recognize, something either culled directly from their own vernacular knowledge/experience or else appealing indirectly, through similarities in structure and form and flavor, to that area of cultural experience that is felt to be (often ineffably) *folk*. This final point—the feeling of folklore, the perception of something's relationship to the folk qualifier—is perhaps the most important dimension of the folkloresque in all its modes. Creatively ignoring scholarly misgivings, the folkloresque foregrounds popular conceptions of folklore that reveal the changing significances people ascribe to it.

REFERENCES

Bird, S. Elizabeth. 2006. "Cultural Studies as Confluence: The Convergence of Folklore and Media Studies." In *Popular Culture Theory and Methodology: A Basic Introduction*, 344–55. Madison: University of Wisconsin Press.

Dean-Smith, Margaret. 1968. "The Pre-disposition to Folkery." *Folklore* 79(3): 161–75. http://dx.doi.org/10.1080/0015587X.1968.9716593.

Koven, Mikel J. 2003. "Folklore Studies and Popular Film and Television: A Necessary Critical Survey." *Journal of American Folklore* 116(460): 176–95. http://dx.doi.org/10.1353/jaf.2003.0027.

Koven, Mikel J. 2008. *Film, Folklore, and Urban Legends*. Lanham, MD: Scarecrow.

Miyazaki, Hayao. 2001. *Spirited Away*.

1

The Folkloresque Circle
Toward a Theory of Fuzzy Allusion

Michael Dylan Foster

> *Undoubtedly something was lost in the translation; watching the parade of wild things flutter, stomp*
> *and crawl though the bathhouse will make you wonder what each represents in Japanese mythology. (At*
> *one point it's as if every item in the Japanese Sanrio line of toys has come to life.) The cultural weight*
> *that the picture bears partly explains why this was the biggest hit ever in Japan, outpacing "Titanic."*
>
> —Elvis Mitchell, *New York Times*

IN 2001, STUDIO GHIBLI RELEASED A FILM CALLED *Sen to Chihiro no kami kakushi*, written and directed by master animator Miyazaki Hayao. It was a blockbuster hit, grossing more than any previous film in Japanese history. In 2002 a translated version was released by Disney with the title *Spirited Away* and it promptly won the Golden Bear at the 2002 Berlin International Film Festival and the Oscar for Best Animated Feature at the seventy-fifth Academy Awards in 2003. The critical and popular success of *Spirited Away* marks not only a watershed moment in the international recognition of the anime genre but also raises provocative questions about the relationship between folklore and popular culture. As the above quotation from the *New York Times* review of the film makes explicit, on this side of the Pacific *Spirited Away* was received as a glorious expression of an enigmatic folkloric tradition ("Japanese mythology") full of "cultural weight." At the same time, the parenthetical aside about Sanrio also suggests that Japanese "mythology" may be all but indistinguishable from (globalized) commercial culture.

It is not my intention here to completely unpack the dynamics of this film; rather, I want to use it as a springboard for contemplating the

DOI: 10.7330/9781607324188.c001

relationship between folklore and popular culture. In particular, I explore the folkloresque as a form of integration that provides insight into any number of popular cultural (and literary) texts. As suggested in the introduction of this volume, the folkloresque can be thought of as the popular, vernacular, folk conception of folklore. A folkloresque text draws on folklore in an often (but not always) conscious manner, using an association with folklore to sell itself, both literally and figuratively, within a commercial venue. Many popular culture products fit into this broad matrix, deploying folklore in a wide variety of ways. In this essay I examine one of these ways, specifically, how allusion to folkloric motifs, characters, and tale types can give a work the semblance of being based on "real" folklore even when there is no direct link with specific referents in a given tradition. Such works operate through a sort of elusive allusion, as it were, or what I call "fuzzy allusion."

This is the case with *Spirited Away*, and one reason for its critical and popular success both domestically and internationally. In order to flesh out these dynamics, I also briefly introduce the way folklore is used in a different Studio Ghibli film, *Heisei tanuki gassen pompoko* (1994), known in English as *Pom Poko*, which directly references beliefs, images, and narratives readily recognizable to most Japanese audiences. Comparing *Pom Poko* with *Spirited Away* provides insight into differences between direct reference to folklore in a creative narrative and the folkloresque operation of fuzzy allusion.[1]

It is hard to pin down in words the quality of *seeming* to be based on folklore that characterizes the folkloresque within popular culture; in the pages that follow I explore a number of metaphors for thinking through this problem. Finally, however, I argue that the very processes involved in the generation of both folklore and the folkloresque are deeply interrelated. While the two can be seen as distinct, they ultimately work in a Möbius strip–like fashion, so that today's folkloresque may become tomorrow's folklore, which in turn supplies the folkloresque of the day after tomorrow. However commercial a folkloresque product may be, it is created through allusion and integration in a process remarkably similar to that by which folklore itself emerges.

ANIMATING FOLKLORE

Animated film (*anime* in Japanese) is a particularly rich vehicle for representing folklore, in part because it allows for the portrayal of physical transformation in a more visually dynamic way than does live-action film or, for that matter, oral or written narrative (see Ortabasi 2013, 257–60). In 1988,

Studio Ghibli, the most internationally successful anime company, released a film called *Tonari no Totoro* (*My Neighbor Totoro*) that tapped into a folkloric nostalgia that would go on to inform many of director Miyazaki Hayao's later films—and which sets the stage for the discussion of the folkloresque that follows.

My Neighbor Totoro concerns a family that moves to the countryside, where the youngest daughter interacts with the natural world, most notably portrayed in the guise of Totoro, a gigantic and charmingly plump creature with perky ears. In many ways, Totoro has the hallmarks of a "traditional" Japanese spirit; it is intimated in the film that the creature is linked to the pristine natural environment and can be seen only by children, who are themselves innocent and pure. There is, as the *New Yorker* notes, "a gentle hint of Shintoism in all this" (Talbot 2005, 68). Indeed, with his portrayal of Totoro and other spirits, Miyazaki seems to reference Japanese folklore and religion, drawing on traditional animistic beliefs about the natural environment. But just as the nostalgic world created in *My Neighbor Totoro* only distantly references its setting in mid-twentieth-century Japan, so too the folkloric allusions connect only vaguely to the Japanese animistic world— nothing more than a "gentle hint." There is in fact no such creature as a totoro in Japanese folk belief; even the moniker *totoro* is likely derived from "troll" rather than from any direct referent within the Japanese countryside. *My Neighbor Totoro* is exemplary of a technique Miyazaki would continue to employ in his work, an emplacement of invented situations and characters into a nostalgically configured landscape and imagined folkloric habitus in a way that seems to "blend Japanese mythology with modern psychological realism" (Talbot 2005, 64–65).[2]

The film exemplifies one way in which folklore informs contemporary cultural production, the mode I call folkloresque integration. To better explore this mode and others, I propose a very simple typology, or rather a continuum with three focal points or touchstones, through which to categorize how popular cultural products employ folklore: (1) version or adaptation, (2) precise allusion (folklorism), and (3) fuzzy allusion (folkloresque integration). I suggest these points for heuristic purposes because they represent three distinct but related (and overlapping) modes through which folkloric materials and motifs are repurposed and remixed. I concentrate here on the latter two by comparing *Pom Poko* with *Spirited Away*. Although my examples are drawn specifically from film, the loose typology I set out in this essay pertains to all popular culture and literary productions that are informed by folklore.[3]

VERSION/ADAPTATION

First, there is the filmic version or cinematic adaptation of a folk narrative. Disney's 1950 production of *Cinderella* is an example of this, an explicit remediation of Charles Perrault's earlier literary version of ATU510A. We might argue that a filmic version fits a definition of folklorism that "assumes that modernity has extracted folklore from its 'original' state and placed it into a 'foreign' context" (Šmidchens 1999, 53).[4] Without confronting questions of "original" and "foreign" and "context," I stress only that we should consider this a (relatively) recent version of ATU510A because it demonstrates a recognizable consistency with earlier texts, both literary and oral, and in this case explicitly expresses allegiance to one (Perrault). Just as screenplays may be based on novels or short stories, so filmic renderings of folk narratives are adaptations for a different medium. Whether we call them remediations, retellings, or re-creations, the prefix "re" emphasizes the notion of again-ness: these narratives have, in some recognizably consistent way, been told before.

PRECISE ALLUSION (*POM POKO*)

Another node in this typology, one step removed from version/adaptation, is a form of creative usage of folklore I call *precise allusion*. This modality might be characterized as a form of folklorism/folklorismus in which "visually and aurally striking or aesthetically pleasing folk materials" are "extracted from their initial contexts and put to new uses for different, often larger audiences" (Bendix 1997, 337). In this case, theme, characters, plot, and other elements of a given folk narrative or belief system are used within an original storyline. Very recent examples include *Red Riding Hood* (2011), *Snow White and the Huntsman* (2012), and *Maleficent* (2014), all of which borrow motifs from tradition but use them in ways different from the tales they explicitly reference. These are original narratives, though the characters and their background are familiar. One pleasure of such films— indeed, the conceit around which many of them are based—is the excitement of seeing how familiar characters or plot twists are creatively reinterpreted in defamiliarizing ways. A common method for doing this is to show a well-worn tale from the perspective of either the antagonist or a minor character. *Maleficent*, for example, was recently described by one critic as "a divertingly different rethink of an awfully old story" (Dargis 2014). It is not the again-ness of these tellings that is primary here but rather the freshness of their construction: the originality of perspective and character, even as older motifs and tale types are explicitly referenced.

To better illustrate this form of folklorism, I focus on the 1994 Studio Ghibli production *Pom Poko*. Directed by Takahata Isao, the film follows a community of *tanuki*—"raccoon dogs" as they are labeled in English—mammals found throughout Japan and other parts of East Asia. Tanuki are real animals, but in Japan they have also long had a reputation as shape-shifting supernatural creatures. In folktales and legends they appear as fun-loving and mischievous (and occasionally murderous) tricksters. Among their distinguishing features is a set of gargantuan testicles they use to perform many of their transformations. Although it is difficult to generalize about any folkloric creature, the prevailing tanuki image since at least the middle of the Edo period (ca. 1600–1868) is of a somewhat bumbling, saké-swilling hedonist—at once a troublemaker and a symbol of fertility and fortune.[5]

Pom Poko takes this deep-seated cultural knowledge as a given for its viewers, and places its protagonists within the specific historical and economic context of the late 1960s, a period of rapid economic growth and (sub)urbanization. A group of tanuki is living in the Tama Hills on the outskirts of Tokyo, where humans are planning to build a new suburb. Desperate to protect their native home from the spread of human civilization, the older tanuki teach the magic of the old days to the younger tanuki so that together they can create illusions and roadblocks to stop construction. As metonyms of the disappearing natural environment, the tanuki invoke their traditional shape-shifting talents in a battle against humans that has a deep ecological and political subtext.[6]

The film is fictional, of course, but it takes place in real historical time in a real geographical setting. It also invokes "real" folklore: we watch the younger tanuki undertaking a kind of basic training in the tactics of shape shifting, learning to perform a range of transformations familiar from folktales and legends (and artwork based on these folktales and legends). Takahata also shows bumbling characters, able only to half transform, a direct reference to the widely distributed "Bunbuku chagama" (The Lucky Teapot) tale, in which a tanuki manages only to half sustain its transformation into a teapot. In one of the final scenes of *Pom Poko*, the tanuki collectively create a gigantic illusion of a parade of demons marching through the new human development; the animated imagery here replicates iconic images from a number of extant picture scrolls.[7]

All these references point directly to specific referents outside the film. They are precise allusions. A teapot with a head and tail sticking out is not a random expression of tanuki ineptitude but a reference to "The Lucky Teapot"—a reference most Japanese viewers (including children) would understand. In a sense, this is a form of folklorism in which identifiable characters, motifs, and narratives from a shared tradition are placed within a new medium and narrative; it is a "rewriting of premodern tanuki lore through sustained sourcing, transplantation, and transformation of familiar iconography" (Ortabasi 2013, 272). Takahata strategically deploys folklore in *Pom Poko* to make a political environmentalist critique of modern Japan. But even as the film reinterprets folklore, putting specific themes and motifs in original juxtaposition, it preserves (and draws on) the direct relationship of these references to the world outside the film: allusions are precise and identifiable. The film is not an adaptation or a new version but a creative "resituating" of folklore (de Caro and Jordan 2004).

In literary criticism, allusion has long been characterized as a rhetorical device by which an author makes reference to an earlier text. Gregory Machacek (2007, 525) argues that allusion, as a form of "diachronic intertextuality," can be divided into two distinct types: "phraseological appropriation" and "learned or indirect reference" (526). The first of these is a kind of quotational practice, an explicit and recognizable borrowing that "incorporate[s] a snippet of someone else's language into the flow of one's own" (525).[8] When a tanuki character in *Pom Poko* only half transforms into a teapot, this is a "phraseological appropriation" from "The Lucky Teapot" folktale: it is a precise allusion to an identifiable set of texts.

FUZZY ALLUSION (*SPIRITED AWAY*)

In comparison, the third touchstone on the continuum demonstrates what Machacek describes as "learned or indirect reference." I call this *fuzzy allusion*. When the source being referenced is folkloric, then the product is a folkloresque text characterized by a process of integration. The product of this process is not a version of a known narrative, nor a remediation, nor even a set of motifs presented in a new format or in unusual juxtaposition. Rather, it is a wholly new creation that is not based on a specific tradition but—and this is what makes it folkloresque—alludes to folkloric elements in a generalized and imprecise way. There is, as it were, an unmistakable odor (Iwabuchi 2002, 27). It smells of folklore, but we can't locate the particular sources of the odor. This is not to say there are no associated referents, but there are no direct correlations; indexical relations are lacking, or at least extremely vague.

I first conceived of the notion of the folkloresque in 2005 when I was asked to give a talk about the folklore in *Spirited Away*. I struggled fruitlessly to identify clear referents outside the text. And yet, even as I watched the film, something about it seemed familiar; I felt this story had been told before, that the motifs and even the plot itself were from some earlier version of something. Through a subtle incorporation and integration of elements from a number of folkloric traditions, the film projects an aura of "authenticity": it seems somehow *based on* folklore or *like* folklore. It is, in a word, folkloresque.

So what is going on here? How is this aura created? In this film (and others, such as *My Neighbor Totoro*) Miyazaki does in fact use folkloric motifs, but they are generally very small fragments from a range of traditions, not just Japanese. Most important, however, his allusions are rarely straightforward or identifiable: they are fuzzy, distorted, inexact. The deities and demons that inhabit his narrative, for example, do not denote "real" deities or demons (with names and histories and known qualities) but rather signify a vague notion of these deities or demons. My own language here, I realize, is also inexact, and that is because I am attempting to describe a very subtle—but critical—distinction. Let me try to flesh it out through the film itself.

Spirited Away opens with a family in a car: a mother and father and Chihiro, a ten-year-old girl. They are moving to a new home and Chihiro, apprehensive about changing schools, lies in the back seat sulking, clutching flowers from a friend. When they lose their way and the road comes to an end, the family exits the car and walks through a long tunnel, emerging on the other side into what looks like an abandoned theme park. Wandering through the deserted streets, they find a stand with some delicious-looking food. The parents begin gorging themselves while Chihiro looks on in disgust, refusing to eat. When twilight falls, her mother and father transform into pigs, and the streets come alive with a cacophony of gods and strange creatures.

To make a long story short, Chihiro finds herself trapped in this alien world. The only way she can help her parents become human again is to go to work at a bathhouse where the gods come to cleanse themselves. It is here that the story unfolds, exploring relationships between several main characters, including Chihiro, Yubāba, the witchlike owner of the bathhouse, her twin sister, Zenība, and Haku, a handsome dragon boy with whom Chihiro falls in love. Throughout the story, Chihiro is tested over and over again. She eventually succeeds in freeing her parents and returning to the human world a little older, a little wiser, and ready for a new life in a new home.

In a sense, of course, this is a classic coming-of-age tale in which the young heroine discovers her true identity. In fact, identity discovery plays out in a literal sense: early in the story Yubāba takes away part of Chihiro's name (one kanji character). By the end, Chihiro has not only rescued her parents but also recovered her full name. Structurally speaking, the film is a classic rite of passage, à la van Gennep, complete with symbolic and literal experiences of separation (preliminal), transition (liminal), and incorporation (postliminal). It is certainly no coincidence that the world Chihiro encounters is full of liminal spaces and times: bridges, tunnels, twilight. These border zones punctuate the geography of the narrative, from the long entrance tunnel to the iconic bridge Chihiro must cross to get to the bathhouse, an in-between space where much of the vital action of the film occurs.

The narrative is also structured around motif H900: "Tasks Assigned. A person's prowess is tested by assigning him certain tasks (usually impossible or extremely difficult) to be performed either to escape punishment or to receive a valuable reward" (Thompson 1955, 3:449). Indeed, the story is filled with motifs from the very beginning, such as "Tabu: eating in fairyland" (C211.1) and "Transformation: man to swine" (D136). This latter motif, of course, has particular resonance because of its fame in the Circe chapter of Homer's *Odyssey* (a narrative that also neatly parallels Chihiro's own quest to get "home").

Such "motif spotting" (Koven 2008, 3) makes clear that, intentionally or not, Miyazaki has integrated familiar elements into his tale. I want to stress, however, the generic nature of these elements. They are not from specific and identifiable Japanese folk narratives. The bridge, for example, is not an identifiable bridge from a known folktale or legend but just a "typical" Japanese-style bridge. It alludes to the semiotic significance of bridges as spaces of transition in Japanese folklore (which they are) and in much folklore around the world, but it does not signify a particular one of these bridges.

The patterns and motifs here can be found in any number of folkloric, literary, or filmic narratives, not limited to Japan. Saijō Tsutomu, for example, lists numerous similar "visits to the otherworld," everything from *Alice in Wonderland* and *The Wizard of Oz* to *Gilgamesh* and the famous Japanese tale "Urashima Tarō" (Saijō 2009, 10–18). His point is that the narrative structure of *Spirited Away* is exceedingly old and common and *therefore interesting* (12). There is no question, of course, that this narrative pattern resonates in any number of cultural contexts. But that is exactly my point: it is so widespread, so flexible in its parameters, and ultimately so open to interpretation as to be all but meaningless as a specific reference. At most we might say that the structure of the film reflects a worldview found in many cultures throughout the globe.

But beyond basic structure, what about characters and actions in *Spirited Away*? Noriko Reider has thoroughly unpacked numerous "covert and overt Japanese folk beliefs, imagery, and symbolism of the film as a text" (Reider 2005, 5). Without replicating her careful readings here, I would emphasize only that most of the examples she reveals are, in fact, "covert." She notes, for instance, that the deities appear "not necessarily in their traditional Japanese form" (11) and that "the 'original' images are evolutionary and not set in stone" (21). I agree that for Miyazaki "Japanese traditional design, rites, and tales are a rich source for the imagination" (9), but I would stress that with the folkloresque, "imagination" often trumps "source."

In other words, Miyazaki may allude to Japanese folklore, but there are no direct citations here. The title itself provides an example of this dynamic. *Sen to Chihiro no kamikakushi* literally means "the kamikakushi of Sen and Chihiro." The term *kamikakushi* refers to kidnapping by a god or, more literally, "hiding by a deity." Records of such supernatural abductions are found throughout Japanese history, especially during the Edo period. These events were most often attributed to the mischief of *tengu* mountain goblins. Details vary, of course, but in many cases a young boy (often it is a boy) suddenly disappears; his family searches frantically but to no avail, until he shows up some time later in a liminal place—in a tree, on a bridge, in the attic of a house—dazed but otherwise unharmed. Sometimes he recounts a story of being abducted by a stranger, often an older man, who takes him to distant places. Japan's most famous folklorist, Yanagita Kunio, tells of a kamikakushi event from 1907. A boy disappears during a festival in which villagers are making offerings of rice to the deities. When he is found in the attic of a house, he explains that an older man took him from house to house to feast on the food provided there, and indeed his mouth is covered with rice (Yanagita 1968, 77). As Carmen Blacker notes, after abductions of this sort, a child might become a seer noted for his wisdom or alternatively end up a "halfwit" or an "idiot" (Blacker 1967, 112).

At first glance Miyazaki's use of the term seems appropriate. Chihiro is a young girl who is abducted by deities and returns to the human world with esoteric knowledge. However, as Komatsu Kazuhiko notes, kamikakushi in the folkloric record are usually (though not always) attributed to tengu; in *Spirited Away*, there are no tengu—nor are there *kitsune* (foxes), *oni* (demons), or any of the other usual suspects for a kamikakushi event (Komatsu 1991, 91). Moreover, it is usually the child who disappears (and partakes of other-worldly food) while his parents desperately search for him. In *Spirited Away* the whole family is abducted, and ultimately it is the child who frees her parents (who have unwisely eaten in the otherworld). Of course, I am not accusing Miyazaki of using the term "incorrectly" but noting rather that through his open-ended invocation of the language of folklore he borrows its authority without limiting his narrative to a given set of precedents. It is exactly this loose interpretation of a specific term that adds to the depth and resonance of the title and furnishes it with a folkloric aura.

A similar example is the theme of cleansing and purity. The main setting of the narrative is a bathhouse of the gods, a multilevel structure where diverse deities from all over Japan come to cleanse themselves. Anybody familiar with Japanese culture will know that ritual cleanliness is associated with Shinto and folk religious practices. Moreover, Japan itself is dotted with natural hot spring spas (*onsen*) used for pleasure as well as medicinal purposes. And although public bathing facilities are increasingly rare, many Japanese communities still have them. In short, bathhouses and communal bathing practices have long been part of Japanese cultural life, and purification through ritual cleansing has played a role in Japanese religion since the earliest mythohistorical texts. It would seem logical that there might also be a tradition, perhaps a legend of some sort, in which deities travel to a sacred bathhouse resort for purification. To the best of my knowledge, however, such an explicit tradition does not exist. Again, then, Miyazaki taps into a worldview, creating resonance with broad patterns of belief but not citing specifics.[9]

Nor are the gods themselves clearly based on the deities of Japan. Kaonashi, or No-Face, for example, is one of the most striking characters in the film. An all but silent figure with a ravenous appetite, Kaonashi, shrouded in black, has a white, masklike face with unmoving black eyes and a mouth but no nose. Certainly Miyazaki was influenced by Japanese Noh drama; indeed, many Noh masks have a ghostly white sheen and an eerie stillness of expression. But despite this vague allusiveness, Kaonashi does not index a specific mask or character. Nor even, for that matter, does it reference Noh drama itself, other than this loose association with its visual aesthetics.

In the long tradition of *yōkai*, or monstrous spirits, there is also a figure called the *nopperabō*, notorious for its featureless face (Foster 2015, 208–10); unlike Kaonashi, however, the nopperabō does not appear as an eerily floating deity shrouded in black but rather as a normal person who is suddenly, startlingly, bereft of facial features. In short, Miyazaki's Kaonashi is striking because of its allusion to and creative amalgamation of several different possible referents and not because it replicates any single one of them. While gesturing to folkloric precedents, it avoids the specificity of tradition.

And a final example: the director of the bathhouse is an old woman named Yubāba. Reider argues persuasively that she is a "descendent" (Reider

2005, 4) of the famous Yamamba character of Japanese folklore; Yubāba's devotion to her strangely large and powerful son, Bō, is certainly reminiscent of the legendary Yamamba's association with motherhood and specifically the raising of the heroic warrior Kintarō (see 11–14). But again, the connection here is never explicit. Yubāba is neither actually called Yamamba nor clearly modeled on one of the many famous Yamamba images. And why is the son called Bō and not Kintarō? Again, my point is that Miyazaki is making a fuzzy allusion, tweaking the viewer's recognition but not making the connection explicit. There is certainly method in this obliqueness: to make the reference unambiguous would limit its semiotic breadth. In fact, Yubāba seems also to be influenced by other, non-Japanese traditions, most obviously (even in her name), the Russian figure of Baba Yaga. Miyazaki has cobbled together scattered fragments from a variety of traditions and invented a memorable new character.[10]

In their ambiguity these references contrast starkly with those in *Pom Poko*. The protagonists of *Pom Poko* are, as noted earlier, a specific species of animal known folklorically to possess certain traits, which are recorded in collected narratives. In the film these traits are explicitly referenced. And in contrast to Miyazaki's Kaonashi figure, *Pom Poko* even features a direct reference to a nopperabō, as the tanuki perform a nopperabō legend in their attempt to frighten away the humans. Other characters in the film, such as kitsune, also behave in accordance with their folkloric identities, appearing more wily and devious than their bumbling tanuki cousins.

It might be argued that by comparing *Pom Poko* with *Spirited Away* I am making a distinction only in terms of degree. At what point, one might ask, does the individual artistic voice overshadow traditional material? Certainly there is a continuum between these two modes of expression. But something more important is going on here. *Pom Poko* is a kind of historical fiction: true to its setting not only with regard to time period and location but also with regard to the folkloric character of its protagonists. *Spirited Away*, in contrast, leaves the constraints of historical time and place the moment Chihiro's family goes through the tunnel into the otherworld, creating a new space that is derived from folkloric patterns and motifs but is not restricted to a specific tradition and does not need to invoke outside, traceable referents. Inversely, it is exactly this ambiguity and untraceablity, the fact that you can almost but not quite figure out where Miyazaki came up with his ideas, that makes *Spirited Away* smell like folklore.

To be clear, the events and characters in *Spirited Away* are not *sui generis*. Miyazaki is indeed making allusions, but they are fuzzy allusions. In contrast to the precise allusion (or "phraseological appropriation") of *Pom Poko*, allusion in *Spirited Away* is, as Machacek would put it, "learned or indirect reference": subtly reliant on shared cultural understandings. Whereas recognizing a "phraseological appropriation" requires both author and reader to be acquainted with the same earlier text (e.g., "The Lucky Teapot"), a "learned or indirect reference" simply presumes a "shared body of knowledge with which poet and reader are acquainted" (Machacek 2007, 526).

I call this *fuzzy allusion* because it does not entail absolute identification of a source (by either the producer or the consumer). Like fuzzy logic in computer science and philosophy, the concept of fuzziness acknowledges the fact that there are infinite degrees between the two opposite points of a binary. A fuzzy allusion works not because it requires you to absolutely recognize or not recognize what is being referenced, but because it acknowledges the space between these absolutes. It allows something to *seem similar* to or *be almost like* something you have experienced before. Viewers watching the filmic Yubāba may be vaguely, perhaps unconsciously, reminded of the folkloric Yamamba without being able to articulate the connection. Similarly, the bathhouse setting makes sense to a viewer who cannot actually cite a single example from tradition of a bathing deity but nonetheless knows that purification and cleanliness are associated with Japanese indigenous religions. In short, fuzzy allusion does not require the reader/viewer/experiencer/consumer (or producer) to pinpoint the source but just to sense that there is one. If precise allusion is a direct quotation or paraphrasing, then fuzzy allusion simply invokes a phrase with a familiar ring to it.

COMMERCIAL ASSEMBLAGE

In the study of material folklore, "assemblage" describes the way an artist assembles items from the man-made world into a new and distinct creative work of "folk" art. The term has origins in the fine art world, where it refers to the combining of scraps or found objects into a single, often three-dimensional work. In folklore, assemblage has been invoked, for example, to describe holiday displays that "use the language of holiday and seasonal symbols to communicate deeper social meaning" (Santino 1992, 27; see also Santino 1986). Assemblage is, as Pravina Shukla (2008, 387) aptly puts it, a form of "creation out of culture" and can even describe the everyday act of dressing, as a person expresses individual identity through a distinctive combination of clothing and accessories. In many cases, folk assemblages reflect a vernacular application and adaptation of commercially produced elements, the creation of something unique and individual through combining mass-generated products. The result is greater than the sum of its

parts: a unified work that comments on or enhances the commercial elements of its construction and also says something about the vernacular
artist who created it.

With this in mind, I suggest that the folkloresque can involve the same
essential processes of assemblage, but with the vectors reversed: a commercial creator selects and sutures together diverse elements of folklore in
order to create a new mass-market product. That is, by assembling motifs,
narrative structures, character types, and so on, a producer crafts a new and
unique (although potentially mass-produced) product. This is a commercial
application and adaptation of vernacular elements, and it is exactly what
Miyazaki does in *Spirited Away*: the bits and pieces of folklore he incorporates are untraceable but allusive, and together they coalesce to form a
product that evokes folklore as essential to its own allure. The folkloresque,
then, is a form of commercial assemblage.

The particular form of folkloresque I am exploring here fits under the
label of *integration* because it integrates (incorporates, interweaves, assembles, combines) motifs, characters, and structures. Unlike a new version—
such as Disney's *Cinderella*—the folkloresque in the integration mode is less
a palimpsest than it is a pastiche of elements, a set of juxtapositions that
has never before existed but that, in the hands of a skilled artist such as
Miyazaki, makes sense. It is cobbled together in an all but seamless fashion
to become an *integrated* whole. The artistry here is important because a more
random, less nuanced suturing of elements would create a farce or a parody
or reek of "artificiality." Miyazaki manages to create something that is, for
many people, plausible as folklore.

DATABASING

Any kind of assemblage, including Miyazaki's, is intertextual, informed by
"the relational orientation of a text to other texts" (Bauman 2004, 4). In
characterizing the kind of intertextual operation performed by Miyazaki, it
is especially helpful to think of intertextuality in a broad semiotic sense, in
which any text is part of the larger cultural discourse. As Roland Barthes
puts it, "The quotations from which a text is constructed are anonymous,
irrecoverable, and yet *already read*" (Barthes 1979, 77). Such an understanding of intertextuality emphasizes an individual text's "participation in the
discursive space of a culture and its relation to the codes which are the
potential formalizations of that space" (Culler 1976, 1382). In Richard
Bauman's words, "Each act of textual production presupposes antecedent
texts and anticipates prospective ones" (Bauman 2004, 4).

With respect to intertextuality between popular cultural texts, Japanese critic Ōtsuka Eiji proposes a theory of "narrative consumption" (Ōtsuka 2001). "Comics or toys," he suggests, "are not consumed in and of themselves; rather, by virtue of the existence of an order behind these products or of a 'grand narrative' of which they comprise a portion, each begins to take on value" (quoted in Azuma 2009, 29). Consumers grasp the grand narrative lurking behind everything they consume and then "freely manufacture 'small narratives' with their own hands" (30). Ōtsuka's theory is not directed toward folklore per se but clearly alludes to folkloristic processes, from the notion of small narratives as fragments of a larger narrative to the active production of new products by fans and "consumers" within a particular folk group. More important, his broader point is simply that certain products succeed because they stimulate consumers' shared (though not necessarily conscious) understanding of the larger narrative (see also Ōtsuka 2001).

Cultural theorist Azuma Hiroki developed this idea into a theory of "database consumption," which emphasizes the nonnarrative aspect of contemporary consumption practices. He suggests that rather than a grand narrative out of which other products are created, there is instead a database containing settings, characters, and so on. Consumer-producers can pick and choose various elements from this database and assemble them to create "new" characters or settings (see Azuma 2009).[11] In this process of mixing and matching and multiple influences, of course, questions of origins ultimately become irrelevant. Such a grand database, in Jonathan Culler's words, would "include the anonymous discursive practices, codes whose origins are lost, which are the conditions of possibility of later texts" (Culler 1976, 1383).

A popular culture product such as *Spirited Away* metaphorically, if not literally, draws on a "cultural inventory," to invoke Trevor Blank's phrase in this volume, a database of elements that have proven durable and resonant—in this case because they are circulating within the folkloric imaginary. Through artful selecting and assembling, Miyazaki constructs a new product that resonates with viewers already familiar with its constituent elements. Just as commercial objects integrated into a folk assemblage create subtle hypertextual links to the contexts out of which they came (even an all but unrecognizable fragment of a Coke bottle still may invoke something about Coca-Cola and all that it stands for), so too the motifs integrated into the commercial assemblage that is *Spirited Away* allude (however fuzzily) to their folkloric predecessors. Miyazaki sutures together a range of appropriate elements archived in the "database" of Japanese and world folklore (and art and literature) to create a folklorically plausible tale and set of characters.

THE POWER OF ALLUSION

Throughout this essay, I have worked to find accurate language to describe this subtle process of integration and its effects on the consumer. Is this form of folkloresque a mode of borrowing, echoing, influencing, remediation, retelling, citation, adaptation, or sampling? All of this, of course, fits broadly within the rubric of intertextuality, but how do we describe the particular relationship between texts that creates the vague but potent form of referentiality of a folkloresque product? Ultimately, it is the notion of allusion, and the contrast between precise and fuzzy, that best characterizes, on a granular level, this type of intertextuality.

Although I focus on Miyazaki here, the dynamics of integration in the folkloresque inform all sorts of popular culture products and literature, such as the work of Lewis Carroll, L. Frank Baum, or Hans Christian Andersen. Neil R. Grobman explains that fantasy and science fiction authors, such as J.R.R. Tolkien and Robert A. Heinlein, often use "materials from mythology, legend, and history to give their novels a 'familiar feel'" (Grobman 1979, 282). What I want to stress here is not the traceability of allusions to such materials but rather how the "familiar feel" is created by their integration; as Grobman explains, Tolkien does not "draw on a specific body of lore" but rather works to "synthesize all of those sources and weave a masterpiece of fantasy" (287). With fuzzy allusion "we are," to quote Culler again, "faced with an infinite intertextuality where conventions and presuppositions cannot be traced to their source and thus positivistically identified" (Culler 1976, 1382). A folkloresque product—despite its genesis within a popular culture or commercial realm—can be understood in terms of what John Miles Foley calls "traditional referentiality," which "entails the invoking of a context that is enormously larger and more echoic than the text or work itself" (Foley 1991, 7).[12]

The process of folkloresque integration is by no means restricted to narrative genres: the same dynamic is found in explicitly capitalist endeavors such as, for example, the consciously "folksy" assemblages of restaurants like Cracker Barrel Old Country Store. Whereas the various objects—farming tools, old signs, washboards—displayed in these restaurants may have once served a practical everyday purpose, in the context of a strip mall restaurant, they signify an idealized, longed-for America of the past.[13] In Cracker Barrel, as in the films of Miyazaki, history becomes nostalgia. And if nostalgia can be thought of as a commercial construct of history, then the folkloresque is to folklore what nostalgia is to history. This is by no means a reason to dismiss the folkloresque as insignificant: just as nostalgia can open up a space for poignant reflection and commentary (see Cashman

2006; Foster 2009a), there is also the possibility of a critical folkloresque that can inspire meaningful social critique.

THE MÖBIUS STRIP OF CULTURE (FAKELORE REDUX)

My description of the folkloresque here may remind readers of *fakelore*, Richard Dorson's famous (now over sixty-year-old) neologism. Dorson's most notorious criticism was of Paul Bunyan lore, which he explains was created to fulfill American desires for a national folk hero: "A mass market existed and writers rushed to supply the need . . . Some writers knew better, some did not, but in either case the product they tendered was ersatz" (Dorson 1971, 9). But of course, this is exactly the sort of commercial assemblage of folk elements I characterize as folkloresque of the integration type. Dorson himself outlines the process: "These writers of folklore tailored their writings to their market. They followed the popular stereotypes of myths, legends, and folklore in the mind of the public" (9). By sharing the same cultural milieu and understanding the "mind of the public," the writers here were making fuzzy allusions, integrating "stereotypes" (characters, motifs, settings from the folkloric database) into their products. They were performing folklore for their readerships.

Ultimately, the processes involved in creating fakelore are the very same as those characterized here as the folkloresque, and in both cases the end product sounds an awful lot like "genuine" folklore, albeit usually generated with commercial objectives and profitability in mind.[14] But this raises some important questions. What if, for example, children growing up in Japan watch a film in which a woodland spirit called a totoro appears? Why should they not believe that this creature is as folklorically real as the deities worshipped at the local shrine, or for that matter the big-balled tanuki portrayed in *Pom Poko*? And after watching *Spirited Away*, why should they not think that there is a tradition of gods going to a bathhouse? To these children, such lore would be a shared part of a broader worldview and cultural archive. And what if these children pass on this lore to their own children, and so on? My point, of course, is simply that it is not farfetched to think of the folkloresque (or fakelore) of today as the folklore of tomorrow.[15]

There is a circular movement here. If there is something we can agree is "authentic" folklore, we can imagine that it can be broken apart into its constituent pieces, disassembled into atomic particles, as it were, and archived in a massive database. (In a sense, of course, this is what Stith Thompson did with folk narratives for his motif index.) Next, a famous writer or a commercial production company sifts through some of these motifs, many of which are almost unidentifiable fragments, and assembles them (perhaps following the contours of a famous tale type) to create a product for sale. The product is mass produced and made for commercial purposes but is constructed almost entirely of "folk" materials. It has the imprimatur of its constituent parts, an authority derived from the folklore out of which it was assembled.

This is a folkloresque product, but like all products—commercial or otherwise—the consumer can also exhibit (some) agency, and there is no reason a creative vernacular artist cannot disassemble and refashion the product itself. Or even if it remains intact, one might imagine that the commercial origins and intentions of the product will someday be forgotten (or ignored) and, "in the mind of the public," it will come to be considered "authentic" folklore . . . which in turn might someday be broken down into a different set of motifs to be reassembled and sold as a new product. And so on. In this circular process, there may be real, identifiable binary oppositions (folk versus commercial; handmade versus mass produced; folklore versus folkloresque), but when we trace them carefully, we find that, like a Möbius strip, the two sides are always also the same.

"CULTURAL WEIGHT" VERSUS "BIZARRE"

Just as there is a diachronic relationship between these sides of the Möbius strip, there is also a relationship across cultures whereby, for example, a product read in Japan as folkloresque may be interpreted by members of another culture as Japanese folklore. In other words, what happens when the folkloresque of one interpretive community is consumed within a different interpretive community? This kind of question, of course, applies to any translation—literary, cultural, or technical—and is certainly also an important issue when a non-Japanese audience watches a folkloresque Japanese anime.

Spirited Away was exceedingly successful on the global stage: it received critical acclaim and was an international moneymaker. *Pom Poko* did not fare so well. Although it was successful in Japan upon its release in 1994, it was not until 2005 that it was distributed worldwide (and then only as a DVD). This difference in reception has a lot to do with the distinction between fuzzy and precise allusion. Simply put, it is because the allusions in *Spirited Away* are fuzzy that the film evinces an aura of authenticity when translated into different cultural contexts; because the references do not point to specific folkloric traditions but to a range of abstract or generic motifs, they are recognizable as folklore to many non-Japanese viewers. The lack of specific references opens up Miyazaki's images and narrative to appreciation by audiences all around the world—no need for any background in Japanese folklore to get a sense of exoticness and, in the words of reviewer Elvis Mitchell (2002), "cultural weight." But at the same time, the film is entirely comprehensible; it does not require viewers to know the folklore, just to sense that there is folklore there.

In contrast, *Pom Poko* demands familiarity with specific folklore; it suffers from the depth and directness of its cultural allusions. These do not give it cultural weight but simply make it incomprehensible to the uninitiated. Skimming through a number of English-language reviews reveals that a common descriptor of the film is "bizarre." Even a reviewer from the *New Yorker* characterizes *Pom Poko* as "one of the most bizarre animated features ever made (even in Japan)" (Sragow 1999). It is not surprising, perhaps, that shape-shifting raccoon dogs with gigantic malleable scrotums might be described as bizarre, but of course in Japan tanuki (and their magical paraphernalia) are common knowledge. And indeed, as one online review pithily notes: "Here's a warning for those interested in watching this movie: unless you are well-versed in Japanese lore, folk tales and history, you will not get nearly as much out of this anime as director Takahata Isao intended. Not even close."[16] Susan Napier, who has written extensively on Japanese anime, explains that Takahata's films in general "are explicitly tied to Japanese settings and themes" and "could only have been made in a Japanese context" (Napier 2001, 491).

In other words, *Pom Poko*'s lack of international success can be attributed to the precision and faithfulness with which it references Japanese folklore, while *Spirited Away* achieved a more international appeal precisely because of the fuzziness of its allusions. Perhaps foreign audiences are particularly subject to the spell of fuzzy allusion: despite, or because of, the vagueness of its references, *Spirited Away* projects "cultural weight" in contexts far removed from Japan. Just as the folkloresque of today may be tomorrow's folklore, the folkloresque of one culture may be perceived as folklore in another.

THE FOLKLORIC CIRCLE

In the introduction to his motif index, Thompson explains that when he uses the term *motif*, "it is always in a very loose sense" (Thompson 1955, 1:19). As for his source material: "In general I have used any narrative, whether popular or literary, so long as it has formed a strong enough tradition to cause its frequent repetition" (1:11). If his language here is fuzzy, it is because the process of breaking down—of reverse engineering—a narrative or text of any sort is not only subjective but requires a certain amount of looseness and imprecision. And if the index attempts in this loose fashion to identify the generic parts of specific narrative engines, then it is easy to imagine a similarly fuzzy process performed in reverse, as an artist (or business) assembles different parts to create new engines. This is what the folkloresque does.

But the moment a folkloresque product achieves a certain cultural stability ("a strong enough tradition to cause its frequent repetition"), it, too, becomes a source of motifs. Indeed, if the folkloresque is constructed through fuzzy allusion, then folklore, with its different versions and variants and transmission across time and cultures, is also created through the same discursive process. Certain elements may remain comprehensible only within the folk group out of which they first emerged, but others, particularly those that are more abstract or less tied to specific places or people, will resonate beyond their local communities of production. They will travel, as it were, to be refashioned and reincorporated into new products. Components may be recombined in original ways, but the movement is cyclical and endless and nothing is ever made from scratch. Constrictive filters, such as copyright laws and plagiarism concerns, may affect different realms of cultural production, but the core processes ignore distinctions between vernacular and commercial culture, between folklore and folkloresque. The process of fuzzy allusion informs the dynamics of invention

Acknowledgments

I thank my good friend Ethan Segal of Michigan State University, who originally invited me to lecture on *Spirited Away* in 2005. His invitation set me off on the explorations that led eventually to this chapter. I also thank the audience at that talk for their perceptive questions and comments in response to my very inchoate presentation. And, as always, I am deeply grateful to my most perceptive and patient reader, Michiko Suzuki.

NOTES

1. I choose examples from Japan because Japanese folklore is my own field and also because Japan has a highly developed popular culture industry producing a dynamic array of material, print, filmic, and digital products, often distributed through so-called media mix strategies and frequently with reference to folklore and history. Moreover, focusing on products that received international distribution allows me to touch on the cross-cultural dimensions of the folkloresque.

2. The film received critical acclaim on its release but did not do well at the box office. In fact, it was not until several years later that Studio Ghibli began making money by licensing

stuffed-animal totoros (Talbot 2005, 72), a merchandising scheme exemplary of the folkloresque dynamic.

3. I am certainly not the first person to attempt to delineate the different ways folklore is used in film, literature, and popular culture. Important explorations include, but are not limited to, Bacchilega 1999, 2013; Benson 2008; de Caro and Jordan 2004; Grobman 1979; Greenhill and Matrix 2010; Greenhill and Rudy 2014; Koven 2003, 2008; Short 2015; Smith 2007; Sullivan 2001; Zipes 2010.

4. Šmidchens is characterizing Hermann Bausinger's early attempt to define the term. I want to acknowledge here and in subsequent references that folklorism (*folklorismus*) is a complex and nuanced concept. A brief discussion cannot do it justice; in fact, the groundbreaking theoretical work of Bausinger, Hans Moser, and other European scholars really set the stage for the discourse on the folkloresque we are exploring today. For more on the German discourse on folklorism, see, e.g., Bausinger 1990; Bendix 1988, 1997; Moser 1964.

5. For more on tanuki folklore, see Foster 2012, 2015, 186–93.

6. For a thoughtful discussion of *Pom Poko*, see Ortabasi 2013.

7. For an English translation of "The Lucky Teapot" tale from Nagano Prefecture, see Mayer 1984, 139–40. For more on monstrous picture scrolls, see Foster 2015, 45–46.

8. For an important discussion of allusion in literary folkloristics, see Dolby (2008, 10), who explains that "within an emic system of narrative performance, the allusion is assumed and relied upon as the fundamental stylistic convention supporting the narrative, its performance, and its reception."

9. Boyd and Nishimura (2004) also argue that "there are many folk and Shrine Shinto perspectives embedded in the cultural vocabulary of this film"; they particularly develop the ideas of purity and cleanliness. Again, although I don't disagree with this assessment, my point is that these are "perspectives," fuzzy references to a worldview and not direct citations of identifiable religious practices.

10. In an undergraduate folklore class I taught at Indiana University in 2014, a student gave a presentation on Baba Yaga in which she explained that the figure is not merely Russian and Slavic but is also found in Japan, where it is called Yubāba—and she showed a screenshot from *Spirited Away*. In a different context, this sort of folkloresque construction of character has been described by Jeffrey Tolbert as "reverse ostention," which "involves the creation of new objects, new disconnected examples of experience; and it involves the combination of these elements into a corpus of 'traditional' narratives, modeled on existing folklore (but not wholly indebted to any specific tradition)" (Tolbert 2013, 3).

11. Strictly speaking, Azuma's work concerns the consumption of certain forms of Japanese popular culture, such as anime and manga, during particular historical moments; he especially emphasizes the *nonnarrative* aspect of contemporary consumption practices. But his basic metaphor of the database can also be applied more broadly to folkloresque products, in Japan and elsewhere.

12. Although developed within the context of oral narrative theories, Foley's concepts of "traditional referentiality" and "immanent art" resonate productively with the notions of allusion discussed here. See Foley 1991.

13. The Cracker Barrel website, in fact, dedicates space to describing the care that goes into restoring these "artifacts," noting, "We like to think of every Cracker Barrel Old Country Store as a museum of Americana." "Restoration Step-by-Step," http://www.crackerbarrel.com/store/explore-our-decor/restoration-step-by-step/ (accessed June 16, 2015).

14. Commerce is not always the objective of the folkloresque; see, for example, Tolbert's discussion of the origins of the Slender Man legend (Tolbert 2013).

15. In fact, this movement of the folkloresque into accepted folklore can be seen with the *yōkai* (monsters, fantastic beings) (re)introduced into the late twentieth-century popular imagination by Mizuki Shigeru, particularly in his famous manga/anime series *Gegege no Kitarō*. See Foster 2009a; 2009b, 164–82; 2015, 61–65.

16. Otaku Center, January 19, 2011, http://www.otakucenter.com/showthread.php?6116 5-Heisei-Tanuki-Gassen-Ponpoko-An-Ichigosan-Review.

REFERENCES

Azuma, Hiroki. 2009. *Otaku: Japan's Database Animals*. Translated by Jonathan Abel and Shion Kono. Minneapolis: University of Minnesota Press.

Bacchilega, Cristina. 1999. *Postmodern Fairy Tales: Gender and Narrative Strategies*. Philadelphia: University of Pennsylvania Press.

Bacchilega, Cristina. 2013. *Fairy Tales Transformed? Twenty-First Century Adaptations and the Politics of Wonder*. Detroit: Wayne State University Press.

Barthes, Roland. 1979. "From Work to Text." In *Textual Strategies: Perspectives in Poststructuralist Criticism*, edited by Josue V. Harari, 73–81. Ithaca: Cornell University Press.

Bauman, Richard. 2004. *A World of Others' Words: Cross-Cultural Perspectives on Intertextuality*. Malden, MA: Blackwell. http://dx.doi.org/10.1002/9780470773895.

Bausinger, Hermann. 1990. *Folk Culture in a World of Technology*. Translated by Elke Dettmer. Bloomington: Indiana University Press.

Bendix, Regina. 1988. "Folklorism: The Challenge of a Concept." *International Folklore Review* 6:5–15.

Bendix, Regina. 1997. "Folklorismus/Folklorism." In *Folklore: An Encyclopedia of Beliefs, Customs, Tales, Music, and Art*, vol. 1, edited by Thomas A. Green, 337–39. Santa Barbara: ABC-CLIO.

Benson, Stephen, ed. 2008. *Contemporary Fiction and the Fairy Tale*. Detroit: Wayne State University Press.

Blacker, Carmen. 1967. "Supernatural Abductions in Japanese Folklore." *Asian Folklore Studies* 26(2): 111–48. http://dx.doi.org/10.2307/1177730.

Boyd, James W., and Tetsuya Nishimura. 2004. "Shinto Perspectives in Miyazaki's Anime Film *Spirited Away*." *Journal of Religion and Film* 8(2). http://www.unomaha.edu/jrf/Vol8No2/boydShinto.htm.

Cashman, Ray. 2006. "Critical Nostalgia and Material Culture in Northern Ireland." *Journal of American Folklore* 119(472): 137–60. http://dx.doi.org/10.1353/jaf.2006.0016.

Culler, Jonathan. 1976. "Presupposition and Intertextuality." *MLN* 91(6): 1380–96. http://dx.doi.org/10.2307/2907142.

Dargis, Manohla. 2014. "Dumped by Her Prince, So Watch Out." *New York Times*, May 29.

de Caro, Frank, and Rosan Augusta Jordan. 2004. *Re-situating Folklore: Folk Contexts and Twentieth-Century Literature and Art*. Knoxville: University of Tennessee Press.

Dolby, Sandra K. (Original work published 1989) 2008. *Literary Folkloristics and the Personal Narrative*. Bloomington: Trickster.

Dorson, Richard M. 1971. *American Folklore and the Historian*. Chicago: University of Chicago Press.

Foley, John Miles. 1991. *Immanent Art: From Structure to Meaning in Traditional Oral Epic*. Bloomington: Indiana University Press.

Foster, Michael Dylan. 2009a. "Haunted Travelogue: Hometowns, Ghost Towns, and Memories of War." *Mechademia* 4(1): 164–81. http://dx.doi.org/10.1353/mec.0.0026.

Foster, Michael Dylan. 2009b. *Pandemonium and Parade: Japanese Monsters and the Culture of Yōkai.* Berkeley: University of California Press.

Foster, Michael Dylan. 2012. "Haunting Modernity: Tanuki, Trains, and Transformation in Japan." *Asian Ethnology* 71(1): 3–29.

Foster, Michael Dylan. 2015. *The Book of Yōkai: Mysterious Creatures of Japanese Folklore.* Oakland: University of California Press.

Greenhill, Pauline, and Sidney Eve Matrix, eds. 2010. *Fairy Tale Films: Visions of Ambiguity.* Logan: Utah State University Press.

Greenhill, Pauline, and Jill Terry Rudy eds. 2014. *Channeling Wonder: Fairy Tales on Television.* Detroit: Wayne State University Press.

Grobman, Neil R. 1979. "A Schema for the Study of the Sources and Literary Simulations of Folkloric Phenomena." *Southern Folklore Quarterly* 43(1–2): 17–37.

Iwabuchi, Koichi. 2002. *Recentering Globalization: Popular Culture and Japanese Transnationalism.* Durham: Duke University Press. http://dx.doi.org/10.1215/9780822384083.

Komatsu Kazuhiko. 1991. *Kamikakushi: Ikai kara no izanai.* Tokyo: Kōbundō.

Koven, Mikel J. 2003. "Folklore Studies and Popular Film and Television: A Necessary Critical Survey." *Journal of American Folklore* 116(460): 176–95. http://dx.doi.org/10.1353/jaf.2003.0027.

Koven, Mikel J. 2008. *Film, Folklore and Urban Legends.* Lanham, MD: Scarecrow.

Machacek, Gregory. 2007. "Allusion." *PMLA* 122(2): 522–36. http://dx.doi.org/10.1632/pmla.2007.122.2.522.

Mayer, Fanny Hagin. 1984. *Ancient Tales in Modern Japan: An Anthology of Japanese Folk Tales.* Bloomington: Indiana University Press.

Mitchell, Elvis. 2002. "*Spirited Away* (2001) Film Review: Conjuring Up Atmosphere Only Anime Can Deliver." *New York Times*, September 20.

Moser, Hans. 1964. "Der Folklorismus als Forschungsproblem der Volkskunde." *Hessische Blätter für Volkskunde* 55:9–57.

Napier, Susan J. 2001. "Confronting Master Narratives: History as Vision in Miyazaki Hayao's Cinema of De-assurance." *Positions* 9(2): 467–93. http://dx.doi.org/10.1215/10679847-9-2-467.

Ortabasi, Melek. 2013. "(Re)animating Folklore: Raccoon Dogs, Foxes, and Other Supernatural Japanese Citizens in Takahata Isao's *Heisei tanuki gassen pompoko.*" *Marvels and Tales* 27(2): 254–75.

Ōtsuka Eiji. 2001. *Teihon monogatari shōhiron.* Tokyo: Kadokawa shoten.

Reider, Noriko T. 2005. "*Spirited Away*: Film of the Fantastic and Evolving Japanese Folk Symbols." *Film Criticism* 29(3): 4–27.

Saijō Tsutomu. 2009. *Sen to Chihiro no shinwagaku.* Tokyo: Shintensha.

Santino, Jack. 1986. "The Folk Assemblage of Autumn: Tradition and Creativity in Halloween Folk Art." In *Folk Art and Art Worlds*, edited by John Michael Vlach and Simon Bronner, 151–69. Ann Arbor: UMI Research Press.

Santino, Jack. 1992. "Yellow Ribbons and Seasonal Flags: The Folk Assemblage of War." *Journal of American Folklore* 105(415): 19–33. http://dx.doi.org/10.2307/541997.

Short, Sue. 2015. *Fairy Tale and Film: Old Tales with a New Spin.* New York: Palgrave Macmillan.

Shukla, Pravina. 2008. *The Grace of Four Moons: Dress, Adornment and the Art of the Body in Modern India.* Bloomington: Indiana University Press.

Šmidchens, Guntis. 1999. "Folklorism Revisited." *Journal of Folklore Research* 36(1): 51–70.

Smith, Kevin Paul. 2007. *The Postmodern Fairy Tale.* New York: Palgrave Macmillan. http://dx.doi.org/10.1057/9780230591707.

Sragow, Michael. 1999. "*Pompoko.*" *New Yorker*, September 20.

Sullivan, C. W. 2001. "Folklore and Fantastic Literature." *Western Folklore* 60(4): 279–96. http://dx.doi.org/10.2307/1500409.

Talbot, Margaret. 2005. "The Auteur of Anime: A Visit with the Elusive Genius Hayao Miyazaki." *New Yorker* (January 17): 64–75.

Thompson, Stith. 1955. *Motif-Index of Folk-Literature: A Classification of Narrative Elements in Folktales, Ballads, Myths, Fables, Mediaeval Romances, Exempla, Fabliaux, Jest-Books, and Local Legends.* 6 vols. Bloomington: Indiana University Press.

Tolbert, Jeffrey A. 2013. "'The Sort of Story That Has You Covering Your Mirrors': The Case of Slender Man." *Semiotic Review.* Issue 2: Monsters. http://www.semiotic review.com.

Yanagita Kunio. 1968. *Teihon Yanagita Kunio shū.* Vol. 4. Tokyo: Chikuma shobō.

Zipes, Jack. 2010. *The Enchanted Screen: A History of Fairy Tales on Film.* Clifton, NJ: Routledge.

2

Folklore, Intertextuality, and the Folkloresque in the Works of Neil Gaiman

Timothy H. Evans

THE MIXING OF OLDER VERNACULAR AND NEW INVENTED traditions in the arts is not, of course, a recent phenomenon. Examples from the nineteenth century include the use and imitation of folk music in the creation of nationalist symphonic music by Grieg and Dvořák (and others) and William Morris's medievalist designs for wallpaper and stained glass, expressions of the turn to handicrafts as part of a critique of industrial capitalism. In such enterprises, folklore has provided a sense of authenticity for its creator's art as well as their political agendas by linking these to a perceived or imagined folk community and to the history and traditions associated with such communities. Similar examples of the folkloresque have proliferated since the nineteenth century, albeit with changing goals and agendas.

The literature now labeled "fantasy" has, like much literature, a history of blending folk traditions with invented traditions. From the reworking of European epics and fairy tales by writers such as J.R.R. Tolkien or Angela Carter to the invented ethnographies of Philip K. Dick or Ursula K. Le Guin to the use of specific folkloric details to create setting or character by such authors as H. P. Lovecraft or Avram Davidson, the use and invention of folklore (that is, the folkloresque) in fantasy literature has a long and complex history. Folklore and the folkloresque may give writers sources of content, structure, texture, setting, characters, and many other elements, but they also provide authenticity, a sense of connection between an author's text and his or her evocation of tradition, which may imply a continuity with the past (e.g., William Morris's evocation of the medieval in *The Wood beyond the World* and his other prose romances) or with cultures with which

DOI: 10.7330/9781607324188.c002

the author feels a connection (i.e., the invented Native American culture of Ursula K. Le Guin's *Always Coming Home*). Such evocations of the authentic, when successful, give a literary work a sense of transcendent realness.[1]

My chapter will focus on the use of folklore and the creation of the folkloresque by British/American writer Neil Gaiman (born 1960). Folklore in Gaiman's fiction is a rather formidable topic because he is a prolific and complex postmodern writer who draws on folklore in almost everything he's published. Gaiman's use of folklore is both intertextual and transtextual, and it is absolutely central to his agenda as a storyteller. The ongoing references and allusions to folklore that characterize his work create a multiplicity of meanings out of the tensions between our common knowledge of these stories and the uses to which Gaiman puts them. Gaiman tells us that "tales of myth and horror are probably the easiest and most effective way to talk about the real world. It's like they are the lies that tell the truth about our lives" (Gaiman 1991a, iv).

As a writer, Gaiman is characterized by his versatility as to form and media (novels, short stories, poetry, comics, illustrated books, film, television, and odd forms such as fictional walking tours) and audience (adult, young adult, children). In addition, his work has a hybrid quality, moving back and forth between genres, often in a single work (fantasy, science fiction, horror, detective stories, literary fairy tales or myths, coming-of-age stories, surrealism, postmodernism), combining fragmented narratives from multiple points of view. His stories can be very complex—perhaps most notably the *Sandman* series of graphic novels—and the genre or audience of specific works is not always easy to categorize. His works are often episodic, somewhere between novels and interconnected short stories. This is especially true of his graphic novels but also characterizes several of his unillustrated novels, such as *American Gods*. Partly this comes out of his background as a writer of comics, which are usually published in installments.

Almost all his work can be characterized as intertextual: it is constructed out of a web of references derived from folklore, popular culture, literature, film, comics, visual arts, architecture, ethnography, travel writing, and other sources, even advertising. From these sources, Gaiman derives and utilizes a complex lexicon of titles and names, characters, settings, plots and fragments of plots, motifs, writing styles, moral and political messages, and cultural commentary.

Just listing all the folklore references in one major work of Gaiman's (*Sandman* or *American Gods*, for example) would in itself be a major undertaking (and is not the purpose of this essay). Throughout his career, folk narratives have been a constant source of material for Gaiman. Sometimes his works are recognizable albeit altered versions of traditional narratives (a film based on *Beowulf*, a graphic retelling of "Orpheus and Eurydice," a short story based on the Grimm Brothers' version of "Snow White" in which Snow White is a vampire). Sometimes, as in the novel *Stardust*, Gaiman writes original literary fairy tales that make use of many traditional motifs (although *Stardust* also draws on early twentieth-century fantasy writers such as Lord Dunsany and Hope Mirlees who, in their turn, also drew on traditional fairy-tale motifs). Sometimes he utilizes canonical works to explore the boundaries between folklore and literature (comics in which Shakespeare writes *A Midsummer Night's Dream* and *The Tempest* at the request of the Sandman). More often, elements of fairy tales, myths, and legends mix in his work with elements from other sources in complex, intertextual ways.[2]

The short story "Murder Mysteries" (Gaiman 2001c) tells a hard-boiled detective story within the larger Christian narrative of the revolt of Lucifer. "Chivalry" (Gaiman 2001b) is a about a nice old lady who finds the Holy Grail at a flea market. In the television series and novel *Neverwhere* (Gaiman 1996), all large cities have monstrous beasts lurking underground, to be challenged by the archetypal character Hunter. In London, the beast is the bull in the labyrinth from classical mythology; in New York City, it is a monstrous alligator in the sewers. Such figures as Titania and Oberon, Loki, Thor, and Odin, the three Fates, Cain and Abel, Lucifer, the Four Horsemen of the Apocalypse, the False Knight on the Road (Child ballad 3), Thomas the Rhymer, Baba Yaga, Iktomi, Anansi the Spider, Harun al-Rashid, and the Sandman (to name just a few) make appearances in his stories, not to mention numerous talking animals and generic characters from legends (and even real life), such as golems, ghosts, ghouls, and serial killers. Gaiman fills his narratives with a variety of references to other folklore genres that are often easy to miss because they go by quickly—songs, nursery rhymes, proverbs, riddles, folk beliefs.[3]

For example, in his novel *Stardust* (Gaiman 1998), the nursery rhyme "How many miles to Babylon" and John Donne's poem "Go and Catch a Falling Star" provide a kind of framework for the narrative. The contrast between the irony and cynicism of the Donne poem and the seeming innocence and unquestioning acceptance of magic in the nursery rhyme embodies a central conflict of the novel. Other stories are based around a sequence of tarot cards ("Fifteen Painted Cards from a Vampire Tarot") or the "Every Good Boy Deserves Favors" mnemonic rhyme (Gaiman 2006a, 2006b). Gaiman's work also contains a number of references to folk theatrical traditions, including Harlequin and Columbine and Punch and Judy—perhaps most notably, the graphic novel *The Tragical Comedy or Comical*

Tragedy of Mr. Punch (Gaiman 1995). References to folklore are inseparable from references not only to literature but to popular culture. Within
the same story, characters from European, Asian, African, Caribbean, or
Native American folktales or legends may interact with heroes from DC
Comics, figures from Christian, Norse, and ancient Egyptian mythology,
and characters from Shakespeare, Lewis Carroll, Arthur Conan Doyle, or
H. P. Lovecraft.[4]

Gaiman's goal, inasmuch as it can be summed up easily, is the pursuit
of human universals through intertextuality. Universals, for Gaiman, do not
reside exclusively in literary or fine art canons or in folklore, but must be
pursued, and re-created from, elements from throughout the world's cultures, genres, and art forms.

In his search for universals, Gaiman not only fills his texts with references but attempts to tell and retell archetypal hero quest stories. He does
this both by drawing on innumerable heroes from world mythology, folklore, literature, and popular culture and by casting ordinary-seeming characters into traditional heroic roles: the meek office workers who become,
essentially, fairy-tale characters in both *Neverwhere* and *Anansi Boys*, the ex-
con who is hired as a bodyguard by Wednesday (an American incarnation
of Odin) in *American Gods*, the conflicted adolescent boy who has to outwit
the troll under the bridge in the short story "Troll Bridge," only to confront
him again as a disillusioned, middle-aged man (Gaiman 2001e). Gaiman's
epic *Sandman* stories end with Sandman's Christlike (or Odinlike) sacrifice
of himself and rebirth.[5]

Gaiman's work is not only intertextual but transtextual: it exhibits, to
quote Gerard Genette, "that relationship of inclusion that links each text
to the various types of discourse it belongs to" (Genette 1992, 82). Gaiman
scholar Chris Dowd refers to this as "metafiction": fiction that emphasizes its
sources and recombinations of sources, its storytelling artifices (Dowd 2007).
It privileges story over storyteller. Clay Smith calls this "protofiction," referring to Gaiman's ability to control a wide range of textuality (Smith 2008, 1).

Gaiman is very self-conscious about his sources and about his place
in the history of the world's narrative traditions. One of the stated goals
of much of his work, including the *Sandman* books, adult novels such
as *American Gods* and *Anansi Boys*, and his many books for children and
young adults, is to educate readers about mythology, fairy tales, and other
forms of folk narrative, a topic about which most modern readers have
little knowledge, according to Gaiman. Gaiman stated in an interview,
"You gain a cultural underpinning to the last 2,500 or 3,000 years, which,
if you lack it, there's an awful lot of stuff that you simply never quite

understand" (*The Dreaming: The Neil Gaiman Page* 2004). He recasts old stories and characters in new cultural settings, but he also lets readers know where they came from.

This interaction of characters, narratives, and assorted folklore from a huge variety of sources is important in many of his novels, perhaps most notably *American Gods* (2001), Gaiman's "attempt to make sense of the country I was living in" after he moved to the United States in 1992. He wanted to write a novel that was American on many levels, including writing style: "I wanted to write *American Gods* in what I thought of as an American style—clean, simple, uncluttered" (Gaiman 2003, 596).

In broad terms, *American Gods* describes a battle of archetypes, pitting Old World gods who have immigrated to America—really they are American incarnations of Old World gods—against America's new gods. The novel begins with a quote from "A Theory for American Folklore," published in 1959 by the prominent mid-twentieth-century folklorist Richard Dorson: "One question that has always intrigued me is what happens to demonic beings when immigrants move from their homelands. Irish-Americans remember the fairies, Norwegian-Americans the *nisser*, Greek-Americans the *vrykólakas*, but only in relation to events remembered in the Old Country. When I once asked why such demons are not seen in America, my informants giggled confusedly and said, 'They're scared to pass the ocean, it's too far,' pointing out that Christ and the apostles never came to America" (Dorson 1971, 36).

A number of the chapter headings in this book borrow from B. A. Botkin's *Treasury of American Folklore* (1944), thus, perhaps unintentionally, bringing together the two great rivals of mid-twentieth-century American folkloristics. Many of the borrowings are uncredited in the novel itself; Gaiman acknowledges their source in his blog (Gaiman 2002). The old gods include Odin, Loki, Anansi, the Slavic god Czernobog, Eostre (Easter), Ibis, Thoth, Anubis, and Kali, several Native American gods or heroes including the Lakota hero Iktomi, and other folkloric figures that are not gods, such as djinns, leprechauns, dwarfs, and Johnny Appleseed. Gaiman's sources for these characters are various, owing as much to popular culture as to scholarly research; Czernobog, for example, is quite an obscure Slavic god—some scholars argue that he never was a god—who is better known for his appearance in the "Night on Bald Mountain" sequence of Disney's *Fantasia* and in several video games. Gaiman apparently derives his information on Johnny Appleseed from Richard Dorson's (1959) *American Folklore*.[6]

American Gods is also a kind of fantastic retelling of the American immigration story. The gods and supernatural beings do not travel on their own.

They are brought to America by immigrants who believe in them and, like the immigrants themselves, they develop distinctly American characteristics. The gods can exist only as long as humans believe in them; American gods exist only as long as Americans believe in them. Included in the book are a number of short stories or vignettes about coming to America, ranging from 14,000 BC to the present, in which immigrants from a variety of places bring their own gods, spirits, or supernatural beings to add to the mix. The protagonists of these stories range from Paleo-Indians to Vikings to English indentured servants to West African slaves to Irish families escaping the potato famine to a gay businessman from Oman residing in twenty-first-century New York City. They each bring with them supernatural belief systems as well as gods, djinns, leprechauns, fairies, and many other folkloric immigrants. Belief makes the supernatural beings real; when Americans tell their stories to one another, their realities are shared with others. "Nobody's American," says Wednesday, "not originally" (Gaiman 2011, 96). The reality of America is made up of the totality of all the stories, all the beliefs, all the gods, no matter how recently they have come to America. The novel's protagonist, Shadow, is continually told to "believe everything" (17).

Along the way, Gaiman gives us close descriptions of a great many other folklore genres, including (but not limited to) proverbs, Wellerisms, jokes and urban legends, sexual folklore, hoodoo beliefs, a variety of foodways, traditional confidence tricks such as the fiddle game, coin tricks and other kinds of stage magic. He does not neglect regional folklore. Much of the novel is set in the upper Midwest (Wisconsin and Michigan): he gives us regional foodways such as pasties (described in some detail) and the texts of a number of upper midwestern tall tales, many of them derived from Richard Dorson's 1952 *Bloodstoppers and Bearwalkers: Folk Traditions of the Upper Peninsula.* Many of the tales are put in the mouth of Richie Hinzelman, a local character and storyteller in the town of Lakeside, Wisconsin. Lakeside is presented as an idyllic, unchanging small town with a real sense of community that displays the continuity of "rural virtue"—an atmosphere made possible by the fact that the town has been enchanted by annual human sacrifices carried out by Hinzelman, who is actually a kobold. Kobolds (immigrants from Germany, now better known as characters in Dungeons & Dragons) are spirits associated with specific places and therefore particularly threatened by the forces of globalization (that is, the new gods).

Such folkloric details give an American character to all of the Old World gods and supernatural beings. The old gods eat American food, tell American jokes and urban legends, argue over Paul Bunyan, tell American tall tales, and perform coin tricks. Wednesday/Odin, for example, is a master of traditional American grifts, several of which, including the "fiddle game" and the "bishop game," he describes to Shadow in some detail (Gaiman 2011, 208–14). Wednesday is also a frequent source of proverbs and Wellerisms (301) and an enthusiast for American regional cuisine. Such details provide texture and authenticity to the sense of place and community that is associated with an older idea of America, an America of both immigrant communities and idyllic farm communities in the Midwest, of ethnicity and place, an image of America that seems to be in opposition to the new gods.

The new gods include the gods of technology, the credit card, the freeway, the Internet, telephone, radio, television, plastic, and neon. The battle is, of course, symbolic—Gaiman isn't maintaining (even as a fictional premise) that any significant numbers of Americans worship Odin or Anubis but rather describing a conflict between old cosmologies and old stories and an emerging globalizing, postmodern world—in other words, a conflict between an older world of face-to-face communities and a new, emerging world wherein communication is largely electronic, and communities are bound not by oral tradition or by old archetypes but by mass media, the Internet, and consumerism. The god of television, manifesting herself to the novel's hero, Shadow, as Lucy Ricardo (from *I Love Lucy*), makes the case for her side: "We are the coming thing. We're shopping malls—your friends are crappy roadside attractions. Hell, we're online malls, while your friends are sitting by the side of the highway selling homegrown produce from a cart" (Gaiman 2011, 156). The old gods, by contrast, are defenders of small towns and small businesses: the Egyptian gods Ibis and Jacquel, proprietors of "a small, family-owned funeral home," are locked in an ongoing battle with chain companies that are taking over the industry (171).

In *American Gods*, American culture is not presented merely as a collection of stories and discrete folklore forms that represent immigration, ethnicity, or region. The work is a road novel, a genre that Gaiman sees as a characteristic, perhaps archetypal, American narrative form. It presents an America in constant motion, an America where communities and identities are fluid. Much of the novel comments on the culture of the American road: it is full of diners, fast-food chains, convenience stores, yard art, small towns that are passed through so quickly that the only memory they leave are signs that say things like "Home of the runner up to the state under-12s speed skating championship" (Gaiman 2011, 144). Everything is shaped by what might be called an older, tackier American vernacular culture, with a crucial scene taking place in the House on the Rock at Spring Green, Wisconsin, and the final battle of the gods playing out in the iconic tourist site of Rock City, Georgia, near Chattanooga. Both places are described in some detail, with the eye of an ethnographer, albeit a somewhat fanciful one. While such roadside attractions are distinct places, they are made up of the detritus of other places—House on the Rock is filled with collections of roadside advertisements, mechanical musical instruments, toys, dolls, antiques, and hundreds of other examples of "Americana." Like Gaiman's stories, such places are made up of elements from all over: from folk culture and popular culture, from the past and the present, from the handmade and the commercial. They are fragmentary and postmodern. They are not places where we settle down or would want to settle down. They are places that we visit on our way from one place to another; they are not our destination.

The culture of roadside attractions and of the road more generally is presented not as opposed to the culture of ethnic- or place-based groups but as inexorably tied to such groups in a larger American identity; it is here that Gaiman's representation of American culture becomes ambiguous. Workers in the folkloresque inevitably are faced with issues of authenticity, and Gaiman tackles this head-on. Gaiman considers the accuracy of his references a "point of honor": the history is "good history," "the mythology is good, accurate mythology" (*The Dreaming: The Neil Gaiman Page* 2004). Citing Richard Dorson, he warns in his blog that writers should be careful to distinguish between actual folklore and commercially produced "fake-lore" (Gaiman 2005b). Things are not that simple in his fiction, however. In *American Gods*, Gaiman puts Dorson's warnings about fakelore into the mouth of Johnny Appleseed. Appleseed compares the inauthenticity of Paul Bunyan to putting out NutraSweet for hummingbirds. "The birds come to the feeders and they drink it. Then they die, because their food contains no calories even though their little tummies are full. That's Paul Bunyan for you. Nobody ever believed in Paul Bunyan. He came staggering out of a New York ad agency in 1910 and filled the nation's myth stomach with empty calories." To which Appleseed's friend Whiskey Jack (a variant of the Lakota hero Iktomi) replies, "I like Paul Bunyan. I went on his ride at the Mall of America, a few years back. You see big old Paul Bunyan at the top, then you come crashing down. Splash! He's okay by me" (Gaiman 2011, 309–10). Whether Bunyan's association with the Mall of America makes him an ally of the new gods and therefore an enemy of the old gods is not made clear. But it seems throughout most of the novel that malls, chain stores, mass media, and multinational corporations are the villains.

This playful debate about authenticity—a commentary on the text that is also part of the text—is, to Gaiman, a way to deepen the transtextual quality of his work: the acknowledgment that some texts may be judged more authentic than others, but also that this judgment is contested. Although he advocates the use of "accurate mythology," this seems to refer to the explicit use of old, traditional stories (legends, folktales, myths, and so on) taken from scholarly sources, to the acknowledgment of these sources, and to the acknowledgment of issues of authenticity associated with them. Questions of authenticity become simply another element in Gaiman's intertextuality, in his web of references, in his process of fabrication. It is okay to bring Paul Bunyan into the story (although in *American* Gods he is a topic for discussion, not a character), but his sources and controversies must also be brought in.

The ambiguous status of Paul Bunyan is a precursor to the novel's ambiguous ending. The dichotomy between the old and new gods seems less clear as the novel moves toward its conclusion. The climactic battle between the old and new gods, to which the novel seems to be leading, never takes place: instead, Wednesday/Odin and "Low Key" Lyesmith (the American incarnation of Loki, the leader of the new gods) are revealed by Shadow to be con artists who are trying to create a sacrifice of blood and chaos to increase their own power. The battle is called off. Shadow tells the assembled old and new gods, "This is a bad land for gods . . . The old gods are ignored. The new gods are as quickly taken up as they are abandoned, cast aside for the next big thing" (Gaiman 2011, 478). The moral dichotomy between old and new was a scam; it begins to appear that the old and new gods aren't really that different. Oral tradition and electronic media are not opposed, they are simply different media for telling stories, for communicating traditions. Both kinds of gods demand sacrifices. Old gods such as Czernobog and Wednesday demand blood sacrifice, even human sacrifice (63, 76, 479). New gods also demand sacrifice: the god of television (in the form of Lucy Ricardo) tells Shadow:

> "The TV's the altar. I'm what people are sacrificing to."
> "What do they sacrifice?" asked Shadow.
> "Their time, mostly," said Lucy. "Sometimes each other." (155)

What characterizes American culture, Gaiman is telling us, is not the battle between old and new gods—that is a false dichotomy—but rather the battle between the multiplicity of voices and the fast-paced, mobile, and transitory nature of American culture. The former is represented by the "Coming to America" stories; the latter by the power of roadside attractions. Wednesday tells Shadow that roadside attractions such as House on the Rock and Rock City are "places of power."

"It's perfectly simple," said Wednesday, "In other countries, over the years, people recognized the places of power. Sometimes it would be a natural formation, sometimes it would be a place that was, somehow, special . . . And so they would build temples, or cathedrals, or erect stone circles . . ."

"There are churches all across the States, though," said Shadow.

"In every town. Sometimes on every block. And about as significant, in this context, as dentists' offices. No, in the USA, people still get the call . . . and they respond to it by building a model out of beer bottles . . . or erecting a gigantic bat-house . . . Roadside attractions: people feel themselves being pulled to places where, in other parts of the world, they would recognize that part of themselves that is truly transcendent, and buy a hot dog and walk around." (Gaiman 2011, 106)

It is all storytelling, no matter the source or the media. This is explicitly stated by Jesus in a conversation with Shadow:

"And then this whole deal of new gods, old gods," said his friend. You ask me, I welcome new gods . . . Have you thought about what it means to be a god? . . . It means you give up your mortal existence to become a meme: something that lives forever in people's minds, like the tune of a nursery rhyme. It means that everyone gets to recreate you in their own minds. You barely have your own identity any more. Instead, you're a thousand aspects of what people need you to be. And everyone wants something different from you. Nothing is fixed, nothing is stable." (Gaiman 2011, 528)[7]

Thus, all cultural forms exhibit the limitless variability of folklore.

In a way, the multiplicity of media for which Gaiman writes—books, comics, television, film, blogs, and so on—is a macrocosm of this world of interlocked narratives found in *American Gods*. The intertextuality and transtextuality of *American Gods* are processes that define the folkloresque as it works in Gaiman's fiction: a complex interweaving of folklore, invented "folklore," popular culture, fine arts, and other sources in an attempt to create a new, invented folklore for the digital age. This process of the folkloresque is an extension of what Dell Hymes called "traditionalizing": the idea that tradition is not a static body of knowledge but rather a process in which all humans continually participate in a quest to find, and create, meaning (Hymes 1975). It extends not only to the author (Gaiman), the illustrators, and the readers; it also extends to the characters. Many of Gaiman's characters, including Sandman in the *Sandman* graphic novels, Tristran in *Stardust*, Wednesday/Odin in *American Gods*, and Mr. Nancy/Anansi in *American Gods* and *Anansi Boys*, seem to be very self-conscious about the stories they tell, take part in, and manipulate (Brown 2010, 219).

The transtextual quality of *American Gods* is present throughout Gaiman's work and is central in his creation of the folkloresque: the citing of texts to create the impression of authenticity. One way this is done is by Gaiman's very frequent use of quotations at the beginnings of books and chapters: these are frequently from folkloristic or folkloresque sources. In *American Gods*, folkloristic examples include academic statements by several scholars of mythology and folklore as well as proverbs, song lyrics, and other folklore texts taken from collections edited by Richard Dorson and B. A. Botkin. Examples of the folkloresque include proverbs from Benjamin Franklin. Gaiman also uses quotes of his own invention, attributed to fictional characters.

Another way that Gaiman uses transtextuality to create the folkloresque is to provide a scholarly apparatus leading his readers to other sources. Gaiman frequently cites his sources, either in introductions or appendixes to his stories, or in his blog, which often has quite detailed explanations of the sources not only of stories and characters but of details such as names, settings, physical props including weapons and magical devices, and other items that Gaiman brings into his stories, such as riddles or proverbs. He does not cite the latest in academic folklore scholarship, but he has a good "layman's" knowledge of older sources (mostly collections) of folk narratives; he cites, among others, J. G. Frazer, Andrew Lang, Robert Graves, Roger Lancelyn Green, Katherine Briggs, B. A. Botkin, Richard Dorson, Ake Hultkranz, Vine Deloria, Jan Brunvand, Roger Abrahams, Mary and Herbert Knapp, and many old collections of folktales and legends. Richard Dorson's work, which Gaiman seems to have read quite extensively, is acknowledged as a primary source and inspiration for *American Gods* (Gaiman 1993a, 3; Gaiman 2002).

Gaiman has also been known to invent citations; for example, the afterword to his graphic novel *The Dream Hunters* cites several texts as sources of his "retelling" of the story. He even tells his readers which versions of the legend influenced different parts of his book and describes the physical appearance of one source, the Reverend B. W. Ashton's *Fairy Tales of Old Japan*. His description of his sources is worth quoting at some length. One version

> is from Y. T. Ozoki's collections of Japanese tales: a strange version in which the King of Dreams is a shadowy figure, barely mentioned . . . and in which the central character is the *Onmyoji*, the Master of Yin-Yang . . . They also found me a Buddhist text in which the tale is alluded to . . . For the rest, I am indebted to the good reverend. As I write this I have my copy of *Fairy Stories of Old Japan* on the table in front of me. The leather binding is flaking and discoloured, the pages are ragged, spotted, and slightly water-stained. (Gaiman 1999, 128)

He goes on for several paragraphs about how he combined and rear-ranged his sources. Later, however, he admitted that these books do not exist (Callahan 2012). This mixing of real and invented folklore, and the invention of citations for the latter as a kind of hoax, characterizes other writers of the fantastic including H. P. Lovecraft, Jorge Luis Borges, and Italo Calvino (to name just three). It creates an illusion of authenticity, ambiguity as to whether the author is really trying to fool us or not, and a kind of game or puzzle for the reader to solve. Hoaxes also may be part of the process of the folkloresque.

A more elaborate example of this is *A Walking Tour of the Shambles*, a collaboration with the writer Gene Wolfe. This short book is a walking tour of a fictional Chicago neighborhood, complete with architectural descriptions, histories of buildings and streets, local legends, and guides to parks, museums, shops, bed-and-breakfasts, restaurants, and bars. The appendixes include "Further Questions," recipes from the restaurants, and an annotated bibliography. There is even a webpage guide to a museum (an actual webpage, that is, not just a reference to one). The entire work is fictional. More obviously tongue-in-cheek than the fictional references in other Gaiman works, *Walking Tour* hovers between parody and hoax (Gaiman and Wolfe 2009).

A consideration of the folkloresque in the work of Neil Gaiman would be incomplete without a discussion of his use of visuals and his relation-ship to visual artists. Since much of his work has taken the form of com-ics, graphic novels, illustrated novels, or children's picture books, in which Gaiman closely collaborates with illustrators, Gaiman's texts often have a peritextual quality (Genette 1997, 8): that is, they cannot be separated from, or understood without, accompanying visuals. Gaiman's relationship with visuality goes beyond comics or illustrated books, however. In his films and television shows (including the films *Mirrormask* and *Beowulf* and the mini-series *Neverwhere*), text is inseparable not only from visuals but from action, motion, and sound.

Gaiman has worked with a great many visual artists in his career, art-ists with a wide variety of styles. In general, the text comes first: these art-ists illustrated Gaiman's texts rather than Gaiman writing the texts for the artists' illustrations. But, as he has said a number of times in interviews, he writes in ways that play to their styles, that "play to their strengths and minimize their weaknesses" (McCabe 2004, 7). It is notable, how-ever, that a number of Gaiman's collaborators, including Charles Vess (illustrator of *Stardust* and many of the *Sandman* stories), and Yoshitaka Amano (illustrator of *The Dream Hunters*), draw quite noticeably on classic, influential, and iconic nineteenth- and early twentieth-century illustrators of fairy tales such as Arthur Rackham, Edmund Dulac, and Kay Nielson (97–103). Kelley Jones, another frequent visual collaborator, cites Gustave Doré and Aubrey Beardsley (Smith 2008, 2). Gaiman and his collaborators are thus using their readers' knowledge not only of the folklore and literary texts on which he is drawing but of illustrations associated with those texts. However, just as Gaiman's texts combine writing styles and materials from a huge variety of sources, his visual collaborators work not only in the styles of such "classic" illustrators but also, for example, in the style of twentieth-century American superhero comics, another source of familiar iconic images.

Stardust and *The Dream Hunter* are possible to follow without illustrations, unlike Gaiman's *Sandman* stories, which are collaborative to the point that neither text nor illustrations alone would be easily comprehensible. Here, Gaiman and his collaborators are taking the literary use of folklore into a peritextual realm in which text and visuals cannot be separated. The visual styles of the ten volumes of the *Sandman* series can only be described as diverse, although many of them do reflect the influence of older, classic fairy-tale illustrators or of other traditional forms of visual storytelling—for example, the style of comic artist Mark Hempel, which resembles stained glass windows (McCabe 2004, 151–58). But no matter how traditional or innovative the visual styles may be, the *Sandman* series, like most of Gaiman's work, uses a variety of media to retell folk narratives to contemporary readers.

The authoritative intertextuality and transtextuality of Gaiman's cultural references thus extend to visuals and to the relationship between texts and visuals: not only familiar narratives from fairy tales or myths but familiar illustrations for those narratives, not only familiar superheroes but familiar comic book images of superheroes. Gaiman's iconography not only bridges textuality and visuality but also bridges folklore and popular culture: Thor is not only a Norse god but also a comic book superhero, Czernobog is not only a Slavic god but a character from *Fantasia*, kobolds are not only supernatural beings from Germanic folklore but monsters in Dungeons & Dragons. This bricolage blending of sources exemplifies the folkloresque.

Cultural critics such as Henry Jenkins (2008) write about the convergence of media in contemporary culture; as different forms of oral communication, written media, mass media, and electronic media are combined in very complicated ways, everyone multitasks between media, and our texts are increasingly multisensual and interactive. The use of folklore in literature (and comics and film) inevitably follows this path of convergence as it becomes ever more difficult to categorize media forms into separate realms such as oral, mass, and electronic media; folk, popular, and elite culture; text and commentary; or entertainment and scholarship. Gaiman's work embraces these trends but, to draw an analogy with roots music, he is attempting to create a kind of roots literature (although literature is too narrow a word) that puts folklore—whether ancient or modern—at the center of contemporary culture. He also places the study of folklore at the center of contemporary culture, in the sense that he includes sources and commentary as part of his text and creatively manipulates these as much as he does any other part of the work.

If Gaiman is using the inherent intertextuality of media convergence to foreground folklore, he is also doing the reverse, using folklore to foreground the intertextuality of media convergence. Gaiman's ambitious enterprise is to make folklore (and the study and discussion of folklore) the structural framework for a literature that transcends nation, genre, and media forms in a way that highlights universal human stories—on whatever pathways the technologies of communication may lead us.

NOTES

1. Amanda Hodgson's (2011) *Romances of William Morris* is an excellent recent study of Morris's medieval sources and their reworking; Jane Chance's (2008) edited collection *Tolkien the Medievalist* is one of several recent works that explore similar issues in Tolkien, for Angela Carter's reworkings of fairy tales, see Bacchilega and Roemer 2001; for Dick, see Evans 2010; for Lovecraft, Evans 2005. Le Guin's (1985) *Always Coming Home* is a fictional ethnography of the Kesh, who live in an alternative northern California. Davidson, an amateur folklorist, frequently reworked folklore of various kinds, especially Jewish folklore, in his novels and short stories. See also Sullivan 2001.

2. For *Beowulf*, see Gaiman and Avary 2007; for "Orpheus and Eurydice," Gaiman 1993b; for "Snow White," Gaiman 2001d; for *A Midsummer Night's Dream*, Gaiman 1991b; for *The Tempest*, Gaiman 1997.

3. For Titania and Oberon, see Gaiman 1991b; for Loki, Odin, and Iktomi, Gaiman 2011; for Thor, Gaiman 1992; for the three Fates, many Gaiman works, including Gaiman 2011 and most of the *Sandman* books; for Lucifer, Gaiman 1991c; Cain and Abel are regular characters in the *Sandman* books; for the Four Horsemen of the Apocalypse, Pratchett and Gaiman 1990; for the false knight on the road, Gaiman 2004; for Thomas the Rhymer and Baba Yaga, Gaiman 2001a; for Anansi, Gaiman 2005a and 2011; for Harun al-Rashid, Gaiman 1993b.

4. Gaiman retells *A Midsummer Nights Dream* (Gaiman 1991b) and *The Tempest* (Gaiman 1997); Shakespeare himself is a recurrent character in *The Sandman*; for Doyle and Lovecraft, see Gaiman 2006c.

5. Several scholars have commented on the importance of hero quests in Gaiman's work, often drawing on Joseph Campbell, although Gaiman has denied being influenced

by Campbell; a good example is Rawlik 2007. Gaiman made his comments on Campbell as respondent in the session "Teaching Neil Gaiman" (chaired by the author) at the International Conference on the Fantastic in the Arts, March 2013 (Gaiman 2013).

6. Gaiman on Dorson: "Dorson's work is where the book's opening quote comes from, and was one of the places that *American Gods* as a whole came from. I'm a writer with an interest in myth, so to understand something I try and understand its folklore, and, over a span of several years, I picked up each of the Dorson titles, read it, learned from it, enjoyed it enormously—and failed to realise until John M. Ford said something about Dorson, that the same man had written all the books I had enjoyed so much and learned so much from. Vigorous, sensible, informative. When I read his account of John Chapman—Johnny Appleseed—I knew that I wanted to put that character in a book one day" (Gaiman 2002).

7. Shadow's conversation with Jesus was edited out of the first edition of *American Gods* but included as an appendix in the "author's preferred text" edition in 2011.

REFERENCES

Bacchilega, Cristina, and Danielle Roemer. 2001. *Angela Carter and the Fairy Tale*. Detroit: Wayne State University Press.

Botkin, B. A. 1944. *A Treasury of American Folklore*. New York: Crown.

Brown, Paula. 2010. "*Stardust* as Allegorical *Bildungsroman*: An Apology for Platonic Idealism." *Extrapolation* 51(2): 216–34. http://dx.doi.org/10.3828/extr.2010.51.2.3.

Callahan, Tim. 2012. "*The Sandman* Reread: *The Dream Hunter*." *Tor.com*. http://www.tor.com/2013/04/17/sandman-reread-the-dream-hunters/.

Chance, Jane, ed. 2008. *Tolkien the Medievalist*. New York: Routledge.

Dorson, Richard M. 1952. *Bloodstoppers and Bearwalkers: Folk Traditions of the Upper Peninsula*. Cambridge, MA: Harvard University Press.

Dorson, Richard M. 1959. *American Folklore*. Chicago: University of Chicago Press.

Dorson, Richard M. (Original work published 1959) 1971. "A Theory for American Folklore." In *American Folklore and the Historian*, by Richard M. Dorson, 15–48. Chicago: University of Chicago Press.

Dowd, Chris. 2007. "An Autopsy of Storytelling: Metafiction and Neil Gaiman." In *The Neil Gaiman Reader*, edited by Darrell Schweiter, 103–20. Rockville: Wildside.

The Dreaming: The Neil Gaiman Page. 2004. "Biographies." http://thedreaming.joefulgham.com/2003/04/04/biographies-contemporary-authors-online-2004-authors-and-artists-for-young-adults/.

Evans, Timothy H. 2005. "A Last Defense against the Dark: Folklore, Horror and the Uses of Tradition in the Works of H. P. Lovecraft." *Journal of Folklore Research* 42(1): 99–135. http://dx.doi.org/10.2979/JFR.2005.42.1.99.

Evans, Timothy H. 2010. "Authenticity, Ethnography, and Colonialism in Philip K. Dick's *The Man in the High Castle*." *Journal of the Fantastic in the Arts* 21(3): 366–83.

Gaiman, Neil. 1991a. *Black Orchid*. New York: DC Comics.

Gaiman, Neil. 1991b. *The Sandman: Dream Country*. New York: DC Comics.

Gaiman, Neil. 1991c. *The Sandman: Preludes and Nocturnes*. New York: DC Comics.

Gaiman, Neil. 1992. *The Sandman: Season of Mists*. New York: DC Comics.

Gaiman, Neil. 1993a. *The Sandman: A Game of You*. New York: DC Comics.

Gaiman, Neil. 1993b. *The Sandman: Fables and Reflections*. New York: DC Comics.

Gaiman, Neil. 1995. *The Tragical Comedy or Comical Tragedy of Mr. Punch*. New York: DC Comics.

Gaiman, Neil. 1996. *Neverwhere*. New York: William Morrow.

Gaiman, Neil. 1997. *The Sandman: The Wake*. New York: DC Comics.

Gaiman, Neil. 1998. *Stardust: Being a Romance within the Realm of Fairie*. New York: DC Comics.

Gaiman, Neil. 1999. *The Sandman: The Dream Hunters*. New York: DC Comics.

Gaiman, Neil. 2001a. *The Books of Magic*. New York: DC Comics.

Gaiman, Neil. 2001b. "Chivalry." In *Smoke and Mirrors: Short Fiction and Illusions*, 33–47. New York: Harper Collins.

Gaiman, Neil. 2001c. "Murder Mysteries." In *Smoke and Mirrors: Short Fiction and Illusions*, 292–324. New York: Harper Collins.

Gaiman, Neil. 2001d. "Snow, Glass, Apples." In *Smoke and Mirrors: Short Fiction and Illusions*, 325–39. New York: Harper Collins.

Gaiman, Neil. 2001e. "Troll Bridge." In *Smoke and Mirrors: Short Fiction and Illusions*, 57–68. New York: Harper Collins.

Gaiman, Neil. 2002. "An Astonishingly Incomplete Bibliography." *Neil Gaiman blog*. http://www.neilgaiman.com/works/Books/American+Gods/in/183/.

Gaiman, Neil. 2003. "An Interview with Neil Gaiman." In *American Gods*, 595–600. New York: Harper Collins.

Gaiman, Neil. 2004. "The False Knight on the Road." In *The Book of Ballads*, illustrated by Charles Vess, 21–29. New York: Tor Books.

Gaiman, Neil. 2005a. *Anansi Boys*. New York: William Morrow.

Gaiman, Neil. 2005b. "Mostly Words." *Neil Gaiman blog*. http://journal.neilgaiman.com/2005/10/mostly-words.html.

Gaiman, Neil. 2006a. "Fifteen Painted Cards from a Vampire Tarot." In *Fragile Things*, 209–18. New York: Harper Collins.

Gaiman, Neil. 2006b. "Good Boys Deserve Favors." In *Fragile Things*, 133–38. New York: Harper Collins.

Gaiman, Neil. 2006c. "A Study in Emerald." In *Fragile Things*, 1–26. New York: Harper Collins.

Gaiman, Neil. (Original work published 2001) 2011. *American Gods*. New York: William Morrow.

Gaiman, Neil. 2013. "Teaching Neil Gaiman." Forum at the International Conference on the Fantastic in the Arts, Orlando, March 15, 2013.

Gaiman, Neil, and Roger Avary. 2007. *Beowulf: The Script*. New York: William Morrow.

Gaiman, Neil, and Gene Wolfe. 2009. *A Walking Tour of the Shambles*. Woodstock, IL: American Fantasy.

Genette, Gerard. (Original work published 1979) 1992. *The Architext: An Introduction*. Translated by Jane E. Lewin. Berkeley: University of California Press.

Genette, Gerard. (Original work published 1987) 1997. *Paratexts: Thresholds of Interpretation*. Translated by Jane E. Lewin. Cambridge: Cambridge University Press. http://dx.doi.org/10.1017/CBO9780511549373.

Hodgson, Amanda. 2011. *The Romances of William Morris*. Cambridge: Cambridge University Press.

Hymes, Dell. 1975. "Folklore's Nature and the Sun's Myth." *Journal of American Folklore* 88(350): 345–69. http://dx.doi.org/10.2307/538651.

Jenkins, Henry. 2008. *Convergence Culture: Where Old and New Media Collide*. New York: New York University Press.

Le Guin, Ursula K. 1985. *Always Coming Home*. New York: Harper and Row.

McCabe, Joseph, ed. 2004. *Hanging Out with the Dream King: Conversations with Neil Gaiman and His Collaborators*. Seattle: Fantagraphic Books.

Pratchett, Terry, and Neil Gaiman. 1990. *Good Omens*. New York: Harper Collins.

Rawlik, Peter S., Jr. 2007. "The King Forsakes His Throne: Campbellian Hero Icons in Neil Gaiman's *Sandman*." In *The Neil Gaiman Reader*, edited by Darrell Schweiter, 30–50. Rockville, MD: Wildside.

Smith, Clay. 2008. "Get Gaiman? PolyMorpheus Perversity in Works by and about Neil Gaiman." *ImageTexT: Interdiciplinary Comics Studies* 4(1): 1–12. http://www.english.ufl .edu/imagetext/archives/v4_1/smith/.

Sullivan, C. W., III. 2001. "Folklore and Fantastic Literature." *Western Folklore* 60(4): 279–96. http://dx.doi.org/10.2307/1500409.

3

Pixies' Progress
How the Pixie Became Part of the Nineteenth-Century Fairy Mythology

Paul Manning

> *Your pixies are pleasant creatures. I know them of old by Coleridge's poem about them, which was written before he and I met in 1794, but your stories were new to me, and have amused my fireside greatly. We have no playful superstitions here, or if there are any, they have not come to my knowledge . . . Large towns and large manufactories destroy all superstitions of this kind.*

> —Robert Southey to Anna Eliza Bray, June 12, 1832

Pixies were a late addition to the British taxonomy of fairies. They could indeed be called "Mrs. Bray's creatures," since it was largely through her writings that pixies entered the canon of British fairy lore. Anna Eliza Bray (1790–1883), protégée of the poet laureate Robert Southey (a Lake Poet along with Wordsworth and Coleridge), was already an accomplished novelist with six published novels by the time she began to write about pixies. Pixies come onto the stage of fairydom in her *A Description of the Part of Devonshire Bordering on the Tamar and the Tavy* of 1836, in which they play a minor but significant role within a larger description of the picturesque locality of Dartmoor; they take on a leading role against the backdrop of the same landscape in her *A Peep at the Pixies* of 1854. In the case of pixies we can see in detail how a local spirit is integrated into the emergent assemblage of British fairy mythology, starting with their adoption in Keightley's *Fairy Mythology* of 1850. While Bray, the first female British collector of folklore *avant la lettre* (Silver 1999, 30), initially brought the "folkloric" pixie into public view, she simultaneously fashioned the "folkloresque" pixie, a creature able to move from the relatively homogeneous oral networks of transmission characterizing local folklore into the extremely heterogeneous,

DOI: 10.7330/9781607324188.c003

multimedia and multiplatform "folkloresque" networks of transmission that sustained the late Victorian to Edwardian popular literary and visual culture of "fairyland" (on which see Gordon 2006, 40–41).

Bray's 1836 description of pixies includes most of the elements that would come to define the pixie ever since, down to their fondness for the color green. Contemporary readers will find her portrayal familiar:

> These tiny elves are said to delight in solitary places, to love pleasant hills and pathless woods; or to disport themselves on the margins of rivers and mountain streams. Of all their amusements, dancing forms their chief delight; and this exercise they are said always to practise, like the Druids of old, in a circle or ring. These dainty beings, though represented as of exceeding beauty in their higher or aristocratic order, are, nevertheless, in some instances, of strange, uncouth and fantastic figure and visage: though such natural deformity need give them very little uneasiness, since they are traditionally averred to possess the power of assuming various shapes at will . . . But whatever changes the outward figure of fairies may undergo, they are, amongst themselves, as constant in their fashions as a Turk; their dress never varies, it is always green. (Bray 1836, 1: 172–73)

This image of the pixie became further solidified in her 1854 illustrated book for children, *A Peep at the Pixies*. Much of this work simply reproduces portions of the earlier work, including the above description copied almost word for word, except for the coda about pixies' preference for the color green (Bray 1854, 12). But despite the fact that it contains a good deal of the same text, this is an entirely different *kind* of book, one belonging to a different print culture. Not only is it a children's book, it is an early example of that prototypical exemplar of late Victorian print culture, a "gift book" with color illustrations by Hablot K. Browne (Felmingham 1988). Such illustrations, made possible by continual advances in color-printing technologies, were becoming increasingly common, transforming late Victorian print culture into a metaphoric visual "fairyland" (Gordon 2006)—characterized, of course, by large numbers of illustrations of actual fairies (Felmingham 1988, 55–68).

The veritable explosion of Victorian and Edwardian representations of fairies cannot be understood without reference to both romantic interest in popular antiquities (folklore) and the exuberant refashioning of folkloric fairies into folkloresque re-presentations across multiple genres and media (theater, print, painting) made possible by new media technologies (theatrical lighting effects, color-printing techniques) (Maas et al. 1997). As pixies move from local folklore to the folkloresque assemblage of British fairy lore, they not only join other fairies in entering into the imagined otherworldly diegetic space of "fairyland" portrayed in illustrated gift books and fairy mythologies, they also leave the confines of oral tradition and enter into the highly mediated cultural assemblage of the late-Victorian folkloresque.[1]

The emergent duality of the term *fairyland*, gesturing at once to a vanishing enchanted pretechnological pastoral world inhabited by fairies and to a set of new media technologies of enchantment that portrayed this world, is reflected, too, in the different "folkloresque" trajectories of the pixie. For writers like John Ruskin in his essay "Fairy Land," "fairyland" seems to represent the otherworldly diegetic space of faerie as well as the "fairyland" of the sundry new technologies and media of representation, from print illustrations to lighting effects, that make the portrayal of this other world possible (Ruskin 1884, 81, 103–5). For contemporary writers of the transnational folkloresque like Lafcadio Hearn, who would later go on to portray Japan as a ghostly fairyland to the West, the term *fairyland* also had two opposed referents, a folkloresque world clearly depicted in new print media like the Victorian illustrated gift book (Felmingham 1988) and another world of vague mysterious landscapes dotted with "picturesque" and "spectral" ruins (Hearn 1919, 45): "a fairyland so clearly and sharply outlined as the artistic fantasies of Christmas picture-books" and "a fairyland of misty landscapes and dim shadows and bright shapes moving through the vagueness of mystery" (43).[2]

The pixie's progress from folklore to the folkloresque also reflects these dualities in understandings of "fairyland." On the one hand, the pixie moved from being a textual figure, a literary transcription of folklore, to become a highly visible, even colorful, illustrated folkloresque figure of the first kind of fairyland, the fairyland of the "Christmas picture-book." On the other, the pixie was associated with the "fairyland of misty landscapes" of Dartmoor, contributing to a kind of "folkloresque landscape," the enduring belief that Dartmoor was among the most haunted places in Britain.

Bray assembled an image of the pixie that would allow it to become a central fixture of the emergent British fairy mythology. Many of the characteristics of these hybrid "folkloric-folkloresque" pixies—their diminutive stature, their ability to shape shift, their love of dancing in circles, their preference for the color green—are reiterated (always citing Bray) in diverse late nineteenth-century accounts of the folklore of the area (Crossing 1890; King 1873, 781). As pixies were swept up into the conventions of the late Victorian fairy aesthetic of fairyland, they underwent iconographic elaborations parallel to those of fairies, ranging from developing pixie-specific features such as pointed caps and eyes upturned at the temple to adopting the standard paraphernalia of the late Victorian fairy, such as elfin pointy ears

Figure 3.1. *The Three Trials* (from Bray 1854, 52).

and butterfly or dragonfly wings (Bown 2001; Mythical Creatures Guide n.d.; Silver 1999).

This popular image of the pixie is so familiar that it is easy to overlook how slender a thread of literary happenstance permitted pixies to move from obscure spirits of local folklore to popular figures of British fairy lore. Popularizing the pixies was, after all, surely not Bray's original intent. As we will see, the pixies move in Bray's work from being minor figures within a comprehensive description of "*every*thing . . . that can be made interesting" in a locality (which was the stated goal of her work of 1836) to becoming the central object of interest in her later work (Bray 1884, 227). Pixies begin as minor figures within the "picturesque assemblage" of the wild and eerie landscape of Dartmoor, which is the central figure of interest, but with the literary reception and revision of her work, they are detached from the picturesque aesthetics of the original work and instead become integrated into what we could call the "folkloresque assemblage" of popular British fairy mythology and print culture. The picturesque pixie that haunts the fairyland of Dartmoor and the folkloresque pixie of the fairyland of the illustrated gift book seem to part ways to take up residence in these different folkloresque ecologies of fairyland: the former pixie stays in Dartmoor and keeps fokloresque company with ghosts and headless wish hounds in the spooky, paranormal, *haunted* landscape of Dartmoor; the latter pixies become portable, national spirits, keeping folkloresque company with winged fairies on the pages of illustrated gift books, animated films, and other media.

LITERARY RELATIONS OF THE PIXIES

The adoption of pixies into this folkloresque assemblage of the British fairy family depended in the first place on their powerful literary allies, specifically, on the literary relations of a small circle of writers, all either central figures among the Lake Poets (Samuel Coleridge, Robert Southey) or direct or indirect protégées of them (Bray, Mary Colling). These were figures whose network of personal literary relations and influence on public popular taste afforded the pixies a means to move from the mouths of local storytellers to the pages of illustrated children's books in the space of a generation. Briefly contextualizing these literary relations and citations, therefore, is my point of departure.

Southey gives the first literary citation (correctly, it appears) to Samuel Coleridge: "I know them of old by Coleridge's poem about them, which was written before he and I met in 1794" (cited in Bray 1884, 252). He is referring to one of Coleridge's early poems, "Songs of the Pixies" (dated 1793), written during a summer vacation with family members in Ottery, Devon. The poem by all accounts consists of mostly literary elaboration with little or no reference to the folklore he was drawing upon, but it is significant that Coleridge at that time could presuppose that none of his reading public would be familiar with pixies, and so it is prefaced with the following context:

The Pixies, in the superstition of Devonshire, are a race of beings invisibly small, and harmless or friendly to man. At a small distance from a village in that county, half-way up a wood-covered hill, is an excavation called the Pixies' Parlour. The roots of old trees form its ceiling; and on its sides are innumerable cyphers, among which the author discovered his own cypher and those of his brothers, cut by the hand of their childhood. At the foot of the hill flows the river Otter. To this place the Author, during the summer months of the year 1793, conducted a party of young ladies; one of whom, of stature elegantly small, and of complexion colourless yet clear, was proclaimed the Faery Queen. On which occasion the following Irregular Ode was written. (Coleridge 1793)

This would remain more or less all the British reading public at large would know about pixies (with one or two minor mentions elsewhere, either under generic names or variant spellings) until Bray undertook her description of the locality. When they are mentioned, it is only in a melancholic manner similar to the Southey quote above, as romantic specters always already vanishing before the onset of industry and urbanization (compare Bown 2001, 163–97; Silver 1999, 185–212): "The age of piskays, like that of chivalry is gone. There is, perhaps, at present hardly a house they are reputed to visit . . . Even the fields and lanes which they formerly frequented seem to be nearly forsaken. Their music is rarely heard" (Hitchins 1824, 1: 98).[3]

While Anna Eliza Bray would later become known primarily as the popularizer of these spirits under the standardized name *pixie*, this is certainly not the project she intended. Bray, an accomplished novelist, seemed to define her life and creative production by reference to her Lake Poet mentor, the poet laureate Robert Southey. Her *Autobiography* (Bray 1884) is, for the most part, a chronicle of her correspondence with Southey, culminating in his one visit to her home in Devonshire, and it is telling that the work terminates abruptly with the death of "her friend and idol" (336) in 1843. Since she presents her whole life in her autobiography as essentially a literary relationship, her correspondence with her mentor explains how she ever came to write about pixies at all.

Southey, in a letter to Bray of February 1831 comparing her recent novels, one (*Fitzford*, 1830) set in Devonshire and one (*The Talba*, 1830) set in Portugal, opines that it seems to him that she had visited the scenes of *Fiztford* but not those of *The Talba*, so that "'Fitzford' has this advantage therefore over 'The Talba,' that in it you describe scenery with which you are well acquainted, and not only your sketches are taken upon the spot, but your coloring also" (Bray 1884, 226). This brings him to the first literary advice he would give her, to undertake a project in which she thoroughly described a locality that she truly knew, her own locality in Devonshire. The advice is worth quoting in full:

> If you would stoop from fancy's realm to truth, I should like to see from
> you what English literature yet wants, a good specimen of local history,
> not the antiquities only, nor the natural history, nor both together . . . nor
> the statistics; but *every*thing about a parish that can be made interesting; all
> of its history, traditions and manners that can be saved from oblivion (for
> every generation sweeps away much), the changes that have been and are
> in progress; everything in short that belongs to the pursuits of historian,
> biographer, naturalist, philosopher, or poet; and not omitting some of
> those "short and simple" annals of domestic life, which ought not to be
> forgotten. (227)

Neither exclusively a natural nor a civic history, the project envisioned would be a large one, with the added proviso that it would also have to be "interesting." Bray describes herself as "honoured and flattered" "on receiving such a letter as this from such a quarter" but simultaneously despairing and hopeless "at the very thoughts of entering upon a work that would require so many talents" (Bray 1884, 228). In the preface of the resulting work she summarized Southey's advice: "Mr. Southey suggested the plan with a view to originality;—namely, to make a local work possess, what it had hitherto been deemed little capable of possessing—a general interest" (Bray 1836, iv).

A Description of the Part of Devonshire Bordering on the Tamar and the Tavy, then, stands at the intersection of multiple sets of imperatives grounding it both in its locality and in a cosmopolitan literary pedigree. The originality of the work was that the parochial details of a locality would have to be presented to provide a "general interest" for the reading public as a whole, a seeming contradiction. The description of the locality would be compendious, far more so than even a typical natural history of the previous century, since it would contain "*every*thing . . . that can be made interesting" (Bray 1836, 2).

And last, the work indexed its own literary context and infrastructural conditions of possibility (arising out of a literary correspondence between mentor and protégée) by taking the form of letters, addressed not to the public that would read it but to Bray's own proximate interlocutor, Southey, so that it draws attention to its own literary pedigree in the telling. The choice to use this particular format was apparently Bray's, and Southey concurred (in a letter dated March 14, 1831) that the epistolary form would be "pleasing and convenient" since it "allows of as much miscellaneous matter as you like to introduce, and transitions are made in it from one subject to another with less difficulty and more grace than in any other mode of composition" (Bray 1884, 229).[4] The resulting work bears an extraordinarily long title that draws together all these different elements of locality and literariness: *A Description of the Part of Devonshire Bordering on the Tamar and the Tavy: Its Natural History, Manners, Customs, Superstitions, Scenery, Antiquities, Biography of Eminent Persons, &c. &c. in a Series of Letters to Robert Southey* (Bray 1836).

In some ways, the title is reminiscent of an eighteenth-century natural history, both in its length and in that it begins with natural history and then moves to civic history (manners, customs, superstitions, and so on).[5] But this apparent similarity hides crucial differences. First of all, her "natural history" is really an extended aestheticized description of the *picturesque* landscape of the region, very different from the rather more utilitarian interests of an eighteenth-century natural historian. Equally important, though subtle, are the different contents of the list of "customs, manners, etc." that comprise the categories of an eighteenth-century civic history, for Bray's list also includes "superstitions." Eighteenth-century natural historians had no place to put *invisible* beings like the pixies, which dwell exclusively in oral folkloric narratives of "superstition," in what was, after all, a science "giving a recital and detail of the whole *visible* creation" (Borlase 1758, iii; emphasis added), and so generally ignored them entirely. This initially subtle change becomes much clearer in the title of the second edition, which places what we would now call "folklore" front and center and expands the "natural history" into "antiquities, scenery, and natural history": *Traditions, Legends, Superstitions, and Sketches of Devonshire: On the Borders of the Tamar and the Tavy, Illustrative of Its Manners, Customs, History, Antiquities, Scenery, and Natural History, in a Series of Letters to Robert Southey, Esq.* (Bray 1838).

Part of the "originality" of her work, then, is registered in this change in title from the 1836 edition to the 1838 edition, where "traditions, legends, and superstitions" (an emergent focus on "folklore" eight years before the term was coined) are the primary focus. This originality, too, can be traced to another piece of advice by Southey. His instructions of October 13, 1831, contain an explicit injunction to attend to "traditions," specifically gesturing to a translation of Danish folklore in Southey's possession as an example:

> Gather up all the traditions you can, and even the nursery songs; no one can tell what value they may prove to an antiquary. The Danes have a collection of such traditions in two volumes—every local story, wise or silly, that could be collected, and a very curious book it is,—my son and I are

just coming to the end of it in our lessons. There is matter enough in such things for fancy and for reflection—to point a moral, or work up into a poem, and not infrequently to elucidate something in the history of former times. Mary may be a very useful helpmate. (Bray 1884, 244)

While both Southey and Bray could be said to be pursuing an object that would later become known as folklore, it is important to recognize that their interest in folklore is primarily literary, either its own literary merits or its potential to be reworked into a literary form. Hence, even the apparent folklore of Bray's account is described with a view to subsequent folkloresque appropriation.

Southey's reference to "Mary" points to the last person of note in this literary genealogy. Mary Colling, a domestic servant and folk poet, might be said to be Bray's own literary protégée as well as Southey's. Southey, knowing her only from her poetry and Bray's letters, judged her to be an "extraordinary person" (Bray 1884, 230), and together Bray and Southey arranged to have her poetry published in 1831 (the proceeds for her own benefit), a volume that Southey reviewed at length and with approbation. The form itself of this volume reflects the complex literary associations of patronage that characterized Bray's relations to her patron, Southey, and her client, Colling: ostensibly a volume of poetry by Colling, the work is actually authored by Bray, again in the form of a series of letters to her patron and privileged addressee, Southey, in which Colling's own poetry and fables appear as quoted excerpts framed within these letters. The same epistolary representation of literary relations would characterize Bray's 1836 *Description*.

The structure of the volume thus denies Mary Colling, a domestic servant, the role of autonomous author and equal. That a domestic servant could share the same body with a gifted poet in itself appeared to be amazing, as Bray observed in her account of the poetess: "Mary Colling the servant, and Mary Colling talking about poetry and flowers, scarcely appears to be one and the same person. If I had not seated her for a couple of hours by my side, I should never have guessed the animated interesting being she could become in conversation" (Bray 1831, 18). As Southey suggested, Mary, having a foot in both the world of the folk and the literary world of the Lake Poets, would serve as a key intermediary in the collection of folklore, particularly tales about pixies: it would be Mary who would take the "pigsie tales" from their original contexts of oral narration between children and grandmothers and allow them to be retold in a literary context. Bray wrote to Southey:

> However, I am digressing, and talking about Drayton and my husband,
> when I ought to be "telling about nothing but a real pigsie tale," as the
> children say here, when they sit around the fire and listen to the legends
> of their grandmothers. In collecting these anecdotes respecting the pixy
> race, I must acknowledge my obligations to Mary Colling, the amiable
> young woman whose little verses you so kindly noticed, and whose artless
> attempts have been so favourably received by her friends and the public.
> Mary, to oblige me, chatted with the village gossips, or listened to their
> long stories; and the information thus gained was no small addition to my
> own stock of traditions and tales "of the olden time." (Bray 1836, 180)

In tracing the literary context of the introduction of the pixies, it appears
that the pixies benefited from the same august literary patronage that Mary
Colling did. The complex chain of literary patronages—Southey's patronage of Bray, and Southey and Bray's patronage of Colling—provided a set
of links by which "real pigsie tales" and Mary Colling's poetry alike could
ascend from local obscurity to recognition by national publics. The production of the pixie as a quasi-folkloric being, then, depended on a gradual
regrounding of the pixie in new genres of representation of localities, from
a first edition whose title suggests that superstitions will be an appendage to
a natural and civic history to a second edition in which "traditions, legends,
and superstitions" are central to the text. Having discussed the literary relations of the text, now I look into the way the text produces pixies as parts
of a locality.

GENRES: HAUNTINGS AND "REAL PIGSIE TALES"

Pixies are presented in Bray's early work as figures embedded in two sorts
of narrative contexts. On the one hand, they are subordinate figures *haunting* a specific picturesque landscape that is the central figure of interest, and
on the other hand they appear as central figures in relatively autonomous
narratives (the "real pigsie tales" mentioned above). The pixie, then, is a
figure whose *disjecta membra* are scattered across the landscape in the place-
names of specific haunted localities and as a separate group of less localized narratives.

The narratives in the former group, what I will call "hauntings," are
strongly *contextualized* within the specific landscape of Dartmoor, in that
the narrative and the context that serves as setting are so connected as
to be inseparable. These hauntings are similar to conventional ghostly
hauntings in that they involve a legend (the ghosts demanding that "their
singular tale be retold and their wrongs acknowledged") associated with

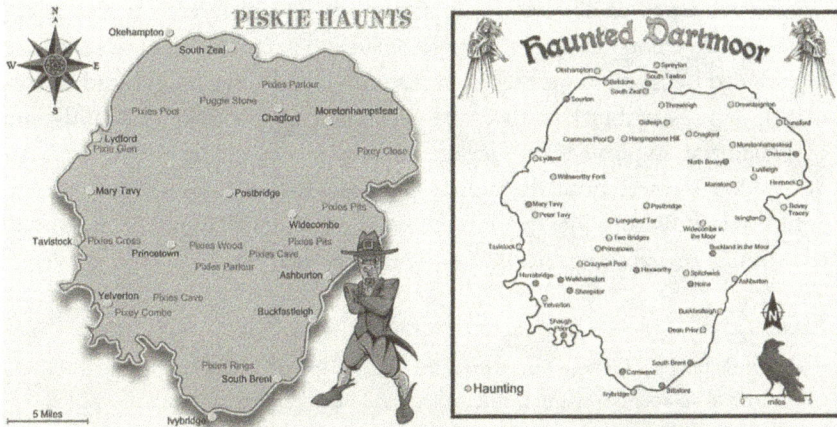

Figure 3.2. Maps of "piskie haunts" and ghostly hauntings (Sandles n.d.).

a specific locale (Luckhurst 2002, 541–42). Aesthetically, such hauntings also locate the pixie as a figure within a "picturesque assemblage" of heterogeneous elements, often including both a singular picturesque material feature of the landscape, including a place-name suggestive of pixies, as well as associated legends or practices.[6] Hauntings are legends entangled with landscapes; their ghosts and fairies are not separable and not portable. As a category of the folkloresque, hauntings by ghosts and pixies confer upon a landscape what Holloway and Kneale call an "uncanny affordance" (Holloway and Kneale 2008, 304). Bray's construction of Dartmoor as a "haunted" landscape emerges out of her desire to recuperate the barren landscapes of Dartmoor within an aesthetic program of the picturesque and sublime. But this has had enduring effects, as Dartmoor has steadily accreted more and more hauntings of both "piskies" and "ghosts" (see figure 3.2), producing a "folkloresque landscape" that draws visitors to the "most haunted" area in Britain. Dartmoor serves as an appropriately "atmospheric and ghostly landscape" for many British ghost stories.[7]

The narratives in the latter group, "real pigsie tales," are much more strongly *entextualized* (Bauman 2004, 4), that is, bounded and self-contained and hence decontextualizable and recontextualizable, iterable and portable. These are legends that do not focus on the relations of the pixies to the landscape as much as on the tenor of relationships between pixies and humans more or less independently of this landscape. Such folkloresque narratives therefore have circulated far afield from the haunted landscapes of Dartmoor, producing an exclusively narrative image of the pixie that is far cheerier than the ones associated with hauntings, a folkloresque

propagated by color illustrations in gift books. The difference in the trajectories of these two kinds of narratives results in part from the ways they are
introduced by Bray: in narratives of haunting, pixies are introduced as animating figures within a picturesque aesthetic framework of the landscape
of Dartmoor; in pigsie tales, they are introduced in a tightly integrated form
devoted to stories about the figures themselves—introduced by what one
could call a folkloresque "pixie mythology" that draws together the different strands of hauntings, tales and the literary citations discussed above.

Hauntings

> In this part of Devonshire a modern "philosopher" might, perhaps, find it
> difficult to recognize the influences of wild land and solitary nature which
> age after age have fostered, if they did not at first create, the local folk-lore
> and traditions. But if he turns southward, and wanders for a time among
> the granite tors of Dartmoor, he will be compelled to acknowledge that the
> whishounds [*sic*] and the pixies have there established themselves in a very
> congenial home . . . Its wide wastes and rocky hill-sides can still produce
> their effect, and, if the season be judiciously chosen, form one of the best
> possible backgrounds for a "tale of ghosts and spirits." (King 1873, 773)

One of Bray's greatest contributions was establishing the singularly
haunted quality of the landscape of Dartmoor. Virtually all later descriptions
of Dartmoor, the home of the pixies, agree with her that the local scenery
is eminently *hauntable* and even grant this landscape a kind of agency over
superstition, in that the "eerie" feeling of the setting seems to foster imag-
inings of hauntings and pixies. Hauntings, then, can be seen as a genre of
the folkloresque that is afforded by a picturesque assemblage of heterogeneous elements in the landscape, including in Dartmoor the rock forma-
tions known as tors, with their "blocks of lichen-stained granite, piled in
fantastic shapes, and growing more and more fantastic in the fading light"
(King 1873, 773). These 'uncanny affordances' of the landscape, to use
Holloway and Kneale's term, combine to produce a set of 'eerie' feelings
conducive to an animating narrative of ghostly haunting.

For Bray, the hauntedness of Dartmoor is almost a secondary effect
of her desire to situate the landscape within the aesthetics of the sublime
and picturesque, and to oppose the picturesque aesthetics of Dartmoor to
the pastoral aesthetics of beauty that predominates elsewhere in Devon.
The landscape of Dartmoor presents itself as a "barren," "rugged wilder-
ness" (Bray 1836, 19), whose treeless "vastness" and "granite masses" lend
it a "rugged and solemn character" contrasted with the "cheerfulness and
placidity of a cultivated or woodland-landscape" (22). Each landscape is

Figure 3.3. Stapletor: one of the tors of Dartmoor (Bray 1836, 240).

associated with a different sensibility or sentiment: "The feelings inspired by visiting Dartmoor are of a very different order from those experienced on viewing our beautiful and cultivated scenery . . . There is nothing in such scenes to raise a thought allied to wonder or fear . . . they delight and soften the mind, but they seldom raise in it those deep and impressive reflections, which scenes such as Dartmoor affords seldom fail to create" (17–18).

Picturesque and sublime landscapes elicit specific kinds of sentiments very different from those elicited by beautiful ones, sentiments such as "agreeable horror" and "pleasing melancholy" (Andrews 1989, 45). Such sentiments are particularly associated with landscape features like ruins, hybrids of nature and culture, which are not only obligatory elements within a picturesque landscape but are individual objects that encapsulate the hybrid aesthetics of the picturesque as a whole (41–50). Accordingly, much of the early part of the *Description* is devoted to a singular pictur-esque aspect of the landscape of Dartmoor, the remarkable granite out-croppings found there called *tors* (from a Celtic word for "tower"). For Bray, the tors of Dartmoor quite explicitly had all the requisite destabiliz-ing aesthetic properties of the picturesque ruin. Though works of nature, they uncannily resembled megalithic ruins ("altars, circles, obelisks, crom-lechs and logans") associated with the druids elsewhere in Britain (Bray 1836, 61), including Stonehenge: "On the plains of Salisbury nature had done nothing for the grandeur of Druidism, and art did all. On Dartmoor the priests of the Britons appropriated the *tors themselves as temples*, erected by the hand of nature" (1:61–62). Like the picturesque landscape of

Dartmoor as a whole, the tors were best viewed with the proper lighting, a broken or fading light that allowed fancy free rein, allowing these rocks to seem to become ruins: "Often I have seen the moor so chequered and broken with light and shade, that it required no stretch of the imagination to convert many a weather-beaten Tor into the towers and ruined walls of a feudal castle" (1:19).

Her emphasis on proper lighting reminds us that tors, like ruins, are defined, in Chloe Chard's elegant phrase, by the conjuncture of "ghosts, moonlight and weeds" (Chard 1999). Taken together, these features can serve as "uncanny affordances" that turn a familiar and normal material geography into a strange and unfamiliar one, a haunting. To populate these already picturesque landscape features with suitable haunting apparitions, Bray imagines the tors as the erstwhile objects of veneration of druids as well as the haunts of pixies. Within such a picturesque assemblage, such haunting human characters play a role similar to what the major theorist of the picturesque, William Gilpin, called *figures* in the adornment of a picturesque landscape painting (Andrews 1989, 25). While Gilpin introduced human figures primarily to demarcate landscapes into foreground and background, he also noted that the specific choice of figure (i.e., a "loitering peasant" rather than an "industrious mechanic") can serve other, *sentimental* purposes of "animating" the landscape (Andrews 1989, 25), of which haunting can be considered a subclass. Situated within a specific "haunting," these "animating" figures do more than demarcate the landscape: they are themselves almost externalizations and figurations of the sentiments inspired by the landscape itself, acting as destabilizing presences that strengthen the sentiment aroused by other affordances of the landscape.

Within the picturesque landscape of Dartmoor, the pixie is encountered occasionally as such a figure within a "haunting" narrative, a singular legend associated with a singular "hauntable" landscape feature that usually incorporates pixies as part of the name or associated legend. An example would be Coleridge's description of the Pixies' Parlour above. In fact, pixies make their first appearance in Bray's published work in a novel set in the locality of Devonshire (*Warleigh,* 1834) in just such a "hauntable" picturesque context:

> "We are now," said the outlaw, "standing before the door of the pix-
> ies' house; for so is this cave called by the few shepherds to whom it
> was known, ere they were scared away from these heights by Grenville's
> men driving off their flocks. The cell is considered the haunt of invisible
> beings: you will hear them at work the moment you enter: but they are

never seen. An old shepherd, who loved not Sir Richard Grenville nor his troopers, first pointed it out to me, and bade me, as I valued good luck or quiet nights, to drop a pin as an offering to the pixie which makes this cave her haunt, else would she torment me ever after.

Bray's learned footnote indicates among other things that "this superstitious offering to the pixies is still observed by the peasantry who venture on a visit to the lofty cave of Sheepstor" (Bray 1834, 277); a following note explains that it is the dripping of water in the grotto that forms the impression that it is haunted by pixies, and that "the pixies are a race of fairies" (278). Her later extensive account of the locality of Sheepstor which—like most of her many descriptions of individual tors, she reproduces from her husband's notes (Bray 1836, 234–35)—contains a description of the same Pixies' House. Specific pixie haunts, however, are fairly rare: in the main pixies generally "congregate together, even by the thousands, in some of those wild and desolate places where there is no church." The list of such places includes only one other specific haunt: "in a field near Down-house, there is a pit which the pixies, not very long ago, appropriated for their ballroom" (182).[8]

Dartmoor *as a whole* is presented as a picturesque landscape that contains an assemblage of picturesque features, including nonhuman features, the ruinlike tors, and the humanlike figures haunting them (druids and the occasional pixie). As a consequence, while pixies have very few specific haunts within Dartmoor, the whole of Dartmoor is said to be their general haunt: "It is reported that in days of yore, as well as in the present time, the wild waste of Dartmoor was much haunted by spirits and pixies in every direction" (Bray 1836, 181).

While Bray's treatment of the scenery of Dartmoor, and the hauntings of pixies within it, as being explicitly framed within the aesthetics of the picturesque is clear, it is arguable that the entire *Description* is a literary version of a picturesque assemblage of heterogeneous elements: although its lengthy title gestures toward the orderly and comprehensive expositions of a natural and civic history like that of William Borlase (1758), its epistolary format lacks orderly transitions from nonhuman nature to human manners. Rather, its very organization is picturesque and chaotic, an exposition that is introduced "in a manner to give variety, and to relieve the more serious portions of the book" (Bray 1836, 1: iii–iv, 2), the style varied and lightened by moving from grave matters to trifling ones, resulting in a picturesque presentation of the picturesque landscape of Dartmoor, in which pixies are subordinated figures or "appendages" that, along with druids, "animate" the landscape.

"Real Pigsie Tales"

The remainder of the material about pixies, including that collected from local gossips by Mary Colling, is less localized in the landscape but much more strongly localized in the text, being found in only one letter (letter 10) devoted more or less entirely to the subject. If the haunts and associated legends of pixies can be understood only as part of a picturesque design of the landscape, then these letters resemble a nascent collection of folklore (for which Bray apologizes at the end). Feeling that she has talked altogether too much about druids (which have occupied her for several of the prior letters) (Bray 1836, 169), Bray devotes one letter to the subject of pixies.

For the most part her discussion here of the fairies is synthetic (a discussion of the "fairy race in general, ere we come to particulars" [Bray 1836, 170]), generalizing across the various narratives, more of a "mythology" than a collection of narratives. Bray is relatively insistent that, while pixies are comparable to fairies, yet they form a distinct race (169, 172), and she spends a good deal of time discussing possible origins and etymologies (170–71). We learn that "the Druids are supposed to have worshipped fairies amongst their deities" (171). She then embarks on a discussion of the properties of pixies in general within a synthetic section one might call a "pixie mythology." She draws a picture of the pixies' haunting relation to the landscape and makes their various antics in relation to humans part of a single overarching mythological plan. In addition to the description quoted above, which outlines their love of solitary places, dancing, and the color green, we learn that these elves dance to the music made by crickets, frogs, and grasshoppers in the light of the moon (173). They are sent on their various errands to torment and trick humans by their ruler: "It is under the cold and chaste light of [the moon's] beams, or amidst the silent shadows of the dark rocks, where the light never penetrates, that on the moor the elfin king of the pixies holds his high court of sovereignty and council" (173–74). This device of an elfin king sending his pixies on errands (which is strongly suggestive of earlier literary elaborations of fairydom's rulers, such as Queen Titania and Oberon) allows her to make a transition to describing their antics vis-à-vis humans, and in telling these stories Bray mixes together Devon fairy lore with copious literary citations from Jonson and especially Drayton (175–80).

But here Bray admonishes herself for citing the writings of Drayton and her own husband when she should be "telling about nothing but a real pigsie tale" (Bray 1836, 180). Here she finally makes the transition from her own literary fancies of elfin kings and citations from Drayton to the varied stories collected by Mary Colling. But Bray is no folkloric purist—after all, the very term *folklore* was not in circulation at the time she was writing. Rather, her meandering discussion here, which moves from literary citation to folkloric transcription, is guided by the same general picturesque principles that guide her discussion of the pixies within the picturesque landscape of Dartmoor. Here, too, her account of pixies is a picturesque assemblage of what would later be considered authentic folklore (the "real pigsie tales" collected by Mary Colling) with folkloresque elaboration, including literary citations of Drayton and her own fancies, producing a pixie that arrives on the scene as both "folkloric" and "folkloresque" from the outset.

PEEPING AT THE PIXIES: RECEPTION AND REVISION

Bray ends her brief recital of pixie legends slightly apologetically, noting that she has given

> enough to prove that the people of this neighborhood, in the lower ranks of life (from whose chit-chat all these were gleaned), possess, in no small degree, a poetical spirit for old tales. The upper, and more educated classes, hold such stories as unworthy notice; and many would laugh at me for having taken the trouble to collect and repeat them; but however wild and simple they may be, there is so much of poetry and imagination in them that I feel convinced you will consider them worthy of being saved, by some written record, from that oblivion, to which, in a few years, they would otherwise be inevitably consigned (Bray 1836, 192).

Her fears appear to be unfounded, for her short account of the pixies, merely a background appendage to a description of the locality, became the centerpiece of attention in the reception of her work. Southey himself, in his lengthy review of her work, devotes his attention to the pixies in particular (Southey 1837, 279–81), with even Bray's much lengthier exposition of the connections of the tors to druidic worship (which he cites with approval) taking second place (281–82). He summarizes in broad strokes her argument about the pixies as follows:

> Mrs. Bray thinks that "the Pixies are certainly a distinct race from the fairies, because the elders among the more knowing peasantry will invariably tell you, if you ask them what Pixies really may be, that they are the souls of infants who were so unhappy as to die unbaptized." Everything, however, which is attributed to fairies in other parts of England is attributed to Pixies in Devonshire. They steal children, they lead travelers astray, they delude

miners, they reward good housewives and punish idle ones, and make rings on the turf where they dance. (Southey 1837, 280)

Moreover, Southey mentions that while others have written such stories about elves and goblins in the area, such writers "never mention the Devonshire fairies by their peculiar name of Pixies." He places Bray's short remarks about the pixies (giving credit once again to Mary Colling's crucial role as collector) in a rather more cosmopolitan context of folklore and folklore studies, suggesting that the tales themselves might be "of Scandinavian or German importation" and comparing her collection to "those which Thiele collected in Denmark, and the brothers Grimm in Germany" (Southey 1837, 303).

The pixies became ever more central in the reception of the work, almost as if the book underwent a reversal of figure and ground, with the pixies moving from decorative appendages of a picturesque scene to the central figures of interest. Thomas Keightley, whose compendious collection *Fairy Mythology* (1833) made no mention of pixies, relies on Bray's description exclusively for his information about these fairies in the second edition of his work (Keightley 1850, 346–47):

> To come to the present times. There is no stronger proof of the neglect of what Mr Thoms has very happily designated "Folk-lore" in this country, than the fact of there having been no account given anywhere of the Pixies or Pisgies of Devonshire and Cornwall, till within these last few years. In the year 1836, Mrs. Bray, a lady well known as the author of several novels, and wife of a clergyman at Tavistock, published, in a series of letters to Robert Southey, interesting descriptions of the part of Devonshire bordering on the Tamar and the Tavy. In this work there is given an account of the Pixies, from which we derive the following information . . .

Whereupon he retells the story of the elfin king giving out offices, which produces a taxonomy of all the major themes of the tales collected by Mary Colling, which he retells afterward.

> The office of some is to steal children; of others, to lead travellers astray, as Will-o'-the-wisps, or to *Pixy-lead* them, as it is termed. Some will make confusion in a house by blowing out the candle, or kissing the maids "with a smack, as they 'shriek Who's this?' as the old poet writes, till their grandams come in and lecture them for allowing unseemly freedoms with their bachelors." Others will make noises in walls, to frighten people. *In short, everything that is done elsewhere by fairies, boggarts, or other like beings, is done in Devon by the Pixies.* (emphasis added)

The wording of his last sentence strongly recalls the comment by Southey that "Devonshire fairies" are known "by their peculiar name of Pixies," and in those words, pixies become a local translational equivalent of a much broader class of beings that are foundational to Keightley's account of "fairy mythology." It is noteworthy that in this retelling, Keightley relies primarily on the "stories": the landscape of Dartmoor and the specific hauntings fall away to produce a pixie that is "portable" and "comparable" to the other fairies—in essence, a delocalized local spirit that quickly became part and parcel of British fairydom.

Certainly the reception of the pixies must have indicated to Bray that perhaps this material about pixies could be reworked, with pixies becoming the heroes, rather than the backdrop, of the story. This Bray did just four years after Keightley's incorporation of pixies into British fairy mythology: *A Peep at the Pixies; or, The Legends of the West* (1854) was written, according to the book's inscription, at the request of Bray's niece for a book for "little people" such as herself.

Bray begins with a truncated description of the scenery of Dartmoor; since the book is intended for children, Bray describes the picturesqueness of the landscape, including the tors, with no suggestion of the "terror" of the sublime—the setting is associated with friendlier, more cheerful sentiments appropriate for children:

> In this most pleasant part of England, the county of Devon, we have many hills and rivers, with plenty of woods, and fields, and birds, and flowers. And we have a large tract of country called Dartmoor, where the hills are so high that some of them are like mountains, with a number of beautiful sparkling streams and waterfalls, and a great many rocks, some standing alone, and others piled on the top of the heights in such an odd way, that they look like the ruins of castles and towers built by the giants in the olden time, and these are called Tors; they are so lofty that the clouds often hang upon them and hide their heads. And what with its being so large and lonely, and its having no trees, except in one or two spots near a river, Dartmoor is altogether, though a wild, a very grand place. (Bray 1854, 1)

Her exposition makes no reference to specific haunts of pixies like Sheepstor; rather, as before, she is content to make the whole landscape of Dartmoor the haunt of pixies, which she describes in general terms.

> Now this wild tract of land, as well as other parts of Devonshire and Cornwall, is considered to be haunted by a set of little creatures, called Pixies. They are not like children; for, though they are small, and can sometimes be seen, it is said they can fly as well as run, and creep through

key-holes, and get into the bells of flowers, and many other places where little boys and girls cannot creep. The Pixies are sometimes good, and do kind acts; but more frequently they are mischievous, and do a great deal of harm to men, women, and children, if they have a spite against them; and often hurt the cattle. (11)

There is little of novelty in the actual content of her revision of her pixie material in this book. As noted above, some of it is actually a line-by-line reproduction of material from her 1836 work. What is important is that Bray produced this book at all. There was by now a general taste for pixies because they were now understood to be local, translational equivalents of the familiar fairies upon which the Victorian public doted. Since Victorian children's literature in particular was filled with fairy lore, it is no surprise that she would choose to repackage letter 10 of her *Description* in an *illustrated* book specifically for children.

In the transition, however, the picturesque and haunted landscape of Dartmoor becomes more cheerful, less eerie, and specific "haunting" narratives like that of Sheepstor, which are heavily localized and embedded in the landscape, disappear. In general, the pixies move from being picturesque haunters subordinated to a description of a locality, which is the primary focus of interest (where the only illustrations are picturesque drawings of tors), to foregrounded figures (illustrated in color!) in stories that are more or less autonomous from this landscape; strikingly, the pixies shift from background to foreground, from their inclusion in a single small section of her three-volume *Description* of 1837, where they are added as more or less a by-product of a compendious plan to catalogue "*every*thing . . . of interest," to become, in effect, the *only* thing of interest.[9]

The subsequent circulation of the folkloresque pixie, then, points in two directions deriving from two sorts of narrative structures in which Bray makes the pixie play a role. On the one hand, in narratives of haunting, pixies act like ghosts in that they lend "an *uncanny affordance* to material geographies" (Holloway and Kneale 2008, 304), producing an entanglement of legend and landscape that has established Dartmoor as a singularly "haunted landscape" that continues to accrete additional folkloresque hauntings and draw tourists of the folkloresque. On the other hand, as characters in entextualized "pixie tales" able to circulate in a media "fantasyscape" (Ruh 2014) outside this haunted landscape, pixies become less spooky and more lighthearted folkloric figures, standard, almost generic figures of British fairy lore, dressed in green, on the pages of color-illustrated children's books, attracting to themselves ever more generic features of the Victorian and Edwardian British fairy (butterfly or dragonfly wings, for example). Both these folkloresque trajectories emerge in part from the way that Bray deploys the pixie within her original design as a figure within a picturesque description of a locality.

Acknowledgments

The author would like to thank the editors, Michael Foster and Jeffrey Tolbert, for their interest, insight, and effort in helping this chapter come to fruition. Among others, the author would also like to thank Ronald James, Rupert Stasch, Charles Stewart, and especially Tim Sandles for permission to use an image from his wonderful Legendary Dartmoor web page.

NOTES

1. Note that illustrated "Christmas gift books" included both those specifically aimed at children as well as books for adults. As Kooistra (2002, 15–16) notes, with specific reference to Rossetti's *Goblin Market*, the tendency to interpret all such illustrated gift books as being marketed to children is part of a twentieth-century tendency to equate picture books, particularly those dealing with fairies, with juvenile audiences.

2. These writings date from Hearn's New Orleans period, but it is clear that Hearn (also a believer in real fairies [Silver 1999, 34]) was fully prepared to see Japan in the light of the folkloresque category of "fairyland" before he even arrived, and the term is one he uses in many places to describe the "preternatural loveliness" of the Japanese landscape, where "Really you are happy because you have entered bodily into Fairyland—into a world that is not, and never could be your own" (Hearn 1997, 29).

3. Hitchins uses a different pronunciation, *piskay*, and there is considerable variation in the folkloric names for these creatures. Bray herself implicitly differentiates her semi-literary "folkloresque" pixies from folkloric *pigsies* ("real pigsie tales") and *piskies* (in place-names), perhaps to keep her own authorial voice separated from the narrators of these tales.

4. Bray surely did not devise this particular format; it is her choice to use it that is significant. She had used the same format five years previously (Bray 1831) to introduce the poetry of a domestic servant, Mary Colling, to a general literary audience personified by Southey.

5. Compare, for example, the paragraph-long full title of the natural history of William Borlase (1758), which shows an orderly progression from natural history (general conditions, minerals, vegetables, animals) to civic history (inhabitants, manners, customs, language, economy, arts): *The Natural History of Cornwall: The Air, Climate, Waters, Rivers, Lakes, Sea and Tides; Of the Stones, Semimetals, Metals, TIN, and the Manner of Mining; The CONSTITUTION of the STANNARIES; Iron, Copper, Silver, Lead and Gold, found in Cornwall; Vegetables, Rare Birds, Fishes, Shells, Reptiles and Quadrupeds; Of the INHABITANTS, their Manners, Customs, Plays or Interludes, Exercises and Festivals; The CORNISH LANGUAGE, Trade, Tenures and Arts.*

6. I am using the commonplace eighteenth- to nineteenth-century collocation "picturesque assemblage" (originally in Gilpin 1792) used to describe a picturesque scene composed of pleasingly heterogeneous irregular or contrasting elements, hybridized with Bruno Latour's well-known collocation "assemblage of heterogeneous elements" both to

suggest a kinship between the "messy" aesthetics of the picturesque and the equally messy aesthetics of actor-network theory and to propose that in many ways the picturesque localities of hauntings can be analyzed in similar fashion.

7. BBC Countryfile.com; for the steady accretion of folkloresque hauntings, see Sandles n.d.

8. Later accounts, like that of Crossing (1890), specifically sought to remedy this dearth of haunts but managed to come up with only one more (Piskie's Holt); nonetheless, like Bray, they generalize from these examples to a generally haunted landscape: "The two grottoes that I have noticed are the principal haunts of the pixies of Dartmoor, but there is not a tor near any of the moorland farms that has not been visited by them occasionally, and every homestead has at some time or other been the scene of the pranks of these merry elves" (5).

9. Bray's work in turn inspired more "folkloresque" elaborations of a similar kind showing similar trajectories (text to illustrated image, adult audience to children): the famous poem *Goblin Market*, penned by her cousin Christina Rossetti in 1859 and published in 1862, was originally titled *A Peep at the Goblins* and appears to be based on a pixie legend in Bray's earlier work (Marsh 1994, 230).

REFERENCES

Andrews, Malcolm. 1989. *The Search for the Picturesque*. Stanford: Stanford University Press.

Bauman, Richard. 2004. *A World of Others' Words: Cross-cultural Perspectives on Intertextuality*. Boston: Blackwell. http://dx.doi.org/10.1002/9780470773895.

Borlase, William. 1758. *The Natural History of Cornwall, &c.* Oxford: W. Jackson.

Bown, Nicola. 2001. *Fairies in Nineteenth Century Art and Literature*. Cambridge: Cambridge University Press.

Bray, Anna Eliza. 1831. *Fables and Other Pieces in Verse by Mary Maria Colling, with Some Account of the Author in Letters to Robert Southey, Esq. Poet Laureate*. London: Longman, Rees, Orme, Brown and Green.

Bray, Anna Eliza. 1834. *Warleigh; or, The Fatal Oak: A Legend of Devon*. London: Longman, Brown, Green and Longmans.

Bray, Anna Eliza. 1836. *A Description of the Part of Devonshire Bordering on the Tamar and the Tavy: Its Natural History, Manners, Customs, Superstitions, Scenery, Antiquities, Biography of Eminent Persons, &c. &c. in a Series of Letters to Robert Southey*. 3 vols. London: John Murray.

Bray, Anna Eliza. 1838. *Traditions, Legends, Superstitions, and Sketches of Devonshire on the Borders of the Tamar and the Tavy, Illustrative of Its Manners, Customs, History, Antiquities, Scenery, and Natural History, in a Series of Letters to Robert Southey, Esq.* 3 vols.. London: John Murray.

Bray, Anna Eliza. 1854. *A Peep at the Pixies; or, Legends of the West*. London: Grant and Griffith.

Bray, Anna Eliza. 1884. *Autobiography of Anna Eliza Bray*. London: Chapman and Hall.

Chard, Chloe. 1999. "The Road to Ruin: Memory, Ghosts, Moonlight and Weeds." In *Roman Presences: Receptions of Rome in European Culture, 1789–1945*, edited by Catharine Edwards, 125–39. Cambridge: Cambridge University Press.

Coleridge, Samuel. 1793. *Songs of the Pixies*. https://en.wikisource.org/wiki/Songs_of_the_Pixies (accessed June 12, 2014).

Crossing, William. 1890. *Tales of the Dartmoor Pixies: Glimpses of Elfin Haunts and Antics*. London: Hood.

Felmingham, Michael. 1988. *The Illustrated Gift Book, 1880–1930*. Aldershot, UK: Scolar.

Gilpin, William. 1792. *Observations on the River Wye, and Several Parts of South Wales, etc. Relative Chiefly to Picturesque Beauty; Made in the Summer of the Year 1770.* http://www.litencyc .com/php/anthology.php?UID=138.

Gordon, Beverly. 2006. *The Saturated World: Aesthetic Meaning, Intimate Objects, Women's Lives, 1890–1940.* Knoxville: University of Tennessee Press.

Hearn, Lafcadio. 1919. *Fantastics and Other Fancies.* Boston: Houghton Mifflin.

Hearn, Lafcadio. (Original work published 1904) 1997. *Lafcadio Hearn's Japan.* Edited by Donald Ritchie. North Clarendon, VT: Tuttle.

Hitchins, F. 1824. *The History of Cornwall from the Earliest Records and Traditions, to the Present Time.* 2 vols. Helston: William Penaluna.

Holloway, Julian, and James Kneale. 2008. "Locating Haunting: A Ghost-Hunter's Guide." *Cultural Geographies* 15(3): 297–312. http://dx.doi.org/10.1177/1474474008091329.

Keightley, Thomas. 1850. *The Fairy Mythology.* 2nd ed. London: H. G. Bohn.

King, Richard John. 1873. "The Folk-lore of Devonshire." *Fraser's Magazine,* n.s. 8 (48): 773–85.

Kooistra, Lorraine Janzen. 2002. *Christina Rossetti and Illustration: A Publishing History.* Athens: Ohio University Press.

Luckhurst, Roger. 2002. "The Contemporary London Gothic and the Limits of the 'Spectral Turn.'" *Textual Practice* 16(3): 527–46. http://dx.doi.org/10.1080/095023602101 63336.

Maas, Jeremy, et al., eds. 1997. *Victorian Fairy Painting.* London: Merrell Holberton.

Marsh, Jan. 1994. *Christina Rossetti: A Writer's Life.* New York: Viking.

Mythical Creatures Guide. n.d. "Pixie." *Mythical Creatures Guide.* http://www.mythical creaturesguide.com/page/Pixie (accessed June 12, 2014).

Ruh, Brian. 2014. "Conceptualizing Anime and the Database Fantasyscape." *Mechademia* 9(1): 164–75. http://dx.doi.org/10.1353/mec.2014.0012.

Ruskin, John. 1884. *The Art of England: Lectures Given in Oxford.* New York: J. Wiley and Sons.

Sandles, Tim. n.d. *Legendary Dartmoor.* http://www.legendarydartmoor.co.uk/index.htm (accessed June 12, 2014).

Silver, Carole. 1999. *Strange and Secret Peoples: Fairies and Victorian Consciousness.* Oxford: Oxford University Press.

Southey, Robert. 1837. Review of *A Description of the Part of Devonshire Bordering on the Tamar and the Tavy,* by Anna Eliza Bray. *Quarterly Review* 59:275–327.

4

Comics as Folklore

Daniel Peretti

COMIC BOOKS ARE NOT FOLKLORE. Or at least they don't qualify as such if we understand folklore according to traditional academic definitions that foreground the dynamics of unmediated human interaction. Nonetheless, writers both inside and outside the discipline of folkloristics have different ideas about what folklore is. This chapter, then, will take a look at some of those ideas, building toward an understanding of the folkloresque in an environment where traditional folklore coexists with the folkloresque in contemporary American culture. The medium of comic books presents too vast an array of possibilities to examine in a single chapter. For the present purposes, I have chosen to look at Superman as an exemplar of the super-hero genre in comics. His genesis and the role ascribed to him by scholars have led to situations where writers find it useful to refer to him as folklore.

The relationship between folklore and technologically mediated forms of storytelling such as comic books is complicated. Each exists on its own terms while simultaneously incorporating elements of the other. Superman presents an interesting case because, regardless of the influences that led to his creation, he existed originally in comic books and newspaper strips. Whereas much folklore does not financially benefit the performer, creators Jerry Siegel and Joe Shuster were very much interested in the commercial possibilities of Superman, going so far as to sketch out what the character might look like on a cereal box (Daniels 1998, 28–30). It is the commercial nature of the character—that he can be found on cereal boxes, in movies and television, on lunch boxes and pajamas—that enabled him to stake a claim to a portion of the larger American cultural landscape. As people, including scholars, work toward understanding the role of the medium of comic books and the superheroes that came to dominate their pages, they

DOI: 10.7330/9781607324188.c004

called upon other, more readily comprehensible aspects of culture, such as folklore. Thus Superman fits well into a discussion of the rhetoric of the folkloresque. In this chapter, the various ways that Superman and comic books have been understood as folklore will build toward an understanding of the interaction between folklore and popular culture. Popular culture does not just operate in a folkloresque mode; it can become folklore.

THE FOLKLORESQUE SUPERMAN

Superman[1] stories fit within the framework of the folkloresque and have done so since the character's genesis. Jerry Siegel's own claim about the conception of Superman—that he stayed awake one night circa 1933, imagining a strong man in the vein of Samson and Hercules—shows us that he had something like integration in mind, resembling the fuzzy allusions and cobbled-together qualities of the folkloresque described by Michael Foster earlier in this volume. Siegel wanted to create a folk hero, though not by following any single tradition (Steranko 1970, 37–39), which is often how the folkloresque integration of folklore into popular culture works. Though the form of a comic book is not precisely the same as oral tradition, we will see below that many writers perceive remarkable similarities between the two. To demonstrate how Superman comics integrate folklore, it's best to begin with some good old-fashioned motif spotting (Koven 2008). Drawing from Stith Thompson's *Motif Index of Folk Literature*[2] (Thompson 1955–1958), Ronald Baker writes of Superman's origin in terms of hero tales, and he points out many traditional motifs: L111.2, Foundling hero; L111.2.1, Future hero found in boat; N825.1, Childless old couple adopt hero; D1540, Magic invulnerability; and Z312, Unique deadly weapon, only one thing will kill a certain man (Baker 1975, 174).

Two specific Superman stories from different decades demonstrate that folkloric motifs can be found beyond the character's origin. I have chosen these because their integration of folklore is readily apparent. In the earlier story, "The Lady and the Lion" (Binder and Boring 2005), Superman drinks a potion created by Circe—diegetically the same Circe from *The Odyssey*—which transforms him into a lion-man. We find in this tale motifs D110, Transformation of man to wild beast (mammal) and D1040, Magic drink. The characters also see a play based on "Beauty and the Beast" (ATU 425C).[3] The more recent series *Absolute All-Star Superman* (Morrison and Quitely 2010) is useful to examine because it incorporates folklore in several different ways. Its writer, Grant Morrison, states his intentions clearly: "Saddled with this slightly odd and archaic title, [penciler Frank] Quitely and

I decided to make it literal and to tell the story of Superman as star, or solar 'deity,' hence our opening shot of Superman framed by solar flares and the structure of the story which traverses one epic 'day'—dipping below the horizon in issue six so that Superman, like all good solar myth heroes, can journey through midwinter's longest Night and the upside-down under-world before rising again in issue nine, revitalized" (Morrison and Quitely 2010).[4] Mythical figures Samson and Atlas show up as foils for Superman in issue 3. Morrison modeled the overarching plot for this series on the twelve labors of Hercules, stating as much himself and going so far as to list them for readers. Furthermore, issue 2 of *All-Star Superman*, "Superman's Forbidden Room," bears an unmistakable resemblance to ATU311/Motif C611 with its reference to a forbidden chamber and the common story in which that motif appears: ATU312—Bluebeard.

Immediately we see that Superman comic books from a variety of eras exhibit a folkloresque integration of folkloric motifs and tale types as part of their never-ending narratives. Writers have also created "folkloric" material within Superman narratives to flesh out the character's backstory. Over the course of Superman's publication history, writers and editors have invented written languages for Superman's home planet along with planetary and cultural history. Elements of that history correspond to many of the traditional genres of folklore. The story "Awake in the Dark" (Simone and Byrne 2006), for example, features a Kryptonian mother telling what seems to be a fairy tale to her son at bedtime. The cover includes the text, "Once upon a time in Krypton" to further the folkloresque depiction of Kryptonian culture. The writers integrate this invented folklore into their stories.

Superman comics have been successful in part because they employ materials resembling folklore. This allows readers to find something that feels familiar and thus draws them into the story. We might consider Superman's superhuman strength outlandish, but it fits within the larger tradition of strong men and becomes acceptable in that context. There might be something to say about the result of the inclusion of specific tale types and motifs (i.e., what Superman identifying with the Beast implies about his relationship with Lois Lane), but this isn't the place to conduct such analysis. Instead, I want to dig into the perception of Superman comics—and comics in general—as folklore.

THE FOLKLORISTIC PERSPECTIVE ON COMIC BOOKS

In an article titled "Print and American Folktales," Richard Dorson discusses the dissemination of oral narrative in American history: "One especial difference, the influence of printing in American life, upsets cherished convictions and established methods of the folklorist. For the ubiquitous printed page becomes an instrument to diffuse and a tablet to record folk tales. Stories in the United States travel interchangeably through the spoken and the printed word; if communities are scattered and fluid and culturally advanced beyond the cement of purely oral tradition, a cohesive force is supplied by commonly read printed matter" (Dorson 1945, 207–8). In recognizing the relationship between oral and technologically produced culture, Dorson sets the tone for the discussion of comics as folkloresque.

Dorson mentions newspapers, weekly magazines, regional periodicals, popular humor publications, local history, and literature itself—but not comic books, though he was writing when comics were at their peak circulation. Folklorists all but ignored comic books before the 1970s. Alex Scobie (1980, 71) enumerates some reasons why: disciplinary dogma, prejudice, lack of availability—all of which concerns are vanishing or nonexistent now.

Five years after Dorson's article, *Southern Folklore Quarterly* published an article by Paul G. Brewster that explores some folkloric motifs and tale types (without reference to the indexes) that appear in comics. Brewster (1950, 97) sets his work within the context of other studies that explore folklore in "more serious art." He finds folklore in a variety of comics; in Superman he sees magical transformation as the operative motif.[5] Brewster's analysis goes no further than identifying folkloric elements. Two years later, in the same journal, Grace Partridge Smith gives a more judgmental analysis. Confining her attention to newspaper strips—humorous ones, not Superman—she opens by arguing that a comic adaptation of a folktale "not only debases the materials of our discipline but also threatens the cultural background of the child" (Smith 1952, 124). She condemns the manner in which the cartoonists stop at nothing in their quest to keep their readers' attention. In the process, she notes some adaptations of specific stories, such as "Cinderella" and the "Pied Piper."

Several folklorists in the 1970s turned their attention to comics. Ellen Rhoads focuses on *Little Orphan Annie*. She conceptualizes comics as folklore and studies them through the method of structuralism—a theory often applied to folklore. Early on, Rhoads includes a quotation by the German literary scholars Reitberger and Fuchs that echoes much of what we have seen regarding the role of comic books: "Comics, together with the other mass media, are a substitute for genuine folklore and culture and have developed into a self-perpetuating institution, and integral part of the American Way of Life" (Rhoads 1973, 346; Rolf Brednich makes the same reference, see below). Rhoads, whose study of *Little Orphan Annie* comics appeared in the *Journal of American Folklore*, considers the words of these scholars as enough to go on when labeling comics as folklore: "As mentioned above, comics constitute a form of folklore, a view shared by Lerner" (346). It's worth noting that neither Lerner nor Reitberger and Fuchs are folklorists. Rhoads makes no attempt to interrogate these statements, nor does she have to; the emic notion of a form as folkloric can be enough for a folklorist to use. Rhoads doesn't return to the notion of how comics might resemble folklore, but it is implicit in her analysis.

Ronald L. Baker's 1975 study places comics within the context of a declining oral tradition and the rise in popularity of dime novels and other mass forms of entertainment. For Baker, comics have replaced *märchen*. He characterizes the hero of the märchen as "unpromising" and "unassuming," and sees the same sort of character in superhero comics. He discusses many of the folk narrative motifs that show up in superhero stories in general, and in Superman stories in particular. Baker's conclusion, however, points to differences between folk tales and superhero stories. Whereas märchen show us ways that limitations can be overcome, according to Baker, "contemporary comic books provide little psychological release from our limitations; they simply reinforce our hangups" (Baker 1975, 174). It's important to note that he's writing about comic books of the 1970s, and that studying the general mood in comics during other time periods might reveal different trends.

A year later, Rolf Wilhlem Brednich begins his folkloristic discussion of comics with the rhetorical move of comparing superheroes and comics in general to older, more venerable forms of art: "Illustrated subjects of narration were found on Egyptian tombs, on Greek vases, Roman victory columns, and so forth. Medieval legend frescoes and altar panels make the connection to the early woodcuts on broadsheets before and after 1500. From that time, a direct path leads to the picture sheets of European image-producers and to the very cradle of comics—America of the late nineteenth century" (Brednich 1976, 45). Brednich stresses the need to examine forms of communication other than oral tradition, forms that are popular and ephemeral, such as comics. He sees no fundamental difference between the popular narrative forms of the previous centuries and the comic book, by which he means that the story is conveyed by a conjunction of words and images. Those elements that have changed— number of copies, distribution, and production techniques—make comics far more influential. He confines his analysis to the content of superhero comics, finding parallels with oral tradition as understood by scholars such as Vladimir Propp and Max Luthi.

Alex Scobie takes a broader perspective in his analysis, which is relevant to the idea of the folkloresque. Whereas most of the other writers here mentioned focus on the content, Scobie attends to the books themselves and their contexts. While acknowledging that the comic book is part of literature, Scobie writes that "as a medium the comic book strives more than any other printed literature to create the intimate rapport between producer and reader which is aimed at by the oral storyteller and his listener-participants" (Scobie 1980, 73). The "pseudo—or quasi—oral nature of the comic book" is achieved, according to Scobie, through the oral editions produced on gramophone records (the equivalent at the time of this writing would be the motion comic) and comics being read aloud. He also finds relevant the migration of certain comic book characters such as Superman into other media where there is a greater oral dimension. But Scobie, following Charles Wooley (1974), also describes aspects of the creation of comic books that resemble oral tradition: anonymity in the production of comics resulting from corporate ownership (though he admits that this varies from comic to comic); a rotating series of creators, resembling the process of multiple narrators for most tales collected from oral tradition; narrative inconsistencies and formulaic expressions, which Scobie attributes to the speed at which comics must be produced; sound effects and idiosyncratic typography that create a semblance of orality on the page. Publishers also try to foster an atmosphere of reader participation through letters pages, and creators earn their living by keeping the audience paying in a way similar to professional storytellers, by teasing the conclusion or next episode at the end of the current one (Scobie 1980, 76–80).

Brednich's call to arms was not really picked up by folklorists until the twenty-first century, when scholars such as Adam Zolkover (2008) and Jeremy Stoll (2011) started paying more attention to comics. Zolkover and Stoll are both interested in the transformation of folk motifs as they become part of comic books, in the American series *Fables* and the Indian Rama stories published in *Amar Chitra Katha*, respectively. They are interested in the operation of the medium itself and the possibilities it opens up when dealing with traditional characters and narratives.

PERSPECTIVES FROM OUTSIDE FOLKLORE

According to Lauretta Bender and Reginald S. Lourie, "Comic books can probably be best understood if they are looked upon as an expression of the folklore of this age. They may be compared with the mythology, fairy tales, and puppet shows, for example, of past ages" (Bender and Lourie

1941, 546). This is perhaps the earliest academic equation of comic books and folklore, and it comes as part of a study of how children use comics. Their goal in this comparison is to demonstrate that comic books can serve the same psychological function that these prior forms of narrative have served, offering adaptive strategies for children. Yet the rhetorical move of comparing comics with other, older forms has taken hold. Scholars in the burgeoning field of comics studies make many references to folklore and folk heroes when discussing Superman. There is an interpretive strategy at work here: understand Superman, these writers seem to say, as you would understand other heroic figures from the past (see also Tim Evans's chapter 2 in this volume). There's an element of the folkloresque in analyses and interpretations that place Superman in the context of ancient heroic figures. I've already noted that in interviews the original Superman writer and creator Jerry Siegel invoked such legendary figures as Samson and Hercules; literary and comics scholars do much the same thing. They do not employ the folkloristic motif or tale-type indexes, but they are sometimes aware of the methods and literature of folkloristics.

M. Thomas Inge (1990) states that the medium closest to comics is probably cinema; nonetheless, he refers to many folk heroes and traditions when discussing comics characters. He devotes a full chapter to Superman and the early years of comic books, and in it he discusses Superman's popularity by taking into account the American interest in heroic folktales and myths, which the technology—and interest in technology—of comic books synthesized into a single genre. Inge places Superman in a line of heroes of western civilization with superhuman strength, such as Ulysses, Hercules, Samson, Beowulf, and King Arthur. The American frontier experience shaped the genesis of the country's heroes, but, Inge states,

> It is important to note that these figures achieved national prominence
> not because of the persistence of oral traditions but because their exploits
> entered the pages of books, dime novels, almanacs, newspaper columns,
> and sheet music (and in some cases were largely created there). A large part
> of the heroic folklore in this century [the twentieth] has survived because
> of the technology of print (and later film and television), and it might be
> argued that this print material is the proper folklore for an industrial soci-
> ety rather than the isolated oral traditions. Folklore purists would disagree
> with such a notion, however (141; see also Levine 1992).

Inge may have had Richard Dorson in mind when thinking of "folklore purists."[6] He cites Dorson's 1939 study of Davy Crockett and references Archer Taylor's study of the hero pattern, applying it to Superman. Inge's application of Taylor's analysis isn't terribly felicitous (he labels Spider-Man a trickster because he is "anti-social" and makes jokes while fighting villains), but his larger point is apt: "Most of the heroes of the world of comic books likewise fit these patterns which are as old as Western Civilization. It seems obvious, then, that the comic books have continued to maintain and develop these patterns, translate them into forms more suitable to a post-industrial society, and educate young readers in a significant part of their cultural heritage" (Inge 1990, 142). "Like folklore," Inge continues, "it [the comic book] gave new life to traditions of heroic and mythic figures that the modern oral tradition cannot sustain in the face of mass communication" (145). Inge's analysis covers some of the same ground as the work of folklorists on comics referenced above.

In "Men of Darkness," C. J. Mackie (2007) compares Superman and Batman to the epic heroes Achilles and Odysseus, respectively. Though his purpose is to show that the superheroes reflect the same patterns and concerns as the epic heroes, one effect is to place the two types of heroes on common ground. Analysis of superheroes in terms of epic heroes works to validate the superhero's role in contemporary culture. Many writers note the Christian overtones in Superman stories (Brewer 2004; Galloway 1973; Garrett 2005; Koslovic 2002; Kozloff 1981; Skelton 2006). Others see echoes of ancient mythologies in Superman stories and other comic book superheroes (Knowles 2007; LoCicero 2008; Saunders 2011). One of the more influential comic book scholars, Richard Reynolds (1992), calls his study *Superheroes: A Modern Mythology.*

These studies are largely literary in their understanding of heroes and mythology—folkloresque in style rather than in substance—but Terrence R. Wandtke (2012) conducts a book-length study of comic book production that is substantially folkloresque in its method. Wandtke explores the idea of the creation of comic book superheroes as analogous to oral tradition (he does not use the term folklore). Though he explores the same ideas that Wooley (1974) and Scobie (1980) address, Wandtke founds his study on the description of oral epic, following scholars such as John Miles Foley, Albert Lord, and Milman Perry. His command of these scholars' work is evident, and his account of the theory of oral composition is compelling in its application to the first several decades of comic books. He marks the difference between oral and literate culture—and thus between literate and secondary orality—as an aesthetic difference as well as a participatory one. He references fan cultures and how they have shaped the comic book industry, and he points to differences in the types of stories comic book fans prefer: "Consumers of comic book stories demonstrate tendencies characteristic of people within an oral culture through their almost pathological desire to return to the superhero's origin; repetition is privileged and this repetition reinforces the basic truths of the story and the fan community" (Wandtke 2012, 25). Here we see the need for a further exploration of those for whom these stories are important, perhaps along the lines of the studies of participatory culture conducted by Janice Radway (1991), Henry Jenkins (1992), and Camille Bacon-Smith (1992).

Wandtke also examines reader participation in the superhero story, noting especially the sense of "collective ownership" facilitated by the actual corporate ownership of the characters: "Through the policy of corporate ownership, the industry erased the individual author (and past versions of the superhero's story) and created a sense of collective ownership that stresses currency over primacy" (Wandtke 2012, 25). This sense of collective ownership, which Wandtke develops to a greater extent than Scobie, is part of his argument that the superhero genre in comic books should be thought of in terms of oral culture rather than literate culture. There's a "different sense of authority" when creators are part of a system rather than championed as individuals: "As a curious consequence of the standard practices of superhero comic book publishers, superheroes came to be regarded as collectively owned, and the story of the superhero transcended the individual writers and illustrators currently working on the superhero titles" (43–44). Wandtke's argument for new traditionality operating in comic books comprises the most extensive statement of comics as folklore. The author shows that the form, distribution, and content operate in a manner remarkably similar to that governing oral traditional epics. His analysis fits nicely in the line of thought that digital media represent a return to something akin to oral tradition. As we have already seen, folklorists began thinking about comic books in terms of oral tradition in the 1950s.

Many books written for a popular audience interpret Superman and other superheroes as characters from a folkloric (or folkloresque) pantheon. Danny Fingeroth's (2004) *Superman on the Couch* includes a chapter titled "It Started with Gilgamesh" that draws comparisons with ancient myth, early American folklore (he calls them tall tales), and the heroes of pulps. In discussing the evolution of stories in the early twentieth century—in particular *The Shadow*, but he applies this to all superheroes from those early decades—he writes that the characters started in a "rough form" but were developed as they spanned media and time: "Like a game of cross-media telephone, the characters evolved in the manner that folk heroes always had, but through modern communications technology, the various incarnations were transmitted simultaneously to thousands and millions of eager readers, viewers and listeners" (Fingeroth 2004, 39).

Dennis O'Neil, writer of Superman comics in the 1970s, characterizes the process of creating comics as a "folk process." "If you read Superman stories in chronological order," writes O'Neil, "you get a sense of guys around a campfire trying to top each other with tall tales; the yarns build from the extravagant to the preposterous and silly" (O'Neil 1987, 51). He compares the creation of Superman stories to a "maniacally accelerated version of the folk process; like fairy tales and myths, the Superman stories were begun by one creator but embellished and altered by many. Because of the need to *produce*, to fill those pages, meet those deadlines, get the stuff out there, what would have taken generations in the preindustrial era took only a few years. And as with folk tales, and particularly myths, the personality of the hero, as perceived by the public, was a residue left in the collective consciousness after audiences and readers were exposed to several different versions of what was presumed to be the same character" (O'Neil 1987, 51–52). Though O'Neil never uses the term folklore, it can be inferred from the phrase "folk process" and the comparison to tall tales. O'Neil's insights fit with much of what folklorists have observed: notice that he describes public perception as the result of exposure to different versions of the same tale. For O'Neil, that the means of production have changed during the industrial age has not fundamentally changed storytelling, at least not as far as comic books are concerned. Stories still come from individual creators (though he glosses over the fact that they work as a team) working toward the same ends; the process is just "accelerated." The implication is that both the ability to reach tremendous numbers of readers and the discovery of precisely what readers are willing to pay for have worked to speed the folkloric process.

In the folkloresque portrayal of Superman, the key issue seems to be technology—specifically, the different modes of storytelling made possible through developing technologies. This goes back several decades, being noticed by folklorists as early as the 1970s. Writers such as O'Neil, Inge, and Wandtke refer to industrial society and its effects as having an impact on storytelling and oral tradition. O'Neil is less specific, stating only that we can understand the creation of comic books as we understand oral tradition; Inge is more detailed, and from his comments we can infer that industrial societies have no place for oral tradition. Superman has permeated the boundaries between technologies since his inception, and no doubt will continue to do so. If we accept Wandtke's view of the trajectory of comic book production, as new media emerge that edge closer and closer to oral tradition, so will Superman.

THE FOLKLORIC SUPERMAN

All of this discussion of comic books as a folkloresque form of popular culture overlooks one simple thing: that Superman also exists as folklore. Aspects of culture are connected, as Lawrence Levine reminds us (Levine 1992, 1372). Artists of one medium borrow from others, and that includes folkloric expression. A great deal of scholarship studies the ways that folklore has become part of popular culture, literature, and the like. Of less prominence have been the ways that popular culture has transformed or migrated into folklore. Levine points out, "What people *can* do and *do* do is to refashion the objects created for them to fit their own values, needs, and expectations" (1373). Much of fan studies has sprung from this realization, that people make stories their own even when they don't produce them. As part of the process by which people make the stories—and the character—their own, the folkloresque reverses the common trend and migrates from popular culture into the more traditionally folkloric channels of oral tradition, festival, and material culture. Superman stories travel through these channels as well. As noted above, Jerry Siegel deliberately modeled Superman on heroes of folklore. As with L. Frank Baum and *The Wonderful Wizard of Oz*, described by Foster in the introduction to this volume, Siegel *aspired* to create a story that was similar to folklore. He succeeded, perhaps even to a greater extent than he had hoped.

Superman has become part of oral folklore in forms such as jokes and folk speech. As an instance of folk speech, the term *kryptonite* refers to a person's weakness (similar to the proverbial "Achilles' heel"). "Bizarro," the name of a villain whom Superman often encounters, has become an adjective that refers to things that are backward or opposite from what they should be. Superman has also become a nickname, applied very frequently to athletes. Superman jokes show that folkloric expressions taken from popular culture are not merely echoes of that form of popular culture; they critique and engage with it (see also the contributions of Trevor Blank in chapter 8 and Greg Kelley in chapter 9 of this volume). Here is a version of the most popular of the jokes:

> A guy walks into a bar on the top of a very tall building. He sits down, orders a huge beer, chugs it, walks over to the window, and jumps out. Five minutes later, the guy walks into the bar again, orders another huge beer,

chugs it, walks over to the window, and jumps out again. Five minutes later, he reappears and repeats the whole thing. About half an hour later, another guy at the bar stops the first guy and says, "Hey, how the heck are you doing that?!" The first guy responds, "Oh, it's really simple physics. When you chug the beer, it makes you all warm inside and since warm air rises, if you just hold your breath you become lighter than air and float down to the sidewalk." "*Wow!*" exclaims the second man, "I gotta try that!" So he orders a huge beer, chugs it, goes over to the window, jumps out, and splats on the sidewalk below. The bartender looks over to the first man and says, "Superman, you're a jerk when you're drunk."[7]

I collected this joke, extant with a great many variants, in oral tradition. Note that it's not merely a joke that happens to have Superman in it; the very qualities that make Superman so appealing to many people—specifically, his powers and morality—make the joke work. According to Ben Saunders (2011, 30), Superman stories represent a continual narrative exploration of the concept of moral virtue; this joke, and others, comprise another way to explore that concept.

Superman can be found in material culture as well, perhaps most commonly as costuming and tattoos. I interviewed and photographed many people who have made their own costumes by hand and machine, using makeup, wigs, and spandex to look like superheroes, including Superman. Scott Boyles, whom I interviewed in 2012, makes superhero costumes for himself, his wife, and his three children. Scott makes the majority of the costumes with a sewing machine, using spandex, gingham, and other fabrics he purchases online. His costumes have won contests, and he has even sold some of them. The family wears the costumes at Halloween, to comic book conventions, and to hospitals where, in character, they visit with children. Scott counts himself as a member of several groups of people organized around costuming and around Superman, such as the Superfriends of Metropolis (http://superfriends.spruz.com/); many of these fan groups organize online but meet regularly in person.

Superman has become an organizing principle for festivals as well, notably the Superman Celebration held annually in Metropolis, Illinois. During this festival, locals and fans from outside the Metropolis community perform what can best be classified as folk drama—a short narrative enacted by men and women in costume that portrays Superman's defeat of several villains—as part of an opening ceremony. There are costume contests (which often include short dramatic exhibitions of costumes), dancing, food, and other customary behaviors typical of small-town American festivals.

Superman brings people together, and whenever people get together, they are likely to engage in the sorts of behavior that we call folklore. Though the study of the relationship between folklore and other aspects of culture has a long history, standard definitions of folklore exclude comic books because they are the result of mass production and thus aren't characterized by the unmediated performance on which so much folkloristic analysis depends. There is genuine creativity involved in their production, and that creativity can resemble the dynamics of oral tradition, but the result goes through the printing press. Because of this mediation, the term *folkloresque* encapsulates the processes involved in creating Superman comics and in the discourses that surround them.

There are comparable examples of contemporary traditions of folklore and official or canonical culture. Francis Lee Utley uses the example of the Adam's apple to demonstrate that a rigidly enforced canon of biblical scripture doesn't preclude a concomitant folk tradition: "Not only is this story [about Adam getting a piece of the fruit stuck in his throat] a product of the folk, but it and others . . . are something more unusual, oral lore ultimately derived from a narrowly localized center and an identifiable written text" (Utley 1945, 1). But why does this sort of phenomenon occur? Why do people supplement a fixed text with their own, more fluid performances? The answer is complicated. For Utley, folklore derived from biblical sources exists because religious folks had to invent it "to adorn a tale when the Bible refused to tell the whole story" (5), thus anticipating participatory fan cultures (Jenkins 1992). Utley notes that much Bible folklore is etiological (i.e., the Adam's apple story); recipients need explanations for things that are left as gaps in the text or, more interestingly, to account for the peculiarities of their own world in terms of the Bible. Utley also reminds us that missionaries are the source of a large amount of folklore (Utley 1945, 14), and though he does not attribute this to the fact that much of their teaching of indigenous populations would have been oral, we can assume that it was. So we must consider many cases in which a story learned from print or other media becomes a part of a storytelling tradition (see Grider 1981). Utley even points out that biblical exegesis "gives rise" to details found in folklore: analysis produces the folkloric text. In the end Utley delineates several uses for the folkloristic exploration of the Bible. Among them is the notion that such research contributes to a well-rounded, if not more complete, understanding of humanity. The same can be said of understanding the folkloresque.

For example, in every instance of a folkloresque description of comic books cited above, we can unequivocally say that a greater depth of research into the folkloric method would have enhanced the findings. What would Inge, who relies on Propp for an entire chapter of his work, have done with Alan Dundes's expansion of Propp's functions into allomotifs and motifemes (Dundes 1964)? And though Wandtke has a command of Ong, McLuhan, Foley, and the oral-formulaic theory of composition, there is a great potential for combining his study with other explorations of comics, oral-formulaic composition, and fieldwork-based studies on creativity by Scobie and Wooley.

Acknowledging that there are concomitant folkloric and folkloresque expressions of Superman allows us a more complete perspective on the character and his role in culture. We have seen the relationship that oral tradition has with popular culture—at once exploring the same ideas and reciprocating content. In fact, what we might argue is that the American experience has blended folklore and popular culture to the extent that to comprehensively study one requires attention to the other. Superman exists as folklore only because of the mass media, and that came into being only because of commercial interests. As Ian Gordon (2001, 182) notes, the commercialization of Superman is responsible for his status as an American icon.

However it is explicated, the folkloresque is a vital concept in the continuing study of folklore in the contemporary world. If we ignore popular conceptualizations of folklore, then we do so to our own detriment. The folkloresque offers folklorists a way to engage with scholars from other disciplines, to the benefit of all involved. By paying attention to how the folk conceptualize folklore, we come to know the folk on their own terms, which has always been one of the most commendable aspects of the folkloristic endeavor. With the case of Superman, we can see that technology is important in conceptualizing the difference between folklore and popular culture. However, we also see that the technology of storytelling is not the primary point of interest; the similarities in content are of greater value when considering Superman's place—and the place of the superhero genre as a whole—within American culture and history. Ultimately, the broad scope of American society provides for a symbiotic relationship between popular culture and folk culture, from which our conceptualizations of these forms of expression arise.

NOTES

1. Superman's intertextuality makes this study possible. There are *Superman* comics, but throughout I have foregone the use of italics so that the word Superman refers to the character as it appears intertextually. References to Superman should be taken to mean the character as he appears across various comic titles such as *Action, Man of Steel*, and the like.

2. Thompson's (1955–1958) *Motif-Index*, like subsequent related works published by other authors, sets out to catalogue and enumerate all the traditional, widespread elements present in a variety of folklore and literature. Its subtitle is perhaps the best explanation: *A Classification of Narrative Elements in Folktales, Ballads, Myths, Fables, Mediaeval Romances, Exempla, Fabliaux, Jest-Books, and Local Legends.* Thompson employs a system of letters and numbers to categorize and reference the elements he found in these sources, with various headings (D, for example, contains magic motifs, while D10–D99 include transformations from "man to different man"; adding further decimal numbers makes the motif more specific). The index provides the sources for these motifs, so that they can be checked and compared.

3. Folklorists often rely on a tale-type index similar to the motif index. Antti Aarne published the first version of this index, which was later expanded by Stith Thompson (at which point folklorists began referring to tale types by their AT number, for Aarne-Thompson). Hans-Jörg Uther expanded the index once again in 2004, and since then the tales have been referred to by their ATU number (Uther 2004).

4. Comics are often published without page numbers. The edition of *All-Star Superman* I used, which contained interviews and notes by the writer, had none. The material I have cited can be found in the notes at the end of that volume.

5. It's hard to pin down the specific motif covering Superman's change to and from his secret identity. It may fall somewhere within motifs D10–D99 and D1050, Magical garments; but more apt may be K1810, Deception by disguise—there's no magic involved in the transformation from Clark Kent to Superman.

6. Levine further examines the early twentieth-century institutional bias against studying folklore and folk music that arose out of popular culture, summing it up nicely: "Folklorists might have been purists; the folk rarely were" (Levine 1992, 1377).

7. I have included this version for brevity—those I collected during interviews were much longer. See http://www.fark.com/comments/665365/Wil-Wheaton-beer-joke-Coors-Miller -surrender (accessed March 13, 2014). As with many online jokes, this one is repeated verbatim on several other sites.

REFERENCES

Bacon-Smith, Camille. 1992. *Enterprising Women: Television Fandom and the Creation of Popular Myth.* Philadelphia: University of Pennsylvania Press.

Baker, Ronald L. 1975. "Folklore Motifs in the Comic Books of Superheroes." *Tennessee Folklore Society Bulletin* 41(4): 170–74.

Bender, Lauretta, and Reginald S. Lourie. 1941. "The Effect of Comic Books on the Ideology of Children." *American Journal of Orthopsychiatry* 11(3): 540–50. http://dx.doi.org /10.1111/j.1939-0025.1941.tb05840.x.

Binder, Otto, and Wayne Boring. (Original work published 1958) 2005. "The Lady and the Lion." *Action Comics* 243. In *Showcase Presents Superman*, 1:85–97. New York: DC Comics.

Brednich, Rolf Wilhelm. 1976. "Comic Strips as a Subject of Folk Narrative Research." Translated by Susanne Siegert. In *Folklore Today: A Festschrift for Richard M. Dorson*, edited by Linda Dégh, Henry Glassie, and Felix J. Oinas, 45–55. Bloomington: Indiana University Press.

Brewer, H. Michael. 2004. *Who Needs a Superhero? Finding Virtue, Vice and What's Holy in the Comics.* Grand Rapids: Baker Books.

Brewster, Paul G. 1950. "Folklore Invades the Comic Strips." *Southern Folklore Quarterly* 14:97–102.

Daniels, Les. 1998. *Superman, the Complete History: The Life and Times of the Man of Steel.* San Francisco: Chronicle Books.

Dorson, Richard M. 1939. *Davy Crocket: American Comic Legend.* New York: Spiral Press for Rockland Editions.

Dorson, Richard M. 1945. "Print and American Folk Tales." *California Folklore Quarterly* 4(3): 207–15. http://dx.doi.org/10.2307/1495815.

Dundes, Alan. 1964. *The Morphology of North American Folktales.* Helsinki: Suomalainen Tiedeakatemia, Academia Scientiarium Fennica.

Fingeroth, Danny. 2004. *Superman on the Couch: What Superheroes Really Tell Us about Ourselves and Our Society.* New York: Continuum.

Galloway, John T., Jr. 1973. *The Gospel According to Superman.* Philadelphia: A. J. Holman.

Garrett, Greg. 2005. *Holy Superheroes! Exploring Faith and Spirituality in Comic Books.* Colorado Springs: Piñon.

Gordon, Ian. 2001. "Nostalgia, Myth, and Ideology: Visions of Superman at the end of the 'American Century.'" In *Comics & Ideology*, edited by Matthew P. McAllister, Edward H. Sewell Jr., and Ian Gordon, 177–93. New York: Peter Lang.

Grider, Sylvia. 1981. "The Media Narraform: Symbiosis of Mass Media and Oral Tradition." *Arv* 37:125–31.

Inge, M. Thomas. 1990. *Comics as Culture.* Jackson: University Press of Mississippi.

Jenkins, Henry. 1992. *Textual Poachers: Television Fans & Participatory Culture.* New York: Routledge.

Knowles, Christopher. 2007. *Our Gods Wear Spandex: The Secret History of Comic Book Heroes.* San Francisco: Weiser Books.

Koslovic, Anton Karl. 2002. "Superman as Christ-Figure: The American Pop Culture Movie Messiah." *Journal of Religion* 6(1): 1–25.

Koven, Mikel J. 2008. *Film, Folklore, and Urban Legends.* Lanham, MD: Scarecrow.

Kozloff, S. R. 1981. "Superman as Saviour: Christian Allegory in the Superman Movies." *Journal of Popular Film and Television* 9(2): 78–82. http://dx.doi.org/10.1080/0195605 1.1981.10001893.

Levine, Lawrence W. 1992. "The Folklore of Industrial Society: Popular Culture and Its Audiences." *American Historical Review* 97(5): 1369–99. http://dx.doi.org/10.2307 /2165941.

LoCicero, Don. 2008. *Superheroes and Gods: A Comparative Study from Babylonia to Batman.* Jefferson, NC: McFarland.

Mackie, C. J. 2007. "Men of Darkness." In *Super/Heroes: From Hercules to Superman*, edited by Wendy Haslem, Angela Nadlianis, and Chris Mackie, 83–95. Washington, DC: New Academia Publishing.

Morrison, Grant, and Frank Quitely. 2010. *Absolute All-Star Superman.* New York: DC Comics.

O'Neil, Dennis. 1987. "The Man of Steel and Me." In *Superman at Fifty! The Persistence of a Legend*, edited by Dennis Dooley and Gary Engle, 46–58. Cleveland: Octavia.

Radway, Janice A. 1991. *Reading the Romance: Women, Patriarchy, and Popular Literature.* Chapel Hill: University of North Carolina Press.

Reynolds, Richard. 1992. *Super Heroes: A Modern Mythology.* London: BT Batsford, Ltd.

Rhoads, Ellen. 1973. "Little Orphan Annie and Levi-Strauss: The Myth and the Method." *Journal of American Folklore* 86(342): 345–57. http://dx.doi.org/10.2307/539358.

Saunders, Ben. 2011. *Do the Gods Wear Capes? Spirituality, Fantasy, and Superheroes.* New York: Continuum.

Scobie, Alex. 1980. "Comics and Folkliterature." *Fabula* 21(1): 70–81. http://dx.doi.org/10 .1515/fabl.1980.21.1.70.

Simone, Gail, and John Byrne. 2006. "Awake in the Dark." *Action Comics* 834. New York: DC Comics.

Skelton, Stephen. 2006. *The Gospel According to the World's Greatest Superhero*. Eugene: Harvest House.

Smith, Grace Partridge. 1952. "The Plight of the Folktale in the Comics." *Southern Folklore Quarterly* 16:124–27.

Steranko, Jim. 1970. *The Steranko History of Comics*. Vol. 1. Reading, PA: Supergraphics.

Stoll, Jeremy. 2011. "Rama for Beginners: Bridging Indian Folk and Comics Cultures." *Folklore Forum* (November). http://folkloreforum.net/2011/11/25/rama-for-beginners-bridging-indian-folk-and-comics-cultures/.

Thompson, Stith. 1955–1958. *Motif-Index of Folk Literature: A Classification of Narrative Elements in Folktales, Ballads, Myths, Fables, Mediaeval Romances, Exempla, Fabliaux, Jest-Books, and Local Legends*. 6 vols. Bloomington: Indiana University Press.

Uther, Hans-Jörg. 2004. *The Types of International Folktales: A Classification and Bibliography, Based on the System of Antti Aarne and Stith Thompson*. Helsinki: Suomalainen Tiedeakatemia, Academia Scientiarium Fennica.

Utley, Francis Lee. 1945. "The Bible of the Folk." *California Folklore Quarterly* 4(1): 1–17. http://dx.doi.org/10.2307/1495452.

Wandtke, Terrence R. 2012. *The Meaning of Superhero Comic Books*. Jefferson, NC: McFarland.

Wooley, Charles. 1974. "An American Mythology." *Harvard Journal of Pictorial Fiction* 1 (Spring): 24–30.

Zolkover, Adam. 2008. "Corporealizing Fairy Tales: The Body, the Bawdy, and the Carnivalesque in the Comic Book *Fables*." *Marvels and Tales* 22(1): 38–51.

Portrayal

Introduction

Jeffrey A. Tolbert

ALL OTHER CONSIDERATIONS ASIDE, THE MOST FUNDAMENTAL aspect of the folkloresque is its capacity to enable critical commentary on any range of topics. By using the available materials of culture, broadly understood, individuals and groups can make clear their positions on issues relevant to their own lives. While all three of the major modes of the folkloresque exhibit this critical capacity, the mode of *portrayal* is directly concerned with demonstrating emic (that is, popular/vernacular) conceptions of what folklore is, how and why it functions within societies, and why contemporary people should concern themselves with it. We can understand it as functioning similarly to what Alan Dundes (1966) called metafolklore, commenting directly on folklore itself.

Folkloresque portrayal concerns the way folklore, as a discipline and as an object of study, is understood within popular culture. Works that employ this mode of the folkloresque may offer commentary not only on folklore itself but also on the role of folklorists as collectors and interpreters of "lore." Through analysis of such works, we discover assumptions about what forms specific folklore genres should take, how they should be performed, and who occupies a position of authority on folkloric matters. In many ways, this folkloresque mode is the most revealing for scholars, in that it provides direct insight into popular thinking about what we sometimes regard as our exclusive intellectual domain. By reminding us that nonacademic audiences and creators of popular culture have their own ideas about the value of culture in general, and of cultural scholarship in particular, folkloresque portrayal forces us to acknowledge differences between the agendas of people inside and outside the academy, and urges us to ponder those moments when our scholarly efforts do not dovetail with extradisciplinary expectations.

The chapters in this section explore these issues as they manifest in popular media as well as more conventional folkloric settings, always with an eye to qualities and characteristics that are thought of as fundamental to folklore itself. Whereas the primary function of folkloresque *integration* is the creation of new forms based on (or at least referencing) existing ones, *portrayal* invokes

DOI: 10.7330/9781607324188.s02

the concept of folklore as such, in some cases calling it by name, in others revealing implicit assumptions about how folklore works.

With these themes in mind, in the first chapter I explore the role of folklore and folklorist characters within a popular horror video game franchise. In my analysis, the focus shifts from the materials and performances that constitute folklore to the individuals who are perceived as folklore authorities, that is, the scholars who make it their business to collect and analyze the lore of the folk. I argue that within these video games the folkloresque elements that are explicitly *referred to as folklore* work to flesh out the narrative and enhance the "fright factor" and also, in the case of the folklorist characters, reveal popular thinking about the role of folklorists as interpreters of lore.

In the next chapter, Chad Buterbaugh approaches the subject of folkloresque performance in the form of highly produced "traditional" storytelling events featuring Irish storyteller Éamon Kelly. Buterbaugh argues that the stylized nature of Kelly's storyteller persona was deemed secondary to his role as preserver and disseminator of traditional narratives. Here, folkloresque portrayal moves from commentary on the "shape" and function of folklore forms to issues of style, aesthetics, and performance, providing a glimpse of the emergent, but usually tacit, rules and guidelines by which audiences judge performances and ascribe authenticity to performers. As Buterbaugh demonstrates, Kelly's portrayal of the "Storyteller" simultaneously reflects and generates a popular culture image of a folk culture character.

In the last chapter of this section, Carlea Holl-Jensen and I explore the role of the fairy-tale genre within another popular franchise, *Harry Potter*. A collection of (fictional) fairy tales from within the *Harry Potter* novels— including "scholarly" analysis in the manner of real-world tale collections— reveals assumptions about implicit truths hidden within "innocent" folklore.

All the chapters in this section engage directly with popular understandings of folklore, considering the ways in which the concept (or its generic components) is applied in various media as well as the reasons for its inclusion. The insights afforded by such investigations are not trivial: they can bridge the intellectual gap between academic pursuits and popular interests, bringing scholars into dialogue with popular audiences who share their interests but not necessarily their terminology (see also Tolbert 2015).

REFERENCES

Dundes, Alan. 1966. "Metafolklore and Oral Literary Criticism." *Monist* 50(4): 505–16. http://dx.doi.org/10.5840/monist196650436.
Tolbert, Jeffrey. 2015. "On Folklore's Appeal: A Personal Essay." *New Directions in Folklore* 13(1/2): 93–113.

5

A Deadly Discipline
Folklore, Folklorists, and the Occult in Fatal Frame

Jeffrey A. Tolbert

It's been at least 10 years since I last came here with my father.
The village still looks exactly the same. Coming here when I was a boy was what made me want to
become a folklorist.

"Green Diary 1," Fatal Frame II

Someone! Anyone! Whoever sees this, look for me. I'm trapped in this village. HELP ME!

"Woman's Notebook 4," Fatal Frame II

THIS CHAPTER CONSIDERS THE RELATIONSHIPS BETWEEN academic and popular attitudes toward folklore as revealed through a close analysis of one franchise within a particular pop culture medium, the video game.[1] Video games have been examined sporadically by folklorists, who have only recently begun to consider digital media worthy of serious attention as forms of expressive culture. The current study is, in part, an attempt to demonstrate the viability of video games as an area for folkloric inquiry. While my focus is on one game series, these observations apply equally to other games and other popular genres.

In addition, this essay is about ghosts. Or, more accurately, about one way in which popular culture has tended to conceptualize folklore both as an academic discipline and as an aspect of social experience in which ghosts—and the supernatural more generally—frequently play a very large part. The category of popular expressive culture that we are calling the folkloresque frequently hinges on the issue of supernatural belief, which is very often portrayed as coterminous with folklore itself: in popular use, *folklore*

DOI: 10.7330/9781607324188.c005

and related terms tend to refer specifically to supernatural legends, magical practices, and "the occult."

The quotes with which this chapter opens are from *Fatal Frame II: Crimson Butterfly* (Shibata 2003), one of the three *Fatal Frame* games to be released on major consoles in the United States (Shibata 2001, 2002, 2003, 2004, 2005). In each game, players take control of a character (usually a young Japanese woman) they must guide through a series of frightening locations inhabited by angry ghosts. The player's only weapon is a magical camera with the power to exorcise evil spirits, a strange but effective gameplay device that gives the player a first-person look at the grotesque spirits attacking him or her. Beyond the novelty of the camera weapon, the games are notable in that, despite their English-language localizations, they are set in Japan. The setting is critical to the games' narratives, as each draws heavily—or seems to—on Japanese traditional culture (see Picard 2009, 97). But by far the most interesting aspect of these games, in terms of their use of folkloresque material, is that they feature characters explicitly identified as folklorists who work with material explicitly labeled as folklore. These characters, though their roles in the narrative are largely enacted "offscreen" (revealed primarily through flashbacks and textual evidence), are nevertheless critical shapers of the plot. The folklorists provide answers to some of the games' most important supernatural mysteries, thereby advancing the plot and helping the protagonists eventually overcome their ghostly adversaries.

By examining the games in the *Fatal Frame* series, I hope to articulate two major points. First, I suggest that in the *Fatal Frame* games folklore, when understood explicitly *as folklore*, deepens the player's experience of terror. Timothy H. Evans (2005) has argued that items of invented folklore in horror literature—what we are calling the folkloresque—"provide background, create an atmosphere of suspense, and prime readers to expect the supernatural." In the *Fatal Frame* universe, clues in the form of fictional scholarly texts, film and audio recordings, and newspaper clippings flesh out the cultural and spiritual frameworks in which the games occur and help players understand the supernatural underpinnings of the frightening environments through which they must navigate. Evans continues, "This body of 'folklore,' along with eerie descriptions of architecture and landscape, provides both ambience and clues for the reader about what is to come" (120). This is particularly true of *Fatal Frame* and similar games, which often require the player to work through intellectual challenges using clues provided within the game narrative. *Fatal Frame* also draws on the aesthetics of Shinto and Buddhist religious practices (or, again, seems to do so) and, like other games in its genre, incorporates generic elements of legends as well as of horror literature and films (Kirkland 2009, 62, 65–68). The first game in the series even claims to be "based on a true story" (Shibata 2002, game box, cited in Nitsche 2009, 202).

The second point I will address is the role of the folklorist characters within the *Fatal Frame* universe. Each game features characters identified as folklorists (as well as journalists, book publishers, and members of related professions with interests in folklore) whose roles are central to the overarching plot. By considering the roles of these characters and examining their own treatments of folkloresque texts within the games, I outline a set of assumptions common to popular culture about the nature and role of the folklorist as a professional.[2] In *Fatal Frame*, most of the folklorist characters are eventually killed in the pursuit of their research, and are directly or indirectly responsible for the supernatural crises which the player now faces. Two of these folklorist characters return as angry ghosts that the player must battle. Simultaneously, and paradoxically, the folklorists' knowledge is the key to defeating the ghosts they helped unleash. This ambiguity reveals another key assumption of the folkloresque: folklorists are often seen as occult experts whose knowledge is both powerful and dangerous. It is powerful because it can be used to combat supernatural evil, and dangerous because it necessitates a precarious proximity to the same supernatural forces it seeks to understand and dispel. The danger of the folklorists' knowledge is often compounded by the fact that the very people who possess it do not accept its supernatural validity but regard it as little more than data to be collected and analyzed (a view that should resonate with anyone familiar with folklore's actual disciplinary history).

Together, these arguments—that folklore as it is used in popular horror fiction heightens a player's/audience's sense of fear and that folklorists, as characters in fictional worlds, possess the means not only of interpreting but of invoking and combating the supernatural—suggest an important area of inquiry for contemporary folklorists. *Fatal Frame* exemplifies the ways in which popular understandings of folklore as a cultural form and as an academic discipline are embedded, sometimes quite self-consciously, in popular media, raising significant questions for those of us in the professional folklore business. Why should folklore create a more engagingly frightening experience? Why is it so frequently connected with the supernatural? Why are folklorists positioned as marginal dabblers in occult rites, in contrast to the dashing exploits of, say, Hollywood archaeologists (see, for example, Baxter 2002)? While it is beyond the scope of this study to address all of these questions in full, it seems important to lay them out here as points of departure for future studies. Considering these questions can shed light on the considerable differences between disciplinary interests and popular or vernacular ones (see also Tolbert 2015).

PHOTOGRAPHING FEAR: THE WORLD OF *FATAL FRAME*

The *Fatal Frame* games were initially released on the PlayStation 2 game console.[3] The first two games were also rereleased on the Microsoft Xbox as "director's cuts." The final game in the main series to see a North American release was *Fatal Frame III: The Tormented*. A fourth game, *Zero: Tsukihami no Kamen* (Shibata and Suda51 2008), was released only in Japan, and a spinoff, *Spirit Camera: The Cursed Memoir* (2012) was released on the Nintendo 3DS portable game console. In addition, a remade version of *Fatal Frame II* was released in Japan and Europe (Shibata 2012). Finally, *Zero: Nuregarasu no Miko* (2014) was released in Japan on the Wii U console. The games are linked in an overarching storyline, albeit a complex one that requires some work on the part of the player to decipher (see Nitsche 2009, 201). The characters available to play in each title are different, but the primary protagonists of each game are young Japanese women. In the present study I focus on the first three games in the series, all of which I have played at length (the second and third games on PlayStation 2 and the first in its Xbox remake).

The first game follows a young woman named Miku Hinasaki as she searches for her missing brother Mafuyu. Mafuyu has gone in search of another missing person, his mentor, the novelist Junsei Takamine. Shortly before the game's timeline begins, Takamine and his editorial team mount an expedition to a dilapidated rural manor house called Himuro Mansion, where the author hopes to find inspiration for his next novel. When Takamine and his staff go missing, Mafuyu takes it upon himself to track them down. After he, too, disappears into Himuro Mansion, his sister Miku decides to follow him.

The player takes control of Miku as she wanders through the mansion in search of her lost brother. She soon discovers an antique camera, and with this mystical object, known throughout the series as the Camera Obscura, Miku is able to fight the angry ghosts that beset her. In the course of her expedition through the sprawling feudal manor house, Miku uncovers the whole grisly story of Himuro Mansion: it was the site of a ritual involving human sacrifice, the goal of which was to prevent a gate to hell, located beneath the mansion, from opening and unleashing a demonic evil into the world. The ritual was successful for many years, until an unexpected development caused it to fail. The result was that the gate to hell opened, releasing a demonic force that caused the deaths of the mansion's inhabitants and bound their spirits to the site as angry ghosts.

The second and third games follow the same formula. In each there are three basic plot elements that remain constant: a failed ritual that leads to a supernatural disaster and creates a haunted site populated by violent spirits; a protagonist (or protagonists) with some close personal link to these events; and the Camera Obscura, a supernatural weapon that enables the ghosts to be held at bay long enough to complete each of the failed rituals.

THE FOUNDATIONS OF FEAR: FOLKLORE, GAMING, AND HORROR

The "Camera Obscura" is a special camera created by Dr. Aso to capture supernatural phenomenon
    [sic] that couldn't be seen with the naked eye.

It was designed to photograph visions of the past and spirit entities, but it was a prototype and its
    functions hadn't been fully tested.

Photographing "things that ordinary people couldn't see" with this camera had an exorcismal effect.

Seijiro Makabe, a folklorist who had come to investigate All God's Village, borrowed this camera
    from Dr. Aso to photograph the village's rumored Forbidden Ritual.

Dr. Kunihiko Aso was a folklorist who studied the spirit world.

He modified the latest gadgets of his time, the camera, radio and projector, trying to create a machine
    that could capture supernatural phenomenon [sic]

He was shunned by the academic world but friends with Makabe.

                                        "Memo: The Camera Obscura," Fatal Frame II

The *Fatal Frame* games are clearly situated within the horror genre. Their focus is on the angry spirits of people killed in horrible or tragic ways that return, under very specific circumstances, to vent their ghostly rage on the living. The games rely on creepy atmosphere, frightening environments, and shocking, unexpected moments ("jump scares") to inspire fear in the player. In the lexicon of gaming, *Fatal Frame* is typically labeled more specifically as *survival horror*. Film studies and new media scholar Ewan Kirkland offers a useful definition of the genre: a survival horror game is *"an action adventure game employing a third person perspective, and drawing on horror film iconography, in which a typically average character navigates a mazelike landscape, solving puzzles and fighting off monsters with limited ammunition, energy and means of replenishing it"* (Kirkland 2005, 172).

As Kirkland indicates, survival horror games draw their inspiration from the larger horror genre. Susan Stewart argues that horror narratives, by virtue of their highly sequential structure, are easily adapted to film "and to the temporality of directed travel through the landscape of the 'house of horrors.' The horror story form thus spans both preindustrial and postindustrial modes of fiction making and provides an important example of the ways in which folklore and literature share a repertoire of narrative devices" (Stewart 1982, 33). The "house of horrors" metaphor is particularly relevant with regard to *Fatal Frame* which, as a video game, is an interactive medium wherein players navigate a haunted site with the express purpose of encountering and vanquishing frightening supernatural beings. It is a house of horrors one step removed—a *virtual* house of horrors—in that the player is not physically present in its world. Simultaneously, the experience of horror is made more intimate by the interactive nature of such games and by virtue of the clever use of folkloresque items throughout each game's narrative.[4]

Folklorists have had less to say about video games than other scholars. In one of the few notable folklore studies of video games, Sharon Sherman (1997) emphasizes the medium's highly intertextual nature. She argues, "Computer games, such as *Mario*, fit within the study of both narrative and game, albeit a genre not constructed to be folk narrative but to model it" (244). In underscoring the importance of *resemblance* to preexisting folklore forms, Sherman's discussion resonates with our basic definition of the folkloresque.

Kiri Miller (2008) makes a similar point in her analysis of Rockstar Games' *Grand Theft Auto: San Andreas* (2004). Echoing Sherman, Miller suggests that the popularity of *Grand Theft Auto* (*GTA*) stems in part "from its satisfying structural affinities with classic children's tales" (262). She continues, "Like folktales and fables, the *GTA* games engage players' attention through intertextual references that rely on prior experience and established values" (275). Previously acquired knowledge of this sort is, I suggest, a prerequisite for the success of the folkloresque and is clearly illustrated by the *Fatal Frame* games, which likewise draw on the familiar conventions of horror and make constant reference to real-world folklore genres such as contemporary legends.[5]

All of these scholars emphasize the highly intertextual nature of the horror genre and the video game medium: in all cases, some prior familiarity with thematically or structurally similar narratives is necessary for the intertextual references to be successful. In *Fatal Frame*, the appearance of familiar folkloric forms such as religious rituals, contemporary legends, and haunted houses works to link the games to larger cultural frameworks with which the audience is familiar both from real-world traditions and from other popular media. These cultural referents give the stories "an air of verisimilitude" (Evans 2005, 117)—that is, the ghostly threats depicted in the games are positioned, through strategic use of folkloresque material, alongside real-world supernatural traditions. On another level, it becomes clear that certain folkloric elements within the games' narratives serve a more overtly metafolkloric function: the word "folklore" is actually used in-game to describe them, thereby revealing one set of assumptions about what folklore "looks like." These elements are portrayed in flashbacks and especially through the documentary evidence found by the player over the course of each game, serving both to explain the games' mysteries and to greatly enhance the cohesiveness and hence the plausibility of their narratives (Kirkland 2009, 68). And in these games, folklore is always *creepy*: human sacrifices and evil spirits abound, elucidated through fragmentary documentary evidence or psychic visions of a given location's tragic past.

FOLKLORE AND THE FOLKLORIST: MEDDLER, MARTYR, SAVIOR

Folklore genres play an important role in the *Fatal Frame* series. Local traditions such as songs and rituals, children's games, and other cultural phenomena that have typically fallen within the jurisdiction of academic folklorists are explicitly mentioned and always figure prominently in the grisly events responsible for the ghosts' existence. These elements usually aid the player in determining how to cope with the supernatural fallout of those events as well. Each game also includes folklorist characters. Typical of popular portrayals of folklore, and as I explore more fully below, the work of folklorists in the *Fatal Frame* universe reflects an outdated mode of folklore scholarship (Kirshenblatt-Gimblett 1998, 296; Tosenberger 2010, 2.4–2.7; see also Holl-Jensen and Tolbert, chapter 7 of this volume).

In all of the games, players guide their character through various frightening locations, searching the rooms they pass through for useful items and clues. On the way they discover documents scattered around the game world, usually presented as notebooks and diaries, newspaper clippings, and audio and video recordings. These primary sources are automatically filed by the game for the player to reference at any time. They range from cries for help from men and women who have found themselves lost in the haunted location to research notes from folklorists studying the local rituals to the strange and disturbing diaries of people affected by the evil presence the rituals were designed to combat. In many cases the documents are connected to individual characters whose backgrounds are critically important to the overarching narrative. There is relatively little dialogue in the games—primarily limited to ghostly utterances before, during, and after battles with the angry spirits, and brief cinematic scenes in which the living characters discuss their situation—and players are left to sort out the plot using the textual evidence they have accumulated. Like the photographic clues the player generates with the help of the Camera Obscura, these documents point the way out of the supernatural perils with which the player must contend (Nitsche 2009, 208). The photographs, audio recordings, folklore texts, and other forms of evidence are pieces of the puzzle the player must assemble—but the interpretive key, the truth underlying the terrifying and mystical events of the games, is the folk tradition that forms the backdrop of the narrative.

As Kirkland notes, "In survival horror, everyone, it seems—research assistants, academics, mercenaries—keeps a journal" (Kirkland 2009, 67). But in *Fatal Frame*, the notes of the folklorists are different, in that they are not only records of "real" events: they are also, in many cases, pieces of scholarly research on a specific topic (typically a ritual). Their language is clearly intended to replicate scholarly analysis. They usually begin by explaining the social functions of the local ritual, but their tone gradually changes as the truth of the ritual is revealed.

An example is found in the notebooks left by folklorist Seijiro Makabe in *Fatal Frame II*:

> Ancient village records have been stored in the Ceremony Master's house.
> Many discuss the legends, folktales or rituals of the village.
> There are sure to be many records of folklore value.
> The Forbidden Ritual is also called the Crimson Sacrifice Ritual.
> Twins are used to help seal the gate to hell. There are two parts.
> The Visible Ceremony, which occurs periodically, and if it fails, a Hidden
>   Ceremony is performed.
> If all the ceremonies fail, the gate to hell will open, the dead will pour out,
>   and the skies will go dark.
> They call this disaster the "Repentance."
>   "Folklorist 4," *Fatal Frame II*

The genres of folklore Makabe names have a specific "value" of their own, and the folklorist is noticeably excited by the opportunity to learn about them. But in the world of *Fatal Frame* the cultural significance of folklore is secondary to its function as a record of, and a set of procedures for dealing with, the supernatural. This is standard in popular treatments of folklore, in which the frameworks for ritual behavior provided by folkloric sources (broadly conceived) are both accurate and necessary for humans to survive interactions with those forces (Holl-Jensen and Tolbert, chapter 7 in this volume; Tosenberger 2010, 1.6). Thus the ceremonies that Makabe describes are not only obscure religious rites but real means to prevent the supernatural catastrophe called the "Repentance." We learn that the main ritual involves one twin killing the other, a sacrifice that will cause the gate to hell to remain closed. The crimson butterflies that are a recurring motif throughout the game are in fact the souls of the ritually murdered twins; their shape reflects the red marks left by the hands of the surviving twins on the throats of their victims.

Likewise, the "Handmaiden's Song" from *Fatal Frame III* takes on a new significance as something more than a fragment of decontextualized folk culture. The ghosts of four girls—shrine maidens whose role in life was to crucify the priestess marked for sacrifice—repeatedly sing the song during the game. One version of the song contains this verse:

Sleep, priestess, lie in peace
Sleep, priestess, lie in peace
If the priestess wakes from her dream
Perform the rite of stakes
Her limbs pinned tight
Lest the doors open wide
and suffering unleashed on all.
                    Fatal Frame III

Within the game's copious notes, the scholar Akito Kashiwagi compares versions of the song from different regions and initially suggests that the song was intended to frighten children to sleep ("Legend of Song 1"). Eventually Kashiwagi links the song to an actual religious ritual practiced in a remote mountain shrine. The player learns that the song is not just a regional survival of some esoteric ceremony, reduced to a children's lullaby (though it is that, too): it is in fact a real, supernaturally potent method for preventing the Tattooed Priestess (the victim of the shrine maidens' sacrifice) from returning and wreaking havoc on the world of the living.

As these examples illustrate, the folkloresque elements within the world of *Fatal Frame* blend with the fictional histories of the haunted locations, deepening the terror of the supernatural threats by situating them within a cultural framework wherein human sacrifice is more than just a custom—it is a true spiritual necessity. Players are tasked with piecing together this information more or less on their own. Stewart suggests that this type of evidence contributes to the "victimization" of the reader or listener: "[This] is particularly clear in those scenes in the written horror story where the reader is presented with a letter to be read at the same moment, within the same temporality, as it is read by the character" (Stewart 1982, 39). It is, I argue, even more apparent in the case of a video game, which requires constant attention and intellectual work on the part of the player not only to make sense of the narrative but to survive it.[6]

But the scholarly nature of many documents in the *Fatal Frame* world also leads to instances of interesting and surprisingly well-informed commentary, both on the various forms of in-game folklore and, at times, on folklore scholarship itself. In *Fatal Frame III*, Kei Amakura provides an example of this type of direct engagement with folkloric material. In a letter to another character, Kei writes:

> Dear Yuu,
>
> Sorry for not writing for so long. How are things with your fiancée? I'm continuing my investigation of the urban legend.
>
> Like I thought, my niece's symptoms bear many similarities to the strange disease associated with the urban legend.
>
> I think most of the story is groundless rumor, but I've heard there was a psychiatric study done. If you have it, I'd like to see it. Maybe it will provide a clue.
>
> I'm taking a break from all my other work to devote myself to studying the urban legend. I'd like your help.
>
> According to the documents I've studied, that camera I sent you is apparently a rare "Camera Obscura."
>
> Given where I found it, it may have some connection to the missing people and the urban legend. If you hear anything, please tell me.
>
> "Letter from Kei 1," *Fatal Frame III*

Kei's letter reveals fascinating ideas about the nature of the legend in question, which he describes as a "groundless rumor" that may nevertheless be partly validated by an academic study. He also draws connections between real missing persons cases and the legend as well as another item of folkloric significance: the Camera Obscura. Further, in the course of the game, Kei participates directly in the urban legend he is studying: by searching for his missing niece Mio (the protagonist of the second game), Kei is cursed himself and drawn into the very ghostly events he was seeking to understand.

Makabe's notes on the Crimson Sacrifice; the "Handmaiden's Song," which contains explicit instructions on how to carry out a human sacrifice; and Kei's commentary on the Manor of Sleep urban legend: we can begin to see from these examples that the folkloresque involves specific assumptions about the truth content of particular folklore genres. A similar set of assumptions is illustrated by Catherine Tosenberger's (2010) discussion of the television series *Supernatural* (Kripke 2005) and its use of folkloric material (specifically fairy tales). Tosenberger suggests that the series alternately replicates and undermines "traditionalist" understandings of folklore (1.2). Following Mikel Koven, Tosenberger focuses on the ostensive dimension of popular television (1.4).[7] She makes the important point that the knowledge contained in folklore is regarded as literal truth within the series, pointing out, "[The protagonists'] methods of defeating [the monsters] are those which folk belief likewise deems 'true': salting and burning remains, performing exorcisms, helping ghosts resolve unfinished business, casting magic spells attested to by the folklore record, and so forth" (1.6).

None of this should suggest that the producers of *Fatal Frame* or other creators of popular culture themselves believe in the supernatural realms they are depicting (but see Koven 2008, 77). Rather, I mean to emphasize the important repeated connections made between folklore as a category of social experience and supernatural belief. Sometimes the assumptions expressed by characters in-game are more concerned with explaining away legendary materials rationally. But in every case, the player learns that skepticism has no place here: the ghosts and demons are real.

Nowhere are these interests and assumptions better illustrated than in the writings of Yuu Asou of *Fatal Frame III*. In response to Kei's requests, Yuu compiles some notes that sound quite familiar to contemporary folklorists, complete with critical commentary on the notion of modernity. Yuu begins by discussing what he calls the "Lost Village" category of urban legends:

> They are often an amalgamation of well-known actual incidents, legend and oral tradition.
>
> Settings such as the "isolated mountain village" or "bygone customs" like night trysts or ceremonies often act to trigger the incidents themselves, and these in turn become the motif [*sic*] for urban legends.
>
> The reason for the popularity of urban legends may lie in the notion of "the view of the country from the city, or the modern bias toward the ancient."
>
> To people in the modern city, the "village" is the wilderness, and those who live there are "different." Perhaps that scorn, or fear, finds expression in the urban legend.
>
> For that reason, the setting of the legend must be the "isolated mountain village." Further, "bygone customs" are attractive elements that end up

acting to provoke the incident. As a case in point, there is the story about
the area around the Minakami dam where Mayu went missing.

"On the Urban Legend," *Fatal Frame III*

Here Yuu is linking what is for him a real-world event—the disappear-
ance of Kei's niece—to a particular type of urban legend. In the remainder
of his essay, Yuu describes the urban legends that form the backdrop for
the first and third games in the series, connecting the disparate stories of
the *Fatal Frame* trilogy along folkloric lines.

The assimilation of these events into the genre of urban legend is a
critical storytelling device: it enables the research that furthers the plot, providing important information to the protagonists; it also greatly heightens
the fear experienced by the player, not only by forcing intellectual engagement with the supernatural events as depicted but by making them seem
more plausible because they are already attested to in local folklore. Stories
like these fictional legends "seem authentic because they appear in appropriate or familiar contexts, are juxtaposed with known folklore, or are bol-
stered with spurious scholarly citations" (Evans 2005, 119). Yuu's essay perfectly illustrates the compelling and creative uses to which the folkloresque
may be put.

But Yuu Asou is rare in the *Fatal Frame* universe in that his study of
folklore does not ultimately lead to his own demise (although he does die,
and like the other characters who study folklore, he returns as a ghost,
albeit not a hostile one). This is in fact the most compelling aspect of *Fatal
Frame*'s use of the folkloresque: not the folkloric content itself—the rituals and legends—but the way in which the games portray the people who
study these phenomena. The folklorist emerges from the game world as a
strangely ambivalent figure, marginalized (in more ways than one) but also,
as I have already suggested, possessing dangerous knowledge and straying
too close to the realm of hostile spiritual beings. Of course, the folklorist
does not know the real truth underlying the strange customs he studies
until it's too late.

In the first game, the player learns that folklorist Ryozo Munakata moved
into the abandoned Himuro Mansion after the failed ritual to study records
left behind by the Himuro family. Eventually the supernatural events at the
mansion lead to the deaths of Munakata and his family ("Ryozo Munakata"
2013). His notes, together with others found by Miku in the game's present,
provide information necessary to understand the ghostly events in the mansion and to combat the evil spirits there. With the help of this knowledge
the player is able to progress further into the mansion and eventually complete the failed ritual, laying the ghosts' angry spirits to rest.

In *Fatal Frame II*, the player discovers that Seijiro Makabe, a folklorist who visited All God's Village to study the Crimson Sacrifice Ritual, was assisted by none other than Ryozo Munakata (prior to his eventual move to Himuro Mansion). It is revealed that Munakata is friends with a young man from the village, Itsuki, who has contacted him to ask for help in rescuing twin sisters Yae and Sae, the intended victims of the next ritual. The villagers welcome the folklorists into their homes, all the while intending to use them as additional sacrifices to appease the supernatural forces threatening their village. With the help of the twins, Munakata escapes the village, taking Yae with him, but his mentor Makabe, who has been captured by the villagers, is sacrificed. Yae's absence causes the village's ritual to fail, opening the gate to hell and throwing the town and its inhabitants into supernatural darkness. Years later, Munakata and Yae marry and move into Himuro Mansion so Munakata may continue his research (folklorists never learn). Thus a major connection is formed between the first two games in the person of a folklorist, Munakata, and his wife, Yae.

Finally, in *Fatal Frame III*, folklorist Akito Kashiwagi falls in love with a woman at the Kuze Shrine named Kyouka, who bears him a son whom she names Kaname. Kaname is smuggled out of the shrine, which men are forbidden to enter. He returns as an adult, meets the priestess Reika, and falls in love with her, again dooming the local ritual to failure. In this case the folklorist's appearance has a delayed effect, but the point is clear: as outsiders who interfere with traditions and forces they don't fully understand, folklore scholars trail disaster in their wake.

The fates of Makabe, Munakata, and Kashiwagi's son are equal parts tragic and horrifying, exemplifying the dangers of folkloristic meddling. Makabe, sacrificed as a temporary measure to appease the evil spirits, in fact becomes a major antagonist, returning as an angry ghost called the Kusabi. Together, the Kusabi and the ghost of Sae, the twin left behind when Yae escaped, slaughter the village's inhabitants and plunge the area into eternal night. Munakata is eventually killed by the first game's main antagonist after the spirits of Himuro Mansion have killed his child and provoked his wife Yae's suicide ("Ryozo Munakata" 2013). The price of studying folklore, in the world of *Fatal Frame*, is very high.

The traditionalist view noted by Tosenberger is clearly evident in the actions of *Fatal Frame*'s folklorists. This view, she suggests, is that which sees folklore as something to be collected by educated outsiders among the backward "folk" (Tosenberger 2010, 2.4–2.10). This is certainly the role of the folklorists in *Fatal Frame*: they are outsiders, and they come to study strange local customs in rural areas. But there is more going on here than a simple reflection of nineteenth-century folklore collecting. Yuu Asou's discussion of urban legends calls into question the validity of romantic modernism and its view of the folk. And the folklorists who collect their materials from the rustic country folk meet with terrible fates as a result, suggesting a darker reality than any cultural theory can encompass.

The *Fatal Frame* series is by no means alone in portraying folklorists (and other scholars) this way. As Stewart notes, "The 'I' in [horror stories] is often the voice of a scientist or scholar, a servant of reason presenting us with the unrealizable and thereby reframing it as the real. Antiquarians and folklorists, those who awaken ambiguous objects into the inappropriate context of the present, are particularly likely to be victimized" (Stewart 1982, 44). In the case of *Fatal Frame*, though, the role of folklorists is quite the opposite: rather than bringing anachronistic folklore into the present, these characters embody the intrusion of rational, urban modernity—from which the supernatural has been largely banished—into a traditional belief complex that, despite its stubborn resistance to the folklorists' scientizing methodologies, conceals a truth that would doom the rational, modern world were it to break free of its ritualistic bindings. It is the very act of study that disturbs an otherwise perfect, closed system, and the introduction of outside influences that causes the supernatural evil to be unleashed. It is tempting to frame this scenario as yet another simple binary, with the contemporary, educated folklorists standing in stark contrast to the backward, rural villagers whom they study; but this would obscure the fact that the "backward" villagers are in possession of true, powerful knowledge that the folklorists at first believe to be of only academic value. This assumption puts them, and indeed the world, in mortal (and immortal) danger. Only when the folklorists' *academic* knowledge is tempered by direct experience of the supernatural—when the villagers' rituals are recognized as more than quaint survivals of ancient beliefs and accepted as *real*—is it transformed into *useful* knowledge. Simultaneously, by entering directly into the system of supernatural belief and ritual practice that they came to document, the folklorists are transformed, in a horrifyingly literal way, into the objects of their own study.[8]

By each game's final scenes, folklore has, in a sense, been vindicated. No longer the stuff of books and abstract cultural theory, no longer mere survivals of ancient custom, the local knowledge of the villagers is reframed as a valid model for containing supernatural forces that would otherwise overrun the living world. Ultimately, then, the question that the folklorist characters tacitly pose to players is not about modernity versus "premodernity" or science versus tradition. It's far simpler, and far more unnerving: what would you do if folklore was not *just* folklore?

CONCLUSION

Fatal Frame's overarching narrative rests on a complex set of folkloresque processes, from the creation of legends within the game world to the portrayal of folklorist characters who interpret (and fall prey to) them. These folkloresque elements help to pull players into a deep narrative universe that features numerous connections to the real world.[9]

As we have seen, one way these connections are established is through the creation of "fictitious" legends (Dégh and Vázsonyi 1983, 25). Drawing as they do on imagery from Shinto and Buddhist religion and thereby linked to larger, real-world systems of supernatural belief, these texts highlight the *integrative* aspect of the folkloresque, specifically what Foster refers to as "fuzzy allusion" (see Foster's chapter 1 in this volume). Through these fuzzy allusions the creators of popular culture generate seemingly authentic folklore that, in fact, has no real-world analogues—a process that I have elsewhere labeled reverse ostension (Tolbert 2013, 2). But more important to the success of *Fatal Frame* as a horror franchise is the folkloresque mode of *portrayal* (see Foster's introduction to this volume), the explicit and self-conscious inclusion of folklore *as* folklore. Folklore is potentially dangerous knowledge, dealing as it does with supernatural truth, and folklorists are therefore dangerous people: this principle is fundamental to the *Fatal Frame* universe. Indeed, in popular culture more generally, folk religion or the "occult" is often understood to be more "real" than official, orthodox faiths or scientific knowledge—real, in the sense that the supernatural forces it articulates have actual, verifiable existence. Together, folkloresque elements in popular fiction and the folklorist (or equivalent) characters who inadvertently unleash the supernatural offer explicit commentary both on the nature and functions of folklore as a social phenomenon and on the role of folklorists as collectors and interpreters of folklore.

The folkloresque in all its forms has tremendous discursive potential, similar to what Ray Cashman (2006) has termed "critical nostalgia" in its capacity to use the concept of tradition inherited from the past to comment critically on aspects of both the past and the present. The difference is that the folkloresque is not the preservation of historical objects or their faithful translation into new media; rather, it is the creative use of folklore-inspired elements to generate new forms. Both critical nostalgia and the folkloresque provide important commentary on any number of social phenomena, intellectual concepts, and scholarly practices. In this sense they function as metafolklore (Dundes 1966), arising in response to particular historical circumstances and traditions and critically examining them in ways that reveal important popular attitudes and concepts.

As a case in point, consider Timothy H. Evans's discussion of H. P. Lovecraft. Evans argues that authors often use folklore to make claims about the loss of tradition in the modern world. "Drawing on legends and beliefs, on the architecture of old houses and the iconic power of religious symbols, horror writers often evoke 'tradition' and the 'past' in order to explore a perceived loss of tradition in the present" (Evans 2005, 99–100). Conversely, Evans highlights the ways in which Lovecraft subtly subverts the quest for authenticity: "In seeking authentic experience, that unobtainable goal of tourists, [Lovecraft's characters] are either destroyed or utterly transformed" (113). This is identical to the experiences of the folklorists in *Fatal Frame*, who likewise come in search of authentic experience only to have the authenticity they seek manifest itself in a horrifically literal way. It is not insignificant that the first three games of the series are set in recognizably "traditional" locations (characterized by distinctive feudal-style Japanese architecture, torii gates and shoji screens, and Buddhist and Shinto iconography), nor that the ghosts are frequently kimono-clad women or Shinto priests. These symbols of "tradition," regardless of the ways in which scholars might problematize their use,[10] highlight the need for figures capable of interpreting the meanings of tradition in the contemporary world. The ghosts also suggest, through their very existence as angry spirits, that meddling with tradition can have dire consequences.

In recent decades folklorists have become increasingly aware that new media provide ample opportunity for study. But the reverse, somewhat surprisingly, is also true: new media are in many cases turning the lens of popular culture onto folklore as a discipline. Film and literature are perhaps the media most obviously engaged in using folklore for contemporary creative purposes. But video games, which can also tell engaging stories, likewise rely on a range of vernacular cultural artifacts to pull players into their worlds.[11] By studying the folkloresque we can better understand what creators of popular culture think about folklore. That such views resonate with popular audiences should be enough to gain the attention of scholars interested in folklore (however defined) in the contemporary world.

Acknowledgments

Thanks to Mitsuko Kawabata for providing helpful feedback on an early version of this essay.

NOTES

1. In this chapter, primary texts from within the *Fatal Frame* games are cited with the document names as provided in-game. I give all Japanese names in the manner in which they are presented in the North American releases of the *Fatal Frame* series: personal name first, then surname.

2. In order to gauge the extent to which my ideas matched the expectations and assumptions of other players, I also started a discussion thread on the forums of the *Fatal Frame* fan page, *Beyond the Camera's Lens* (Emi-chan 2013). Unfortunately a server crash deleted the forums and all responses to my original questions. I posted new questions in November 2013, but as of this writing I have not received any responses in the new thread.

3. Throughout this chapter I rely on the *Zero Wiki* ("Zero Wiki" 2014), located at http://bcl.rpen.us/zerowiki/index.php?title=Main_Page. This Wiki contains a compilation of all of the found texts from the *Fatal Frame* series as well as information on specific characters, rituals, objects, and contributors' interpretations of each game's plot.

4. For an important discussion of the relationship of haunted house attractions to the legend genre, see Dégh and Vázsonyi 1983, 22–26. On the "virtual" aspect of horror video games, in particular as it pertains to the concept of ostension, see Tolbert 2013, 13–14.

5. In addition to these folkloristic treatments of video games, game theory scholars have contributed a number of useful texts. Ewan Kirkland (2009) discusses narrative technique in the horror genre. In the same volume as Kirkland's piece, Michael Nitsche's (2009) "Complete Horror in Fatal Frame" focuses on the *Fatal Frame* series specifically. Besides Nitsche's article, one of the few academic works to focus solely on *Fatal Frame* is Hoeger and Huber's (2007) essay "Ghastly Multiplication: *Fatal Frame II* and the Videogame Uncanny." Hoeger and Huber argue that the fear in *Fatal Frame* is a function of the "videogame uncanny" in which "the textual elements are deeply entwined with the mechanical and spatial aspects" (153). They also emphasize the mechanics of gameplay as a source of fear, such as the player's fixed visual perspective on the game world or the player's incomplete control over his or her character (155–56).

6. Discussing the horror film *Candyman* (Rose 1992), Mikel Koven (2008, 139) argues that the portrayal of urban legends in popular film constitutes a kind of ostension—the acting out of folklore texts—that draws audiences into the debate about the veracity of the folkloric material presented. Like *Candyman*, *Fatal Frame* presents the events leading to the central hauntings as the stuff of folklore, as outgrowths of old beliefs and stories that the player must now navigate. And both the games and the film feature characters who engage in explicitly folkloristic research. Candyman's victims and the numerous people killed by the angry ghosts in *Fatal Frame* are the proof that folkloric knowledge is not trivial. Studying folklore puts the folklorists dangerously close to a realm of paranormal evil, and in most cases they do not survive their encounters with that realm.

7. See Koven's (2008) treatment of ostension in popular media.

8. Thanks to Mitsuko Kawabata for pointing out the irony of the folklorists' transformations.

9. In the spirit of reflexivity, I should also note in closing that I am an avid gamer and have played all of the *Fatal Frame* games that have been released in the United States. I was also influenced by their portrayal of folklore in not insignificant ways. Ryozo Munakata, the fictional folklorist's assistant (later a folklorist himself) quoted in the first epigraph at the opening of this chapter, observed that it was a particular rural village that encouraged his interest in folklore. My own interest in folklore was spurred in part by the *Fatal Frame*

games themselves. That video games can motivate an entire course of study is yet another reason why academic folklorists should consider popular perspectives on their discipline. Consequently, a final goal of this study is to offer a model for bringing disciplinary and popular understandings a bit closer together, encouraging dialogue between them and, ideally, fostering within the discipline a greater concern with what people outside of it think about it.

10. Martin Picard (2009) is uncomfortable with the presence of such icons of Japanese "traditional" identity. "In these games," he writes, "many national cultural icons serve as background, for instance, feudal Japan, legends and folktales, ghosts, monsters, and film stars. However, far from purely representing a nation, this marketing device is used to sell products and they need the 'Japanese signature' to sell well, in Japan or abroad" (113). Picard seems to imply here that only culture produced spontaneously, naively, and without economic motive is viable as culture—an argument that should sound familiar to contemporary folklorists. Despite Picard's concerns, the folkloresque as we employ the concept in this volume helps remind us not only that "pure" representation is an impossibility but also that the processes of commodification and localization, so central to the globalizing tendencies of contemporary media, are not necessarily any less creative, less meaningful to participants, or less worthy of study than any other form of cultural expression.

11. This point is dramatically underscored by a game on the Sony PlayStation 3 whose title, *Folklore* (Okamoto and Shono 2007), has drawn less attention from disciplinary folklorists than one would perhaps expect.

REFERENCES

Baxter, Jane Eva. 2002. "Popular Images and Popular Stereotypes: Images of Archaeologists in Popular and Documentary Film." *SAA Archaeological Record* 2(4): 16–17, 40.

Cashman, Ray. 2006. "Critical Nostalgia and Material Culture in Northern Ireland." *Journal of American Folklore* 119(472): 137–60. http://dx.doi.org/10.1353/jaf.2006.0016.

Dégh, Linda, and Andrew Vázsonyi. 1983. "Does the Word 'Dog' Bite? Ostensive Action: A Means of Legend-Telling." *Journal of Folklore Research* 20(1): 5–34.

Dundes, Alan. 1966. "Metafolklore and Oral Literary Criticism." *Monist* 50(4): 505–16. http://dx.doi.org/10.5840/monist196650436.

Emi-chan. 2013. "Beyond the Camera's Lens." www.cameraslens.com.

Evans, Timothy H. 2005. "A Last Defense against the Dark: Folklore, Horror, and the Uses of Tradition in the Works of H. P. Lovecraft." *Journal of Folklore Research* 42(1): 99–135. http://dx.doi.org/10.2979/JFR.2005.42.1.99.

Grand Theft Auto: San Andreas. 2004. PlayStation 2. New York: Rockstar Games.

Hoeger, Laura, and William Huber. 2007. "Ghastly Multiplication: *Fatal Frame II* and the Videogame Uncanny." In *Situated Play: Proceedings of DiGRA 2007 Conference*, 152–56. Tokyo: University of Tokyo. http://www.digra.org/digital-library/publications/ghastly-multiplication-fatal-frame-ii-and-the-videogame-uncanny/.

Kirkland, Ewan. 2005. "Restless Dreams in Silent Hill: Approaches to Video Game Analysis." *Journal of Media Practice* 6(3): 167–78. http://dx.doi.org/10.1386/jmpr.6.3.167/1.

Kirkland, Ewan. 2009. "Storytelling in Survival Horror Video Games." In *Horror Video Games: Essays on the Fusion of Fear and Play*, edited by Bernard Perron, 62–78. Jefferson, NC: McFarland.

Kirshenblatt-Gimblett, Barbara. 1998. "Folklore's Crisis." *Journal of American Folklore* 111(441): 281–327. http://dx.doi.org/10.2307/541312.

Koven, Mikel J. 2008. *Film, Folklore, and Urban Legends*. Lanham, MD: Scarecrow.

Kripke, Eric. 2005. *Supernatural.* Warner Brothers.

Miller, Kiri. 2008. "Grove Street Grimm: *Grand Theft Auto* and Digital Folklore." *Journal of American Folklore* 121(481): 255–85. http://dx.doi.org/10.1353/jaf.0.0017.

Nitsche, Michael. 2009. "Complete Horror in Fatal Frame." In *Horror Video Games: Essays on the Fusion of Fear and Play*, edited by Bernard Perron, 200–219. Jefferson, NC: McFarland.

Okamoto, Yoshiki, and Takashi Shono. 2007. *Folklore.* Sony PlayStation 3. Tokyo: Sony Computer Entertainment.

Picard, Martin. 2009. "Haunting Backgrounds: Transnationality and Intermediality in Japanese Survival Horror Video Games." In *Horror Video Games: Essays on the Fusion of Fear and Play*, edited by Bernard Perron, 95–120. Jefferson, NC: McFarland.

Rose, Bernard. 1992. *Candyman.* TriStar Pictures.

"Ryozo Munakata." 2013. *Zero Wiki.* http://bcl.rpen.us/zerowiki/index.php?title=Ryozo_Munakata.

Sherman, Sharon R. 1997. "Perils of the Princess: Gender and Genre in Video Games." *Western Folklore* 56(3–4): 243–58. http://dx.doi.org/10.2307/1500277.

Shibata, Makoto. 2001. *Fatal Frame.* PlayStation 2. Tokyo: Tecmo Koei.

Shibata, Makoto. 2002. *Fatal Frame: Director's Cut.* Microsoft Xbox. Tokyo: Tecmo Koei.

Shibata, Makoto. 2003. *Fatal Frame II: Crimson Butterfly.* PlayStation 2. Tokyo: Tecmo Koei.

Shibata, Makoto. 2004. *Fatal Frame II: Crimson Butterfly: Director's Cut.* Microsoft Xbox. Tokyo: Tecmo Koei.

Shibata, Makoto. 2005. *Fatal Frame III: The Tormented.* PlayStation 2. Tokyo: Tecmo Koei.

Shibata, Makoto. 2012. *Fatal Frame II: Deep Crimson Butterfly.* Nintendo Wii. Tokyo: Tecmo Koei.

Shibata, Makoto, and Suda51. 2008. *Zero: Tsukihiami No Kamen.* Nintendo Wii. Tokyo: Tecmo Koei, Grasshopper Manufacture.

Spirit Camera: The Cursed Memoir. 2012. Nintendo 3DS. Tokyo: Tecmo Koei, Nintendo.

Stewart, Susan. 1982. "The Epistemology of the Horror Story." *Journal of American Folklore* 95(375): 33–50. http://dx.doi.org/10.2307/540021.

Tolbert, Jeffrey A. 2013. "'The Sort of Story That Has You Covering Your Mirrors': The Case of Slender Man." *Semiotic Review,* no. 2: Monsters. http://semioticreview.com/index.php/thematic-issues/issue-monsters/22-the-sort-of-story-that-has-you-covering-your-mirrors-the-case-of-slender-man.

Tolbert, Jeffrey A. 2015. "On Folklore's Appeal: A Personal Essay." *New Directions in Folklore* 13(1/2): 93–113.

Tosenberger, Catherine. 2010. "'Kinda Like the Folklore of Its Day': *Supernatural,* Fairy Tales, and Ostension." *Transformative Works and Cultures* 4. http://journal.transformativeworks.org/index.php/twc/article/viewArticle/174.

Zero: Nuregarasu No Miko. 2014. Wii U. Japan: Koei Tecmo.

Zero Wiki. 2014. Last modified July 17. http://bcl.rpen.us/zerowiki/index.php?title=Main_Page.

6

They Say Éamon Kelly was Ireland's Greatest Storyteller

Chad Buterbaugh

IRELAND'S VERSION OF THE U.S. TALENT show *American Idol* was called *Glas Vegas*—*glas* being Irish Gaelic for green.[1] Its panel of three judges included actress Molly Bhreathnach, television personality Tom O'Brannigan, and Eoghan Harris, a longtime writer, political columnist, and former member of the Irish Senate. During an episode of *Glas Vegas* in 2008, the three judges relaxed at their podium as the onstage emcee informed them that the next performer would "slow the pace a bit." As the emcee stepped aside, out came Tim Evans, a slim young man wearing a roomy black top-coat and crooked-brimmed fedora. Tonight, Evans announced, he would be performing "a fierce lie." So began his rendering of a story called "The Tayman," a humorous anecdote about thickheaded farmers, traveling sales-men, and Ireland's national drink, tea—or *tay*, as Evans pronounced it in an affected County Kerry accent. The tale was a hit with the judges. Even Eoghan Harris, peering out from under his arched eyebrows, congratulated Evans on the performance. "When Éamonn Kelly died, there was a con-siderable void in Irish culture. Tonight, that gap was filled" (Evans 2008).[2]

The man Harris was referring to is the late actor Éamon Kelly, who, despite his diverse accomplishments on stage and screen, is most famous for playing the role of a storyteller.[3] Not only that, Kelly is popularly remembered *as* a storyteller, with the gap between the man and the role having shrunk to nonexistence over decades of public appreciation (see Bauman 2011). Donning a heavy coat and hat, and leaning deeply into the Kerry accent that he grew up with, Kelly spent the latter half of the twentieth century telling stories onstage, on the radio, and on television.

DOI: 10.7330/9781607324188.c006

"The Tayman" formed part of his repertoire, much of which recounted the local customs and eccentricities of a rural Ireland of the past. Kelly inhabited the storytelling role with such appeal that the artifice of his performance—its scripted nature, its position as a single role among many that he played as an actor—receded in importance under the quality of the narrative entertainment that he provided. Today, Kelly is widely remembered as a *seanchaí*, or loremaster, and his work is famous the length and breadth of Ireland.[4]

The concept of the folkloresque offers a productive rubric for interrogating the popular application of labels like seanchaí.[5] Although this breed of narrative artist seems to belong to a tradition that has dwindled or disappeared, the seanchaí proved a successful vehicle for Kelly because his performances guided audiences' attention to a storytelling custom of the past—that of the rambling house, which I will discuss in detail later. The main purpose of the following pages is to examine the public adulation that Kelly enjoyed as a result of his storytelling work as well as the influence he has had on contemporary narrative performance practices in Ireland. This discussion unfolds in the following order: first, I consider the folkloresque as a recent addition to the critical vocabulary of folkloristics. Next, I explore the personal and professional lives of Éamon Kelly, including the mechanisms by which audiences conflated him with the character he portrayed. Finally, I theorize public authentication in terms of its potential to influence popular and academic conceptions of folklore. Throughout the essay, I posit Kelly's work as a folkloresque portrayal of Irish storytelling that amalgamates elements of oral tradition, theatrical performance, and mass mediation. While it strayed from the conception of Irish storytelling as an extemporaneous form, Kelly's storyteller character also seeded subsequent patterns of narrative performance that invite folklorists to reimagine the boundaries of vernacular narrative art.

A DICTIONARY OF MUTATIONS

Like biologists, folklorists must take care to separate the name of our discipline from the name of the material that we study. *Folkloristics* is useful for referring to the academic field, while *folklore* itself refers to the everyday words, objects, and customs that express the identity and culture of people or groups. This essay adopts such terminology for ease of understanding, especially in light of the *folkloresque*, a new term being used to study expressions that derive their folkloric character from popular, though not necessarily scholarly, perspectives.

The introduction of the folkloresque is folkloristics' latest recognition of the ever-changing dynamics of vernacular expression. As people find new ways to interact with one another, folklore changes in tandem. Critical vocabulary must change likewise if there is any hope of understanding how people label and index the material of everyday communication. A brief look into the terminological evolution of the word *folklore* reveals many changes in critical vocabulary over time. The word was born as a linguistic mutation in William Thoms's 1846 letter to the *Athenaeum* magazine, in which he debates the meaning of popular literature: "It is more a Lore than a Literature, and would be most aptly described by a good Saxon compound, Folklore" (Thoms 1999, 11). Though it has since lost the novelty of Thoms's original construction—"Remember that I claim the honor of introducing the epithet Folklore," he writes (12)—the word at the heart of our discipline seems to have retained a spirit of linguistic innovation.

Mutation often occurs as part of a scholarly effort to grapple with folklore's appearance in previously unfamiliar contexts. For example, *folklorismus* is folklore divested of an informal community performance dynamic. In her roundup of scholarly uses of the word, Newall (1987) provides a glimpse of folklore held captive by commodification, tourism, and product packaging. The suggestion is that folklorismus functions less as a meaningful cultural expression and more as a quaint accessory to the trade of goods and services. A devolutionary streak characterizes this interpretation of folklorismus. It is the shade of folklore that has drifted away, at its own peril, from its perceived point of origin. Another mutation, the word *folklorization*, takes a more measured look at folklore in unfamiliar contexts. Specifically, folklorization recognizes folklore's ability to engage with multiple media (see McDowell 2010). While oral storytelling might be the most apt medium for expressing a particular narrative, it is not impossible for the story to shift back and forth among oral, sung, journalistic, or televised accounts (see Dégh 1994; Paredes 1974). Furthermore, nonoral forms might provide constructive counterpoints to the story as it is rendered orally, as with the hero-making function of a Texas border legend (McDowell 2005; Paredes 2003). In short, discussions of folklorization tend not to suggest that the folklorized form is a devolved copy of an authentic ancestor. Instead, they recognize the multimedia interchange through which folklore may take on new and unexpected forms.[6]

Though philosophically distinct, both folklorismus and folklorization place the analytical focus on folklore as it appears in new contexts. The form is at the center of the discussion. The folkloresque expands the analytical focus to include both the form and the audience. It meditates on how producers/consumers of popular culture interpret folklore and consciously draw on it for the sense of authenticity and authority it offers" (see Michael Foster's introduction to this volume). The folkloresque expression encourages audiences to think about what folklore is. Accordingly, folkloresque analysis asks the question: What do people think about when they think about folklore?

Academic study of the folkloresque begins with a modicum of comparative work. Presumably, the folkloresque expression contains elements that recall previously studied forms of folklore. The folklorist must identify these features in order to determine what exactly is folkloric about the expression at issue. However, what gives the folkloresque its true conceptual momentum is the part of the expression that is unfamiliar in terms of previous folkloristic inquiry. To fully understand the folkloresque is to study lore that is being expressed in ways that have few or no historical antecedents. Therefore, the analytical task is to interrogate the familiar and the unfamiliar with equal vigor, with the goal of understanding how they cooperate. In Éamon Kelly's case, a trained actor's painstakingly crafted performances reminded audiences of an Irish storytelling tradition of the past. But what was it about Kelly's craftsmanship that created such a successful metonym for days gone by? Moreover, how did his stories exceed the function of inducing nostalgia and come to provide a template for what Irish narrative folklore should look like today? These are the questions that I attempt to answer here.

Folkloresque *portrayal*, the subject of this essay, creates an impression of folklore through embodied performance. Kelly, a professional actor playing the part of a storyteller, gestured toward the vernacular speech and customs of County Kerry by wearing the costume of an elderly raconteur, speaking in a practiced dialect, and telling stories that were carefully scripted to mimic the affect of storytellers he had encountered in his youth.[7] These elements, combined with a theatrical set built to look like a country kitchen, created an impression of rambling house storytelling, a form of rural Irish entertainment based on patterns of evening visitation among near neighbors. Kelly's childhood home was a rambling house in the village of Carrigeen, County Kerry. The people of the locality often gathered there to spend an evening chatting, playing music, or telling stories. Kelly remembers, "When people came visiting to the house, the men would come and sit down and talk. They would tell it as a story, whatever it was, if they'd been to market, a wedding, a wake, whatever it was" (Hickey 2004, 106). There is no evidence to suggest that Kelly was known as an expert storyteller in his childhood rambling house, so it is plausible that his involvement in this tradition consisted mainly of youthful observation. To this extent, the storyteller character of his adulthood (hereafter "Storyteller") is a fiction. The Storyteller's performances portrayed a stylized version of what Kelly remembered of the rambling house. On the other hand, if the social customs of Carrigeen informed Kelly's early years, then the Storyteller is more accurately described as a theatrical invention that is partly informed by exposure to narrative and customary folklore. Its "remediated" quality depends on some amount of personal experience (Bauman 2011). The following section attempts a short biography of Kelly in the interest of locating the thread that connects the young man of Carrigeen with the professional actor who is presently embedded in the Irish popular imagination as a master storyteller.

THE LIFE AND WORK OF ÉAMON KELLY

Éamon Kelly was born in 1914 in County Kerry in the final years of British rule. Growing up in rural Carrigeen, he learned woodworking from his father, Edmund, a carpenter and wheelwright. Kelly pursued this trade through his young adulthood as he studied to become a carpentry teacher. After serving a short time as an itinerant instructor, he took a full-time teaching appointment at a technical school in Listowel, a town in north Kerry. Listowel at the time was a hub for the dramatic arts.[8] Kelly joined the local drama group and appeared in various plays by Irish playwrights. In a production of J. M. Synge's *The Playboy of the Western World*, Kelly both won a national acting award and played opposite his future wife, Maura O'Sullivan.

Following their marriage and after receiving numerous accolades for their acting work in Listowel, Kelly and O'Sullivan moved to Dublin. There they continued their dramatic work on the national radio service *Raidió Teilifís Éireann* (RTÉ) and at the Abbey Theatre. Kelly soon became acquainted with the role for which he is most remembered today, apart from storytelling: that of S. B. O'Donnell, an austere father figure in the Brian Friel play *Philadelphia, Here I Come*. In this tale of an emigrant's last night in Ireland, Kelly's O'Donnell cannot bring himself to show emotion in the hours before his son's departure. Audiences embraced the production. The Irish run of *Philadelphia, Here I Come* enjoyed such success that it led to additional tours in England, the United States, and Canada as well as an eventual film adaptation. For his performances in the United States, Kelly received a Tony Award nomination in 1966.

The Storyteller's first appearance came before the success of *Philadelphia, Here I Come*. Audiences met him in 1957 on the RTÉ radio production *Take the Floor*, a scripted variety show that carefully affected the rambling house tradition. *Take the Floor* portrayed multiple forms of folk entertainment, including storytelling, traditional music, and even dance. Kelly explains: "Dancing on the air seemed in no way odd at the time. The rat-a-tat-tat sound of the Rory O'Connor troupe was refreshing, and was achieved by the tapping of well-shod dancing feet on thin wooden laths backed with strips of canvas—a little like an extended roll-top desk cover" (Kelly 1999, 68). The program's imaginative writers also scripted lines for supporting characters to recite in the background, a nuance that made it seem as if neighbors were being welcomed into a real home. Listeners delighted in the illusion. *Take the Floor* received favorable reviews, particularly in Kelly's native region. A letter to the editor in the December 29, 1957, edition of the *Sunday Independent* notes: "We here in the West largely look forward to it every Saturday night; in fact, it is a tonic in these days of satellites, atomic missiles, etc."[9] In response, RTÉ producers developed *The Rambling House* in 1961 to give the character a greater share of the airtime. The reaction to that program was similarly positive, though it was taken off the air after one of its cast members, the poet and storyteller Éamon Keane, was fired following an argument with a government official (Kelly 1999, 69–70). The Storyteller's activities then slowed somewhat, as Kelly tended to the international success of *Philadelphia, Here I Come*. However, the public's appetite for storytelling had been whetted, and Kelly's reputation for delivering it began to grow.

A high point in the Storyteller's career came in 1975, when Kelly took the character from the radio to the stage with a one-man play titled *In My Father's Time*. This theatrical production gave the Storyteller two full hours to perform. Enriched by the costume of a rural Kerryman and a set built to resemble a rambling house kitchen, he engaged audiences visually as well as verbally. He mortared his stories together with brief asides, and wandered around the kitchen set as he spoke, making cups of tea or tending the fire in the open hearth. The end product portrayed the rambling house with remarkable detail, and public response was tremendous. Irish audiences lauded *In My Father's Time*, and international excitement led to tours of the United States and Canada. It was the beginning of a time of plenty. The demand for new material reached such heights that Kelly was able to develop a new one-man play for the Storyteller every June for seven years, starting in 1975. Each production was a theatrical success, and they also accelerated Kelly's media presence. The actor's face began to appear on the covers of LPs and paperbacks, on playbills advertising his work, and in newspapers and magazines.

Much of the success of the Storyteller grew from the stylistic attention that Kelly gave the character in terms of verbal artistry. Barring a linguistic analysis, the only adequate description of the Storyteller's voice is that it demonstrates a pronounced Kerry accent rendered in a crisp baritone. Only a blurry border could be said to separate Kelly's own inherited accent from that of the Storyteller. His familiars, including his son Eoin, say that he leaned more heavily into the accent during his early performances; as he aged, he began to let the exaggeration fade (Kelly 2013). From the point of view of appreciative audiences, the source of the accent mattered little in comparison to the images that it stirred. Storytelling promoter Bob Jennings, who grew up in a local rambling house in Richfordstown, County Cork,[10] said that the Storyteller's voice reminded him of the *seanchaithe* he knew as a boy. "I could hear their voice in his voice," Jennings recalls. "He spoke very much like the older people I knew" (Jennings 2013).

In terms of idiom, the Storyteller was fluent in a form of speech play that adorned simple statements with artful syntax. Describing a woman's desire to curb her husband's bad behavior on his album *Stories from Ireland, with Eamon Kelly*, he does not say that she will "stop him" but opts instead to assure that she will "soon put a halt to his gallop." Similarly, rather than stating that the hired farm laborer gets only a brief night's sleep, he notes: "He had hardly the impression of his body made in the feather tick when he was called again to go out and tackle the horse" (Kelly 1998, 310). Such constructions, coupled with the Kerry accent, constituted a form of Hiberno-English that proved familiar and playful for fans. Carefully crafted scripts dictated the Storyteller's speech play. A diligent wordsmith, Kelly drafted his stories first by hand, then revised them to cross out straightforward phrases in favor of the sorts of flourishes described above. A final typed version would serve as the source for performance, although this, too, was often marked up with additional revisions. Some contemporary storytellers criticize Kelly for scripting his work rather than performing extemporaneously, but the method proved successful in crafting a stylized image of rambling house storytelling for the public's entertainment. In an April 4, 1986, interview with the *Kerryman/Corkman* newspaper, Kelly explained why he wrote his stories down: "If I was born in an era before television or radio and before the masses of printed material we all consume, I wouldn't have to write them down. I knew unlettered men who had the freshness of mind which made it like blotting paper. They could recite whole sermons from memory. But I'm obliged to write them down as a matter of record."

The Storyteller's costume visually accentuated his personality onstage and in later filmed productions (see, for example, the 1987 VHS release

Stories from Ireland, as Told by Eamon Kelly). With little variation, the character appeared in a weathered fedora, a dark topcoat, and a waistcoat worn over a collarless white button-down known in Ireland as a grandfather shirt. The fedora became the Storyteller's most identifiable accessory. Battered to near shapelessness, it sat askance on the Storyteller's head and was often drafted into the action of the performance. A segment of *In My Father's Time* uses the hat as a prop for making conversation with the audience: "As well as covering the head the hat is a handy receptacle. If you are caught short you can give a feed of oats to a horse out of a hat. You can gather apples in the orchard or bring in new laid eggs from the hayshed" (Kelly 1976, 5). The Storyteller's sustained popularity in Ireland has turned the costume to a symbol of his performances. Contemporary storytellers appearing in hats, waistcoats, or grandfather shirts are priming their audiences for the sort of humorous, linguistically playful narratives made popular by Éamon Kelly. Those who wear the costume but do not deliver the narratives risk estranging the audience, which is well able to read the visual code for this particular style of narrative performance.

Part of the Storyteller's sizeable repertoire comes from the Irish genre of *scéalaíocht*, or what would folkloristically be categorized as folk tales and myths. However, fans most prized the Storyteller for his local character anecdotes (see Cashman 2008). These humorous stories recounted the exploits of characters from an unnamed location that was coded, through the Storyteller's verbal and visual style, as a rural Kerry of the past. Like all the Storyteller's narratives, his local character anecdotes were scripted. They were also fictitious, in contrast to anecdotes collected elsewhere (see Cashman 2008; Glassie 1982, 2006). Characters such as Mick the Fiddler, Pegg the Damsel, and Father MacGillacuddy never existed as such, but they were composited from figures Kelly encountered in his own life, as suggested by his remark in *Inside Tribune* magazine on August 7, 1983: "I always go back to someone I knew, to some sort of basic reality rather than something that was out of the realms of fantasy, of imagined characters."

Built into the Storyteller's kindly affect was a pinch of criticism for those who do not behave appropriately in the context of family and community life. For example, emigration anecdotes addressed the smallness of Ireland relative to destinations such as the United States, and characters marveled at returned emigrants' reports of Manhattan skyscrapers. At the same time, the returnees risked criticism if they allowed their American experience to feed their ego. Such was the case with the blacksmith's wife, who returned to Ireland with the hope of schooling her husband in elocution and table manners: "Ah, she was used to the good thing in America, where she was a lady's companion, wintering it in New York and summering it in Spring Falls. She was full of airs and graces, which she tried to transfer to the blacksmith" (Kelly 1980).

Priests also played a significant role in the Storyteller's repertoire, and they were not spared his criticism. Though introduced as a source of authority, the priest often enough exited the narrative as the object of fun. In "The Looking Glass," a country bumpkin looks into a mirror for the first time and thinks it is a picture of his father as a young man. The parish priest, called in to resolve the matter, appears doubly foolish: he sees a picture of the priest who served before him at the local church. Such gentle prodding destabilized the religious authority that was understood to hold the final word in community matters in rural Ireland. "People were kind of downtrodden by powers that be, but Éamon's stories always subverted that," says Dublin storyteller Nuala Hayes. "He used humor to laugh at the pomposity, the misuse of power, the folly of it all" (Hayes 2013).

Finally, the Storyteller narrated the local customs of his home place. A story titled "The Season of Light" describes the rural Christmas holiday in meticulous detail, right down to the thickness of the candles to be set in each window of the house (Kelly 1998, 193–97). Lacking any discernible plot, this story does not seek to entertain so much as inform. Notably, similar information appears in Kelly's memoirs as part of his childhood holiday recollections (Kelly 1995, 125–39). That the material appears in both places suggests its relatively accurate portrayal of the customs of a rural Kerry Christmas. Newspaper reporters recognized stories like "The Season of Light" as legitimate exhibitions of folk custom. A June 20, 1976, review in the *Irish Press* notes the pleasing effect of such narration. Apart from more formal narratives, "Kelly also draws on old themes of the wake, the chamber pot, the bridal bed or the fear of hell, and when the laughs come, they come easy. His intonation is refined but his show is vulgar in the best sense of theatre: it is entertainment by the people for the people."

Kelly continued to perform as the Storyteller until his passing on October 24, 2001. His last appearance was in September of that year at the Courtmacsherry Storytelling Carnival in County Cork. The audio recording of this performance provides an intimate glimpse into Kelly's final weeks. The bell-clear voice that defined his early work is gone, replaced by the mellowed tones of a man in his eighty-seventh year. On the other hand, the joy of the crowd is undiminished. The Storyteller's narratives, familiar though they might be, still earn raucous laughter and hearty applause. Maura O'Sullivan remembers the night fondly: "The minute he went onstage, the adrenaline started to flow. People couldn't believe it. He was like a young man again, telling the stories" (O'Sullivan 2013). The success of the evening inspired festival organizer Bob Jennings to look ahead: "I said to him, 'Maybe you'll come again next year.' And the answer he made me was, 'I'll be eighty-eight next year, you know'" (Jennings 2013). Five weeks later, Kelly passed away.

DISTINGUISHING THE ACTOR FROM THE ROLE

When Éamon Kelly and Maura O'Sullivan arrived at the Courtmacsherry Storytelling Carnival, the site of the Storyteller's final performance, Cork storyteller Pat Speight was already in the middle of a set. Speight is affectionately known as Pat the Hat because he seldom performs without headwear. So it was on this day: a fine hat from Christys' of London rested atop his head. Speight says that some fans assume he is trying to mimic the style of the Storyteller, but he thinks of the accessory as an homage. He grew up listening to the Storyteller on the radio, and he never fails to attribute Éamon Kelly when performing one of his pieces in public. Upon noticing Kelly's arrival, Speight made the rare gesture of removing his hat before a live audience. "I stopped in the middle of a story," he recalls, "and I said, 'Ladies and gentlemen, we're very privileged to have Maura and Éamon Kelly here. As far as I'm concerned, this room is only big enough for one hat.' And I took off my hat and handed it to Éamon" (Speight 2013b). Again, the hat was a luxury item crafted by a London haberdasher. However, the fiction of the Storyteller quickly engulfed it. As Kelly made his way to the front of the room, he quietly slipped into character. Taking Speight's hat in his hands, he inspected the inner band, where the Christys' label was imprinted. He then announced that this was a good Cork hat, made at O'Gorman Hat Company near Shandon on the north side of Cork City.

In this episode, fact and fiction collide, and the audience is left to sort out the pieces. The hat objectively belongs to the world inhabited by Pat Speight and Éamon Kelly. It was manufactured in the distant metropolis of London, and Speight purchased it for a considerable sum. Nonetheless, these facts do not suit the needs of the Storyteller. To prime the audience members for his particular brand of storytelling, he must guide their attention away from distant places and situate it firmly in the local landscape of County Cork. This requires Kelly the actor to withdraw so that the Storyteller may attach the hat to a fictitious narrative that keys the subsequent performance as an expression of local wit and wisdom (see Bauman 1977). Kelly's shift into character eschewed theatrical conventions. No curtains or spotlight preceded the Storyteller's appearance; he simply arrived, looking much like Éamon Kelly. Who is who, then? In fairness, this example might be frivolous. It could signify little more than the desire of two experienced performers to fill the dead air between sets. On the other hand, if this moment confuses the issue of who the Storyteller is relative to the actor who is playing him, then it has done its job. Onstage, in the press, and in product packaging, audiences more commonly observed a conflation of Kelly and the Storyteller than a distinct separation between the two.

Journalists equated Kelly with the Storyteller by attributing the actor's storytelling skill to his Kerry upbringing. Reviewing the character's 1980 one-man play, a reporter for the *Sunday Tribune* notes that "the loosely-connected stories in the Abbey production of *English That for Me!* are rooted in rural ways and places, the true feel of which is something of conjecture today for most people under 40." Similarly, a review in the *Stage and Television Today* newspaper on September 22, 1977, provides little indication that *In My Father's Time* was a stage performance: "Mary and Jesus hang resolutely on the wall, sacks of spuds lie propped against the sideboard. Shoes under the table, socks in front of the fire, and, on a chair in the middle of this contemporary Co. Kerry Kitchen, hat pushed back on head, legs spread in patched pants, sits our storyteller." Some reviews are more nuanced, but even these invoke something other than stagecraft as a contributing factor to the Storyteller's success. An article in the *Hot Press* reports: "Some of it is the actor's skill—and Eamon Kelly is a fine actor—but there's also a native wisdom at work, a priceless lack of credulity at whatever is pompous, insincere, and phoney." These remarks reveal something of the logic behind the popular perception of the actor playing the Storyteller. Because Kelly grew up in a place known to be rich in folklore, his stage success must draw on "native wisdom" at least as much as it relies on dramatic skill. Actor and character can never be wholly separate when the material being staged so successfully portrays something of rural folk culture.

Product packaging also mingled the identities of Kelly and the Storyteller, though less articulately. Playbills, book covers, and recording inserts generally did not identify Kelly as an actor playing a storyteller; they simply identified him *as* a storyteller in releases like *Éamon Kelly: Ireland's Master Storyteller* (1998) or *Eamon Kelly: The Irish Storyteller* (1980). Thus advertised, products assured consumers that their purchase would get them closer to both the character and the man. As the poet Brendan Kennelly (1980) explains in the program for *English That for Me!*, "Eamon Kelly is unique. He is a delight to witness and listen to; he would be a disaster to imitate. He has arrived at the rare and happy position of being completely

himself. Paradoxically, he is never *merely* himself because there are generations of storytellers in his bones."

Kelly resisted the trappings of his character. In his reckoning, he was
not the Storyteller so loved by audiences. He was a dramatic craftsman
whose youthful experiences allowed him to refit the rambling house tradition for the stage. Responding to the notion that he was a seanchaí,
Kelly made these remarks in a 1976 interview with the *Irish Times*: "The
seanachaí was a man with all the time in the world to ramble the highways
and byeways in his account; so I have to pare it down and incapsulate the
stories into a smaller slot—and it improves it. He had the intimacy of the
firelight and the candlelight, and the small group of people who would
go to the 'visiting' house until he eventually deserted it for another place,
and they followed like a swarm of bees. He was very static and stared into
eternity as he spoke—something I cannot do onstage of course. I add the
actor's craft."

Despite these protestations, the Storyteller was never popularly identified as a theatrical invention. The actor and the character were ascribed the
same identity: a rural Kerryman with a gift for words. Although the name
Éamon Kelly was used to identify both the public figure and the private
citizen, it more strongly connoted the public figure, whose social network
far outstripped the associations of family and friends. In this way, an appreciative public determined the pace and extent of discourses identifying the
position and importance of a theatrical character in the popular imagination. Kelly was a storyteller mainly because people said he was, and although
he made statements to the contrary, even he catered to this label somewhat.
He could shift into character in an instant, as he did when he proclaimed
the Cork provenance of a London-made hat. Such improvisational mastery
depends on more than theatrical wherewithal alone. The Storyteller's voice,
gesture, and affect were contingent on a vast local knowledge. He had to
be able to produce folk speech, custom, and local landmarks at will. Kelly
seems to have been attuned to all of these elements. While he might not
have accepted the label of seanchaí, he did accept the responsibility of nur-
turing a popular conception of the seanchaí storytelling style, and he used
his awareness of local traditions to do it.

In this case study, the folkloric and the folkloresque are alternating
currents, always switching between the rambling house tradition and the
representation of that tradition onstage and through mass media. The
folkloric elements of this equation include narrative and customary traditions that Kelly modified for public performance. The folkloresque elements rest with the Storyteller's audiences, whose overwhelming approval

of the character and his work contributed to a contemporary conception of rural Irish storytelling. The following section addresses this oscillation between folklore and the folkloresque. Specifically, it seeks to explain what happens when the public authentication of the folkloresque portrayal reaches cultural proportions.

INTERPRETING THE WORK OF ÉAMON KELLY THROUGH THE LENS OF THE FOLKLORESQUE

Éamon Kelly's storytelling work espoused many of the conventions of theater and mass media. Its use of scripts, sets, costumes, and broadcast technology placed it outside the purview of folk narrative studies in Ireland in Kelly's time. The local Irish storyteller "who cannot do justice to his material in an unfriendly or strange environment" would consider the stage a foreign place (Ó Duilearga 1945, 16). His stories exist on the vernacular side of a gap between oral tradition and the accouterments of professional entertainment. Indeed, the local storyteller's very existence is something of an anomaly, as his art represents "a continuation and survival of a very ancient way of thinking" (Ó Súilleabháin 1967, 8). Yet, as the essays in this book demonstrate, the folkloric and the folkloresque may complement each other. Kelly's storytelling work illustrates the successful transition of rambling house storytelling from the fireside to the stage. This movement encourages a critical exploration of the space between what has traditionally interested folklorists—the oral, the local, and the seemingly informal—and the contexts in which stylistically vernacular communication arises today—the mediated, the commodified, and the international (see Foster's introduction to this volume). The following interpretations attempt such an exploration, with the goal of highlighting how folkloresque portrayal may gain so much cultural momentum that it begins to alter the definition of folklore.

The Storyteller and his repertoire arose in part from Kelly's personal experience with the narrative and customary folklore of rural Kerry in the early decades of the twentieth century. The character's performances borrow from these traditions; they paint a gestalt of rural life in a certain time and place. Despite the new contexts in which the Storyteller performed, something of the rambling house tradition survived the journey from Kerry to the stage—according to audiences, at least. At the same time, the Storyteller's performances obscured the original position of the rambling house in everyday life. Kelly's character was an invented persona that ceased to exist outside the storytelling performance. By contrast, the rambling house storyteller was a local person for whom storytelling was an evening diversion rather than a full-time career.[11] This difference presented no dilemma for Kelly. He did not consider himself a storyteller; he was an actor playing the part of a storyteller. By this logic, the Storyteller's work is largely commemorative in that its chief function is to stimulate nostalgic remembering (McDowell 1992). The hearth, mantle, kettle, *súgán* chair, and inventive speech play drew listeners toward a storytelling imaginary of the past, when rural people had to make their own entertainment. On the other hand, this commemorative function could not be manufactured in the same way as a theatrical set. Within the theater's artifice, a special element was needed to successfully remind the audience of folk tradition. This responsibility rested with Kelly, whose childhood experiences in the rambling house carried forward into his stagecraft as an adult. As one critic observed in the August 21, 1988, edition of the *Sunday Independent,* "Kerry long ago is always with him." Herein lies the turbulent center of this case study. It contains folklore, but it is not folklore alone. The tradition has been drawn from its original performance context, scripted, advertised, and offered sans the community dynamics that contextualized it in the past. In these circumstances, the Storyteller's work becomes folkloresque *bricolage* (see Foster's introduction to this volume). It offers the most entertaining elements of rambling house storytelling—engaging stories, humor, speech play, and a well-loved storyteller—without any of the blemishes—poor stories, interruptions, or the difficult conditions that many rural Kerry people endured during the transition from British to Irish rule (see, for example, Tom Doyle's 2008 book *The Civil War in Kerry*). In sum, the Storyteller's performances rock back and forth, folkloric from one angle and folkloresque from another.

Yet the preceding thoughts offer a conservative folkloristic perspective only. The public perception of the Storyteller's work offers a wider ranging and potentially more influential take on what is or is not rambling house storytelling. Audiences have long authenticated Kelly as a premier storyteller, as shown earlier. This admiration is especially crucial in the professional storytelling community today, where some performers treat the character as a template for narrative performance, and his stories as a repository of folk narrative. Any performer who achieves Kelly's level of popularity must expect imitators—or, in kinder terms, tribute acts. For example, many blues musicians might cover the B. B. King standard "The Thrill Is Gone." The difference between Kelly and King is that Kelly's artistic product is based on a form of art that is generally understood to be public property: the folk narrative. Authorless and intimate, the folk narrative belongs to the people, even though its appearance in the work of the Storyteller placed it partly under the rubric of high art (the theater), mass media (radio and television), and copyright law (books and recordings sold in shops). If audiences had treated the Storyteller's work as stagecraft, it would have become easier to recognize as Kelly's intellectual property. However, the overwhelming public authentication of Kelly as a teller of folk narratives meant that his stories became a form of folklore, which knows no single owner. Thus, professional storytellers have for decades mimicked Kelly's style and drawn from his repertoire in aid of their own careers. Sometimes the mimesis is total, as with the story, accent, and costuming of Tim Evans, whose example began this essay. At other times the borrowing is gentler, as with Dublin storyteller Jack Lynch, who personally asked permission to use Kelly's "Mick the Fiddler" in his own work. "I was going to America, and I wanted to bring the story with me," Lynch remembers. "So I wrote to him, and he rang me up and said, 'Sure, you're welcome. Thanks for asking. Not many would'" (Lynch 2013).[12] In certain realms, Kelly's stories have assumed the hue of folklore almost completely. County Donegal storyteller Aussie Bryson performs "The Mirror," which describes a hapless farmer's encounter with a gewgaw merchant. The basic narrative arc of "The Mirror" resembles that of "The Looking Glass," which appears on Kelly's album *Stories from Ireland, with Eamon Kelly*. However, Bryson's version changes the characters, setting, tone, and accent to appeal to a Donegal audience. It is not difficult to imagine "The Looking Glass" as a kind of ur-text for "The Mirror," which acts and sounds like a variant of the sort that might be collected by a folklorist completing historic-geographic research.[13] The crux of the folkloresque lies in such narrative movement. If audiences treat a certain form of art as folklore, and the results of this treatment produce new forms of art that possess the qualities of folklore, it is reasonable for folklorists to treat the art likewise, at least on an experimental basis. We must amend our critical vocabulary in order to understand the difference between what we think folklore is and what it is for those who hear it, enjoy it, and perform it.

If folklore and the folkloresque are indeed "never intersecting because they are always already intersecting" (see Foster's introduction to this volume), then it follows that one may subsume the other, depending on the perspective of the critical observer. This case study suggests that the folkloresque portrayal of storytelling may produce embryonic forms of folklore that engage with institutional support, professional training, and electronic mediation as means of everyday communication. If this is true, then the folkloresque, as a term, has a shelf life. In 10 years' time—or perhaps 50 or 100—it will no longer be necessary to differentiate folkloresque communication from folkloric communication, because the popular conception of what folklore is will have changed. The folkloresque will have been absorbed into a new definition of folklore that matches its moment in history. It is easy to argue that Éamon Kelly's storytelling commemorates the old rambling house tradition, but if this is true, then those who tell his stories today are commemorating a commemoration. At some stage, it makes more sense to release the stories from the restrictions of commemoration and recognize them as mercurial narrative expressions that stubbornly insinuate themselves into the changing dynamics of everyday life.

CONCLUSION

Artistic expression of any kind reflects the society from which it emerges. The popularity of Éamon Kelly's Storyteller character appealed to an Irish public that sought much of its entertainment in the theater and on the radio. The impact of this cultural and technological milieu was that storytelling, perhaps once understood as a local, rural form, began to reach audiences through other means. Parts of this process drew on folkloric tradition. Kelly's memories of rural Kerry inspired his folkloresque portrayal of the rambling house. Other parts of this process diverge from previously understood methods of folkloric expression. Theater, radio, and television have been less common subjects of folkloristic inquiry. The folkloresque is a tool for parsing out the differences and similarities between such divergent forms of communication. It allows us to follow the vernacular on its journey into new realms. This essay does not exhaust all folkloresque interpretations of the Storyteller's work. Further study of his electronic media presence would consider the relatively recent release of his audio and video recordings online, where comment sections and product review posts create a disjointed master narrative about the Storyteller's importance in Irish society. There is also more work to be done in terms of how the Storyteller's work is treated as folklore. Performers like Tim Evans, Jack Lynch, and Aussie Bryson are aware of the connection of their work with that of the Storyteller. Other performers are unaware of such connections, however, and they continue to tell the Storyteller's stories as if they were drawn from a storied oral tradition.

Of the many uses of folkloresque analysis suggested in this volume's introduction, one with significant theoretical potential is the effort to understand emic conceptions of folklore. While the work of the Storyteller might not correlate with previous folkloristic ideas of how folk narrative works, popular voices speak more loudly. The title of this essay alludes to the importance of popular authentication. For the Storyteller's audiences, scholarly annotation is less vital than their own aesthetic reaction to his work (see Kirshenblatt-Gimblett 1998, 17–78, 203–39). This attention toward public opinion has the potential to rattle foundational scholarly concepts of what folklore is. However, for a discipline concerned with vernacular expression, it is appropriate to pay attention to what people are talking about when they talk about folklore: to interrogate the stories but also "to figure out what the devil they think they are up to" (Geertz 2000, 58).

Acknowledgments

Many people have generously given their time and energy to this study of the work of Éamon Kelly, notably his elder son, Eoin, and his widow, Maura O'Sullivan. I am indebted to them both. I also thank two members of the storytelling community in County Cork, Bob Jennings and Pat Speight, whose sparkling anecdotes illustrate Éamon Kelly's importance in contemporary Irish narrative performance. However, particular appreciation must be reserved for Dublin storyteller Jack Lynch, who eagerly made contacts and procured resources for my use in this project. Jack Lynch's enthusiasm for the work of Éamon Kelly and for folkloristic interest in this subject have contributed greatly to the quality of the present essay. He must share in whatever recognition it receives, while any faults rest with me alone.

NOTES

1. Few sources provide information on the defunct *Glas Vegas*, though some information is archived on the Internet Movie Database at http://www.imdb.com/title/tt1459625/.

2. This quote comes from the subtitles shown on an episode of *Glas Vegas*, which is broadcast in Irish Gaelic. The words, along with the irregular spelling "Éamonn," match the subtitles displayed for Eoghan Harris's commentary.

3. This essay uses the spelling "Éamon," which is how Kelly identifies himself in his memoirs. Alternate spellings are used only as part of quoted material.

4. This essay uses the standard Irish Gaelic spelling "seanchaí," as it appears in *Brewer's Dictionary of Irish Phrase and Fable*. Alternate spellings are used in quoted material only.

5. The word *seanchaí* is the subject of a terminological debate regarding its synonymy with the word *storyteller* (see Harvey 1992). I do not use seanchaí denotatively in this essay. I use it in keeping with the label that audiences have given to Kelly's storyteller character.

6. An adjacent term is *folkloricization*, defined as the recontextualization of expressive culture from an everyday or "folk" existence to an alternative frame (Hagedorn 2001, 67–68).

7. Anecdotal evidence points to local storyteller Batt Shea of Castlecove, County Kerry, as a major influence on the Storyteller's style. Kelly credits Shea in a November 9, 1957, interview with the *Kerryman*, and contemporary storyteller Batt Burns noted the connection between Kelly and Shea in a recent informal conversation.

8. Playwrights Bryan MacMahon and John B. Keane, both Listowel natives, lived in the town when Kelly arrived.

9. Journalistic sources cited in the running text come from the National Library of Ireland's Eamon Kelly Papers, compiled by Éilís Ní Dhuibhne (2003) and cited in the references

section here. This compilation is a collection of Éamon Kelly's personal papers donated to the library after his death. It includes many newspaper clippings. I have made an effort to cite each such source independent of its particularity as an item in the Eamon Kelly Papers. My intention is to provide as much contextualizing information as possible while still allowing for the replication of my research by consulting the Eamon Kelly Papers alone.

10. In Richfordstown, as in the rest of County Cork, this would have been called a *scoriaochting* house, but its function is the same as a rambling house—a local home reserved for regular verbal and musical entertainment.

11. I draw this conclusion from personal interviews with various contemporary storytellers and storytelling promoters, most notably Pat Speight (2013a, 2013b) and Bob Jennings (2013).

12. Jack Lynch does not imitate the Storyteller in terms of costume or accent, and the Storyteller's stories make up only a small part of his repertoire.

13. Further comparative inquiry reveals that "The Looking Glass" has roots in Japan, where it is known as "The Mirror of Matsuyama" (see Ozaki 1905).

REFERENCES

Bauman, Richard. 1977. *Verbal Art as Performance*. Rowley, MA: Newbury House.

Bauman, Richard. 2011. "The 'Talking Machine Storyteller': Cal Stewart and the Remediation of Storytelling." In *The Individual and Tradition: Folkloristic Perspectives*, edited by Ray Cashman, Tom Mould, and Pravina Shukla, 71–92. Bloomington: Indiana University Press.

Cashman, Ray. 2008. *Storytelling on the Northern Irish Border*. Bloomington: Indiana University Press.

Dégh, Linda. 1994. *American Folklore and the Mass Media*. Bloomington: Indiana University Press.

Doyle, Tom. 2008. *The Civil War in Kerry*. Cork: Mercier.

Evans, Tim. 2008. "Irish Storyteller. Famous Seanachaí from Kerry." November 7. Online video clip. http://www.youtube.com/watch?v=jWTrJ1id3jo.

Geertz, Clifford. (Original work published 1983) 2000. *Local Knowledge: Further Essays in Interpretive Anthropology*. New York: Basic Books.

Glassie, Henry. 1982. *Passing the Time in Ballymenone: Culture and History of an Ulster Community*. Philadelphia: University of Pennsylvania Press.

Glassie, Henry, 2006. *The Stars of Ballymenone*. Bloomington: Indiana University Press.

Hagedorn, Katherine J. 2001. *Divine Utterances: The Performance of Afro-Cuban Santería*. Washington, DC: Smithsonian Institution Press.

Harvey, Clodagh Brennan. 1992. *Contemporary Irish Traditional Narrative: The English Language Tradition*. Berkeley: University of California Press.

Hayes, Nuala. 2013. Interview with the author. Dublin, Ireland, September 4.

Hickey, Margaret. 2004. *Irish Days: Oral Histories of the Twentieth Century*. London: Kyle Cathie.

Jennings, Bob. 2013. Interview with the author. Cork, Ireland, June 26.

Kelly, Eamon. 1976. "*In My Father's Time* . . .": A Night of Storytelling with Eamon Kelly. Dublin: Mercier.

Kelly, Eamon. 1980. *Eamon Kelly: The Irish Storyteller*. Compact disc. Naas: Chart Label.

Kelly, Eamon. 1987. *Stories from Ireland, with Eamon Kelly*. Compact disc. Naas: Chart Label.

Kelly, Éamon. 1995. *The Apprentice*. Dublin: Marino Books.

Kelly, Éamon. 1998. *Ireland's Master Storyteller: The Collected Stories of Éamon Kelly*. Dublin: Marino Books.

Kelly, Éamon. 1999. *The Journeyman.* Dublin: Marino Books.

Kelly, Eoin. 2013. Interview with the author. Shandon, Cork, Ireland, August 27.

Kennelly, Brendan. 1980. "Introduction." In *English That for Me!* Peacock Theatre program.

Kirshenblatt-Gimblett. 1998. *Destination Culture: Tourism, Museums, and Heritage.* Berkeley: University of California Press.

Lynch, Jack. 2013. Interview with the author. Smithfield, Dublin, Ireland, July 5.

McDowell, John H. 1992. "Folklore as Commemorative Discourse." *Journal of American Folklore* 105(418): 403–23. http://dx.doi.org/10.2307/541619.

McDowell, John H. 2005. "Chante Luna and the Commemoration of Actual Events." *Western Folklore* 64:39–64.

McDowell, John H. 2010. "Rethinking Folklorization in Ecuador: Multivocality in the Expressive Contact Zone." *Western Folklore* 69:181–209.

Newall, Venetia. 1987. "The Adaptation of Folklore and Tradition (Folklorismus)." *Folklore* 98(2): 131–51. http://dx.doi.org/10.1080/0015587X.1987.9716408.

Ní Dhuibhne, Éilís. 2003. Collection List No. 72: Eamon Kelly Papers, Manuscript 37018. Leabharlann Náisiúnta na hÉireann (National Library of Ireland), Dublin.

Ó Duilearga, Seamus [James Delargy]. 1945. *The Gaelic Story-teller: With Some Notes on Gaelic Folk-tales.* London: Geoffrey Cumberlege Amen House.

Ó Súilleabháin, Seán [Sean O'Sullivan]. 1967. *Irish Folk Custom and Belief [Nósanna agus Pis-eoga na nGael].* Dublin: Three Candles.

O'Sullivan, Maura. 2013. Interview with the author. Coolock, Dublin, Ireland, September 3.

Ozaki, Yei Theodora. 1905. *Japanese Fairy Tales.* New York: A. L. Burt.

Paredes, Américo. 1974. "José Mosqueda and the Folklorization of Actual Events." *Aztlán: International Journal of Chicano Studies Research* 4(1): 1–30.

Paredes, Américo. (Original work published 1958) 2003. *With His Pistol in His Hand.* Austin: University of Texas Press.

Speight, Pat. 2013a. Interview with the author. Cork, Ireland, June 25.

Speight, Pat. 2013b. Interview with the author. Shandon, Cork, Ireland, June 27.

Thoms, William. (Original work published in 1846) 1999. "Folk-Lore and the Origin of the Word." In *International Folkloristics*, edited by Alan Dundes, 9–14. Lanham: Rowman & Littlefield.

7

"New-Minted from the Brothers Grimm"

Folklore's Purpose and the Folkloresque in The Tales of Beedle the Bard

Carlea Holl-Jensen and Jeffrey A. Tolbert

IN THE FINAL VOLUME OF J. K. ROWLING'S *Harry Potter* series, the boy wizard and his friends receive a battered old volume of fairy tales, willed to Hermione Granger by the late Hogwarts headmaster Albus Dumbledore. Though the children initially dismiss the tales as "just . . . things you tell kids to teach them lessons" (Rowling 2007, 414), it eventually transpires that the fairy tales conceal secret information that proves crucial to Harry's quest to defeat the dark wizard Voldemort.

This is by no means an unfamiliar premise: popular media are full of stories predicated on the idea that folklore contains literal truths about real events, people, and creatures (see Tolbert, chapter 5 in this volume). Many books and films take up the premise that mythological figures are real or historical personages. For instance, Neil Gaiman's *American Gods* (2001; see also Evans's chapter 3 in this volume) finds deities like Odin and Thoth struggling to find their place in a twentieth-century America that does not believe in them, and Rick Riordan's children's novel *The Lightning Thief* (2005) imagines its protagonists as the demigod children of the Greek pantheon. In many instances, myths and legends are understood to contain secret clues that must be decoded before the protagonists can solve some urgent modern problem. *The Da Vinci Code* (2003) supposes that Judeo-Christian tradition has encoded historical facts about Jesus's lineage, and in the television show *Grimm* (NBC 2011), Jacob and Wilhelm Grimm's fairy-tale collections are revealed to be bestiaries of actual creatures. In short, for many contemporary audiences, folklore is not understood simply as traditional literature. While folklore's literary merit and potential to reflect cultural values

DOI: 10.7330/9781607324188.c007

may be readily acknowledged, it is also often suspected of harboring arcane truths, its purpose not simply to entertain or educate but to transmit secret factual information. Strange as this may seem to folklorists committed to studying expressive culture, these attitudes imply a conscious assessment of folklore—a process closely related to what Alan Dundes (1966) calls meta-folklore. Examining works of popular culture that represent folklore in this way may help shed light not only on the popular perception of folklore but also on our own folkloristic perspective. In the interest of exploring these popular attitudes about folklore in more depth, we've taken J. K. Rowling's *Harry Potter* series as a case study. Her treatment of fairy tales in *The Tales of Beedle the Bard* (Rowling 2008), in particular, represents a complex portrayal of folklore that both resonates with and challenges folklorists' understanding of the genre.

Published in 2008, *The Tales of Beedle the Bard* is a collection of wizarding fairy tales that features in the final *Potter* novel, *Harry Potter and the Deathly Hallows* (Rowling 2007). In the collection, Rowling critically engages the fairy tales, making choices regarding form and function based on her own understanding of how the genre works. Styled after well-known European fairy-tale collections, *Beedle* contains five tales as well as a lengthy introduction from Rowling and a "commentary" by Dumbledore. As such, it is presented not only as a collection of imaginary fairy tales but also as a mock-scholarly venture, a fictional analysis of fictional tales. In writing her own fairy tales, Rowling both makes conscious use of the fairy-tale genre and advances explicit commentary on that genre. This commentary not only reflects Rowling's views but also indicates a larger pattern of social thought about fairy tales: they are apparently silly, irrelevant texts with little meaning beyond their obvious moral messages, and yet they hint at obscure truths that modern readers would do well to root out.

This attitude is clearly illustrated by the role *The Tales of Beedle the Bard* plays in the broader fictional universe Rowling has created. It is by reading *Beedle* that Harry learns of the existence of three magical artifacts, the titular Deathly Hallows, which ultimately provide the key to his success against Voldemort. In reading the novel, Rowling's audience must tacitly accept her use of folkloric and folkloresque material: we are guided through the same reading of *Beedle* that leads the protagonists of *Deathly Hallows* to their conclusions. For Harry to succeed he must acknowledge the literal truth that underlies these stories, and for the novel to succeed we as readers must also acknowledge this. This reading of *Beedle* is the only one that works in the context of the *Harry Potter* universe—performance theory and deconstruction are ineffective against the Dark Lord—and the extensive annotations offered in *Beedle* help ensure that Rowling's readers arrive at the inevitable conclusion that the fairy tales presented in the novel actually contain solutions to specific problems of Harry's world.

The overwhelming success of the *Harry Potter* franchise suggests that Rowling is not alone in her thinking. The last installment of the series sold 15 million copies in the first twenty-four hours of its release alone, and more than 450 million *Harry Potter* books were in circulation as of July 2013 (*Time* 2013). *Beedle* enjoyed similar success, and critical responses to the collection explicitly corroborated Rowling's understanding of fairy tales. Several reviews compared *Beedle* to real-world fairy tale collections (Cooper 2009; Wilson 2008), and one reviewer eagerly claimed that Rowling's tales "could have come new-minted from the Brothers Grimm" (Craig 2008). Another wrote, "Muggles grow up with Grimm's fairy tales; wizarding children grow up with *Tales of Beedle the Bard*" (Gioia 2009, 152). Clearly, Rowling is not the only one who views fairy tales in this light.

Given these connections between the fictional tales of *Beedle* and real-world fairy tales, validated both by Rowling in the construction of her novels and by the response of her readers, it seems reasonable to conclude that Rowling's work may be used "to reconstruct people's attitudes, values, and reactions" regarding traditional literature (Levine 1992, 1372). That is, Rowling treats fairy tales in the *Harry Potter* universe in ways that are generally intelligible and commonly acceptable to contemporary audiences.

So how, precisely, does Rowling use fairy tales? We suggest two primary modes of engagement with folklore in Rowling's work, which we see replicated in many works of popular media: one, the use of existing folklore to enrich a world of a fiction through intertextual reference (an aspect of the folkloresque mode of *integration*) and two, the metafictional use of created folklore (folkloresque *portrayal*) to comment on her perceptions of the genre. Our discussion of these modes is based in part on the work of Neil Grobman (1979), who provides a comprehensive system for classifying the uses of folklore in literature.

At the most basic level, creators of popular culture use folklore intertextually. Intertextuality depends on the "relational orientation of a text to other texts," especially "the ways in which each act of textual production presupposes antecedent texts and anticipates prospective ones" (Bauman 2004, 4). In popular culture, intertextual uses of folklore typically consist of the inclusion of "real-world" folkloric images and motifs in new cultural forms and media. Grobman calls this the "redacted, reworked, reconstruction" of folklore, which he says involves the conscious reworking of folkloric phenomena "usually in order to establish a point or make the traditions more universally and popularly understood" (Grobman 1979, 29). This use naturally assumes the audiences' familiarity with the material to which authors allude.

Another use of folklore in popular culture is what Alan Dundes famously referred to as "metafolklore," a term he applied to "folkloristic statements about folklore" (Dundes 1966, 509). For Dundes, this specifically indicates a commentary on one item of folklore—a myth, fairy tale, or proverb—by another. But the term applies equally well to the creation and deployment of folkloric material in a fictional universe, because such use of folklore serves as commentary not only on the forms folklore may take but also on the work folklore does in the world. Grobman labels this "imitation," which he defines as the creation of new folklore "in direct imitation of old folk patterns or what is thought to be the folk pattern" (Grobman 1979, 29). The tales *Beedle* contains clearly do imitate existing folk narratives, a point made explicit by Rowling herself in the text of *Beedle* (and to which we will return). They also function in the mode of portrayal through the terms in which they are presented and discussed within the *Harry Potter* universe.

Unlike Grobman, who is interested primarily in the identification and interpretation of the folkloric material that authors integrate into their texts, our interest here is in noting the specific implicit and explicit assumptions authors make when choosing to include such material. Ultimately, though we note two distinct folkloresque modes at work in *Beedle*, both work metafolklorically, since both reveal these assumptions about folklore's forms and functions. Though our purpose is not to enumerate items of real-world folklore that find their way into Rowling's work, it is worth noting that the strategic use of folkloric elements implies a conscious evaluation of folklore, a tacit commentary on the relative appropriateness of different genres and motifs. Rowling herself has said, "I've used things from folklore . . . just to add a certain flavor, but I've always twisted them to suit my own ends. I mean, I've taken liberties with folklore . . . to suit my plot" (A&E 2002). In acknowledging these borrowings, Rowling is also highlighting the conscious process of evaluation that guides her writing. These borrowings add "flavor" because, as C. W. Sullivan writes, they "[allow readers] to recognize, in elemental and perhaps subconscious ways, the reality and cultural depth of the impossible worlds these authors have created" (Sullivan 2001, 279). For Rowling, folklore becomes a resource to be dipped into and cherry-picked, then manipulated to suit her needs. What makes these allusions successful as a source of color and texture for Rowling's fictional world is the fact that her readers share her set of references.

This strategic reliance on the rhetorical power of folklore is what Priscilla Denby describes as the use of "folklore as foundation" (Denby

1971, 115–16). Denby likewise argues that "anything founded in folk tradition is by nature not esoteric and is likely to be understood by most of the masses" (116). For instance, for a reader familiar with Western mythology, Rowling's references to Arthurian legend not only enrich her fictional universe but also reinforce the currency of Arthurian tradition itself. These facts are all taken into consideration by creators of popular culture, who also recognize that the success of these creative strategies depends on the audience's familiarity with the material being referenced: if a reader fails to recognize the intertextual cues, then their evocative power is lost. Authors and other creators of popular culture must choose the folkloric elements that are best suited to their audiences and their ends.

While intertextual readings help to tease out the strategies employed by creators of popular culture, they do so indirectly. Clearly an author includes intertextual elements deliberately, but the specific motivations behind such inclusions can be gleaned only by an analysis of the work as a whole, its reception by its audience, and other factors external to the folkloric material itself. A consideration of folkloresque portrayal offers a more direct view of an author's understanding of folklore and strategies for capitalizing on it. Though in Dundes's use, the term metafolklore refers to oral critiques of folklore, we argue that popular works that mimic traditional forms may also be read as commentary on the material they are patterned after. Fictional constructions of folk literature, the real focus of the present study, function as intertexts that seek less to replicate the content of familiar tales than to mimic their forms.

The conscious construction of new material based on folkloric forms is significant because it reveals assumptions about the nature of specific folkloric material: its functions, origins, and relevance to contemporary life. Implicated here are both the author's own assumptions and those of his or her audience, anticipated by the author as he or she undertakes the process of world-building. When an author offers overt commentary on this material, the strategies that guide its inclusion become all the more apparent. In *The Postmodern Fairytale*, Kevin Paul Smith labels the process by which an author constructs a new tale using recognizable generic markers as "fabulation" (Smith 2007, 42); commentary on the genre within a fictional work, he suggests, constitutes a "metafictional" use of folklore (45). *The Tales of Beedle the Bard* exemplifies both the fabulation of new tales and metafictional commentary on them. Like Rowling's intertextual references to folklore, this reflects a highly self-conscious use of folkloric narrative. However, her use of fairy tales in *Beedle* goes beyond intertextual uses by offering a direct explanation of the attitudes that have informed a particular work. *Beedle*, with its "scholarly" commentary, is particularly useful to a discussion of metafolklore.

Many formal comparisons can be made between the tales in *Beedle* and European fairy tales. Most of the tales exhibit trebling (Propp 1968, 74). In "The Fountain of Fair Fortune," for instance, three witches and a Muggle (human) knight embark on a quest to find a wish-granting fountain and must overcome three trials. In "The Tale of the Three Brothers," three wizards try to thwart Death using three magical items, and only one, the youngest, succeeds. "The Wizard and the Hopping Pot" relates the consequence of violating an interdiction (Propp 1968, 26–27): when a young wizard refuses to use his magic for the good of his nonmagical neighbors, he is punished by an enchanted cauldron that comes to life and constantly reminds him of the ailments of those he has refused to aid. In an inversion of "Beauty and the Beast," the main character of "The Warlock's Hairy Heart," desiring immortality, removes his own heart and keeps it hidden away. Love, rather than breaking his curse, reveals the evil that has destroyed his humanity.

Jeana Jorgensen calls tales like those in *Beedle* "fairy-tale pastiches" (Jorgensen 2007, 218) and emphasizes their ability to convey new messages through familiar forms (224). Authors and other creators of popular culture choose these forms for specific reasons. As Merja Makinen says, "Fictionalized representations of fairy tales say as much about the culture within which they are written as about the fairy tale per se" (Makinen 2008, 155). Thus, Rowling's pastiche of the fairy tales in *Beedle* serves as a telling mirror for the author's attitudes about the genre's defining qualities.

Discerning Rowling's ideas about folklore and its functions in society necessitates not just an analysis of the text of *Beedle* but an examination of the relationship between the tales in *Beedle* and the plot of the *Harry Potter* novels. In *Deathly Hallows*, Hermione explicitly calls "The Tale of the Three Brothers" "just a morality tale," and Ron identifies Beedle's tales as part of a larger body of wizarding folklore, including superstitions and proverbs. It is clear that Rowling imagines the wizarding and Muggle (or nonmagical) worlds as parallel cultures with parallel bodies of folklore. As Hermione points out, "Harry and I were raised by Muggles . . . We were taught different superstitions" (Rowling 2007, 414). The tales in *Beedle*, as they first appear in *Deathly Hallows*, represent cultural artifacts that transmit traditional values.

Rowling expresses this attitude about fairy tales in her introduction to *Beedle* and in Dumbledore's commentaries, where she explicitly describes the parallels that she sees between her invented tales and existing European fairy tales. She writes, "Beedle's stories resemble our fairy tales in many respects; for instance, virtue is usually rewarded, and wickedness punished" (Rowling 2008, vii). On the other hand, she suggests that one "notable difference between these fables and their Muggle counterparts is that Beedle's witches are much more active in seeking their fortunes than our fairy-tale heroines" (viii–ix). Here Rowling is identifying the kinds of cultural values she sees expressed in European folklore, and imagining how a different set of values might arise from a different culture, that of the wizarding world. Regardless of the accuracy of Rowling's observations on fairy tales, they seem to reflect larger social perspectives about the nature of traditional narrative.

Rowling's attitudes also typify two opposing perspectives regarding the veracity of folklore. The first views folklore as false, a sentiment that characterizes the attitude of most wizards toward the tales in *Beedle*. For them, *Beedle*'s fairy tales are useful, if somewhat antiquated, didactic tools, but are of little value otherwise, and certainly have no connection to "real life" beyond their pithy moral lessons. As Hermione says of *Beedle*, "I never heard such a lot of nonsense in my life" (Rowling 2007, 426). For Hermione, while the stories in *Beedle* may be entertaining and educational, they are "just" stories, consigned to the realm of fantasy.

The second view, held by other characters in *Harry Potter*, is that folklore contains fragments of literal truth. For these characters, traditional narratives "encode real and important data" (Barber and Barber 2004, 2). This encoded literal truth must then be decoded by an audience removed from the context in which the tale was initially told. This view is explicitly espoused by Xenophilius Lovegood in *Deathly Hallows*: "That is a children's tale, told to amuse rather than to instruct. Those of us who understand these matters, however, recognize that the ancient story refers to three objects, or Hallows, which, if united, will make the possessor master of Death" (Rowling 2007, 409).

Of course, as *Potter* fans know, it is Lovegood's reading of *Beedle* that turns out to be accurate. It is eventually revealed that the last story in *Beedle*, "The Tale of the Three Brothers," does actually contain literal truth. In this tale, three brothers each receive a magical item from Death: an unbeatable magic wand, a stone capable of resurrecting the dead, and an invisibility cloak. Over the course of *Deathly Hallows*, the heroes learn that the three brothers were not only real people but Harry's ancestors. The boons they received from Death are real objects, the titular Deathly Hallows. The verifiable existence of these supposedly imaginary objects proves central to the plot of the novel. In order to defeat Voldemort, Harry must accept the possibility that fairy tales contain hidden ancient knowledge.

The picture of folklore that develops from Rowling's work is one that is strikingly familiar but also remarkably out of date. As we have seen, it has more in common with folklore scholarship of a hundred years ago than it does with the state of the discipline today (Kirshenblatt-Gimblett 1998, 296; Tosenberger 2010, 2.4–2.7; see also Tolbert's chapter 5 in this volume). Rowling's assessments of folklore might appear superficial to the trained folklorist but, as Merja Makinen acknowledges, "Writers are not necessarily folklore scholars or interested in being so" (Makinen 2008, 155). As a writer, Rowling's goal is to tell an engaging story, and she likely sees herself as having little responsibility to scholarly perspectives about the material she borrows from.

What's more, Rowling's assertions about folklore have probably reached a much larger audience than any work of contemporary folklore scholarship. With 450 million copies of the *Harry Potter* novels currently in print, Rowling's ideas are far more visible than academic theories. Put simply, Rowling's works and the popular views they encapsulate are simply more available and more accessible than esoteric scholarship. It seems fair to say that Rowling has represented folklore and folkloristics in a way that is immanently comprehensible to her audience. When critics compare Rowling's work to that of the Brothers Grimm, they enthusiastically validate it by likening it to the "real thing."

In the past, folklorists have been inclined to dismiss popular uses of folkloric material out of hand. Richard Dorson famously rejected "fakelore" as nothing but contemporary artifice masquerading as tradition (see, for example, Dorson 1969). While Rowling makes no claims about the authenticity of her own work, she does assert that her stories exhibit the characteristics of genuine folklore.

In discussing Dorson's concept of fakelore, Alan Dundes argues that these fabrications fulfill a "national psychic need" (Dundes 1985, 13), and we are inclined to argue that Rowling's work is serving a similar purpose for her readers. Nationality is not at stake here, of course; the point is that "authenticity," contrary to what Dorson might suggest, is not necessary for folkloric material in literature to resonate with its audiences, who readily invest such material with meanings based on their shared understandings of how folklore works. Folklorists should be especially interested in the conscious use of folkloric material that authors like Rowling engage in, the express purpose of which is to elicit this type of audience response. As Dundes argues, rather than dismiss it as "impure or bastardized folklore, let us study it as folklorists, using the tools of folkloristics" (15–16).

It is important that we as academics acknowledge that nonscholars engage critically with folklore in ways that may not coincide with our

own theories and methods. Metafolklore and metafictional uses of folkloric material provide direct insight into what people think about folklore.
Regardless of the source of these views, be it commercial advertising or
pulp fiction, they persist, and scholars cannot dismiss them because they
contrast with contemporary disciplinary models. By considering works
like Rowling's, folklorists can endeavor to bridge this divide. However, as
Richard Bauman puts it, "It can't happen if folklorists shelter their work
behind disciplinary walls" (Bauman 1996, 19). Until the discipline can provide a balanced consideration of both scholarly and popular perspectives,
it will continue to struggle to communicate contemporary thinking about
folklore to those outside academia (see Tolbert 2015).

NOTE

Earlier versions of this chapter were presented at the 2009 Indiana University / Ohio
State University Folklore Conference in Bloomington, Indiana, and at the 2009 Annual
Meeting of the American Folklore Society in Boise, Idaho.

REFERENCES

A&E. 2002. *Biography: Harry Potter and Me.* November 13. Transcript of video recording.
    http://www.accio-quote.org/articles/2002/1102-aebiography.htm.
Barber, E., and Paul Barber. 2004. *When They Severed Earth from Sky: How the Human Mind
    Shapes Myth.* Princeton: Princeton University Press.
Bauman, Richard. 1996. "Folklore as Transdisciplinary Dialogue." *Journal of Folklore Research*
    33(1): 15–20.
Bauman, Richard. 2004. *A World of Others' Words: Cross-Cultural Perspectives on Intertextuality.*
    Hoboken, NJ: Blackwell. http://dx.doi.org/10.1002/9780470773895.
Cooper, Ilene. 2009. "The Tales of Beedle the Bard." *Booklist* 105(9–10): 84.
Craig, Amanda. 2008. "Review: The Tales of Beedle the Bard by J K Rowling." *The Times*
    (London). December 4. http://www.thetimes.co.uk/tto/arts/books/article24
    53642.ece.
Denby, Priscilla. 1971. "Folklore in the Mass Media." *Folklore Forum* 4 (5): 113–25.
Dorson, Richard. 1969. "Fakelore." *Zeitschrift Für Volkskunde* 65: 56–64.
Dundes, Alan. 1966. "Metafolklore and Oral Literary Criticism." *Monist* 50(4): 505–16.
    http://dx.doi.org/10.5840/monist196650436.
Dundes, Alan. 1985. "Nationalistic Inferiority Complexes and the Fabrication of Fakelore:
    A Reconsideration of Ossian, the *Kinder- und Hausmärchen,* the *Kalevala,* and Paul
    Bunyan." *Journal of Folklore Research* 22(1): 5–18.
Gioia, Robyn. 2009. "The Tales of Beedle the Bard." *School Library Journal* 55(3): 152–54.
Grobman, Neil R. 1979. "A Schema for the Study of the Sources and Literary Simulations
    of Folkloric Phenomena." *Southern Folklore Quarterly* 43(1–2): 17–37.
Jorgensen, Jeana. 2007. "A Wave of the Magic Wand: Fairy Godmothers in Contemporary
    American Media." *Marvels and Tales* 21(2): 216–27.
Kirshenblatt-Gimblett, Barbara. 1998. "Folklore's Crisis." *Journal of American Folklore*
    111(441): 281–327. http://dx.doi.org/10.2307/541312.

Levine, Lawrence W. 1992. "The Folklore of Industrial Society: Popular Culture and Its Audiences." *American Historical Review* 97(5): 1369–99. http://dx.doi.org/10.2307/2165941.

Makinen, Merja. 2008. "Theorizing Fairy-tale Fiction, Reading Jeanette Winterson." In *Contemporary Fiction and the Fairy Tale*, edited by Stephen Benson, 144–77. Detroit: Wayne State University Press.

Propp, Vladimir. 1968. *Morphology of the Folktale*. 2nd ed. Edited by Louis Wagner. Translated by Laurence Scott. Austin: University of Texas Press.

Rowling, J. K. 2007. *Harry Potter and the Deathly Hallows*. New York: Arthur A. Levine Books.

Rowling, J. K. 2008. *The Tales of Beedle the Bard*. New York: Children's High Level Group in association with Arthur A. Levine Books.

Smith, Kevin Paul. 2007. *The Postmodern Fairytale: Folkloric Intertexts in Contemporary Fiction*. London: Palgrave Macmillan. http://dx.doi.org/10.1057/9780230591707.

Sullivan, C. W. 2001. "Folklore and Fantastic Literature." *Western Folklore* 60(4): 279–96. http://dx.doi.org/10.2307/1500409.

Time. 2013. "Because It's His Birthday: Harry Potter, by the Numbers." July 31. http://entertainment.time.com/2013/07/31/because-its-his-birthday-harry-potter-by-the-numbers/.

Tolbert, Jeffrey A. 2015. "On Folklore's Appeal: A Personal Essay." *New Directions in Folklore* 13(1/2): 93–113.

Tosenberger, Catherine. 2010. "'Kinda Like the Folklore of Its Day': *Supernatural*, Fairy Tales, and Ostension." *Transformative Works and Cultures* 4. http://journal.transformativeworks.org/index.php/twc/article/viewArticle/174.

Wilson, Frances. 2008. "Keeping Us under Her Spell: Harry Potter May Have Finally Hung Up His Wand, but in Her New Collection of Hogwarts Tales J K Rowling Shows She Hasn't Lost the Magic Touch." *Sunday Times*, December 14.

SECTION 3
Parody

Introduction

Jeffrey A. Tolbert

THE FOLKLORESQUE MODE OF PARODY COULD BE VIEWED as a natural out-
growth or subset of both folkloresque integration and portrayal. As we
envision it, folkloresque parody relies not only on the appearance of "folkness" but also on a tacit acknowledgment that both creators and audiences
"get" the folkness thus invoked. This is, of course, a hallmark of all parody.
As David Bennett (1985, 29) has noted,

> The term parody, in contemporary usage, designates a form of literary
> satire distinguishable from other kinds of satire by its imitative mode, its
> internal dependence on the devices and conventions of its satiric target.
> Treating discourse as performance, parody enacts its critique of literature
> from within literature, foregrounding the artifice or factitiousness of its
> model's representation of reality, reversing the formal self-effacement on
> which the parodied discourse depends for its claims to mimesis or truth.
> The principal device parody relies on for this exposure is incongruity.

Bennett, eager to privilege the reader of a literary text as a site of meaning, moves on to discuss how parody necessitates one of two critical models: "Logically speaking, a parodic reading is either intentionalist or volun-
tarist: either it presupposes a complicity between the reader and the author
in their critical apprehension of the way the parodied discourse misfigures
reality, or it is motivated by interests extrinsic to the text for which the
reader is accountable" (Bennett 1985, 30). Bennett's point seems to be that
parody works primarily to undermine taken-for-granted notions of textuality, authority, and the reader's role in ascribing meaning to a text.

Folkloresque parody collapses Bennett's "intentionalist" and "volun-
tarist" readings into a single, albeit a complex, textual process. Successful
folkloresque parody requires both the creative redeployment or wholesale
creation of folkloric images and motifs, and a subtler recognition of the
processes underlying "real" folklore—issues such as tradition and variation, generic structure and form, vernacular language, and so on—which

DOI: 10.7330/9781607324188.s03

are themselves often critiqued through the parody in question. (Conversely, folkloresque parody may be situated more fully on the popular culture side of the equation, creatively recycling forms and structures from popular media and reentering vernacular discourse as a self-contained but highly allusive new entity.) Thus both complicity between the creator of a text and its audience and extrinsic factors that depend wholly on the reader (i.e., a knowledge of contemporary events) are articulated through the parodic form. Simultaneously, folkloresque parody demonstrates the recombinative and demonstrative qualities associated with the other two folkloresque modes.

Jokes and joking are among the most obvious arenas for the deployment of folkloresque parody. As a folklore genre, jokes are of course already inclined toward satire; they likewise depend upon what Elliott Oring has called "appropriate incongruity" and on shared knowledge on the part of their audiences (Oring 1987, 277–78), and thus resonate quite strongly with Bennett's definition of parody. Moreover, as an often topically based genre, jokes particularly highlight the integral and contingent nature of folklore and popular culture; in some cases it is impossible, and ultimately perhaps meaningless, to separate the two or to speak of "origins."

Trevor J. Blank, in the first chapter of this section, discusses the cycle of jokes that arose in response to the recent Penn State sex abuse scandal. These jokes display the satirical qualities typical of the genre, demonstrating Oring's notions of "speakability" versus "unspeakability": "Jokes are forms par excellence that deal with situations of unspeakability, because they may conjoin an unspeakable, and hence incongruous, universe of discourse to a speakable one" (Oring 1987, 282). But they can go beyond the level of simple commentary, providing a window onto the processes whereby individuals creatively repurpose existing joke materials, adapting them to emerging social situations, traumatic events, and distressing news accounts.

Greg Kelley, in the second chapter, examines jokes about jokes: that is, jokes that draw on shared knowledge and expectations about how jokes should be, and then employ that knowledge and those expectations to humorous or critical effect. This is parody in its truest sense, clearly echoing Bennett's claims about the artifice of texts as well as the incongruity that both Bennett and Oring emphasize. In the jokes that Blank and Kelley examine, parody is achieved implicitly, by swapping punch lines and thus tacitly equating significantly different current events. It is also achieved explicitly, through the overt lampooning of celebrities and other public figures. In both cases, the comedic and critical aspects of jokes rely on a shared knowledge not only of the circumstances or events referenced but also on preexisting jokes and joke forms. Kelley's elucidation of "joke metonyms" represents, in fact, an intensely distilled form of folkloresque parody, in which a reference to a joke becomes the joke, and nothing more needs to be said.

Jokes and other humorous genres are only the most obvious form that folkloresque parody may take. Bill Ellis discusses the process through which characters in a popular anime series become aware of their own role in a larger fairy-tale-like narrative; by gaining this awareness of storytelling conventions, the characters are empowered to alter the course of their own story. The new text that the characters generate can be viewed as a parody in the sense that it simultaneously critiques and pays homage to the form out of which it emerges, engendering a more desirable story that discards the negative aspects of existing narrative threads and incorporates new ones more appropriate to the characters' own agendas. Ellis dubs this type of process "fairy-telling," a label that usefully calls our attention to the particular strategies by which certain types of narrative can be constructed and reconstructed, deployed and redeployed, both drawing on and subtly subverting established formal conventions.

Another subtlety of the parodic mode is its capacity to emerge not only in the creation of a text but in its reading. It is entirely possible for a new text to unconsciously mimic known folkloric forms. This appears especially likely in those instances when the creators of a new text attempt to position their product as antithetical to an existing folkloric tradition.[1] In the final chapter of this section, Gregory Schrempp demonstrates how popular science writers, despite debunking traditional depictions of monstrous creatures, actually create a mythological narrative of their own, deploying the same conventions they claim to reject as they attempt to conceptualize undiscovered forms of life.

In a certain sense a culmination of the other modes of folkloresque expression, parody is also the most elusive. It requires the most specialized knowledge, the most critical thinking on the part of its creators and its audiences—without which it ceases to be parody and becomes instead simple imitation. Beyond jokes and joking, it can be located in numerous other areas of popular expression, including the "fairy-tale pastiches" that Jeana Jorgensen (2007, 218) identifies, and such popular media as the "Fractured Fairy Tales" segment of *The Bullwinkle Show* (Ward, Anderson, and Scott 1959–1964). Certainly the most self-aware of folkloresque modes, parody is, perhaps, also the area in which popular and scholarly voices can most fruitfully interact, as both seek to understand the conventions with which the popular and vernacular worlds furnish them.

NOTE

1. One is reminded of Richard Dawkins's (2008, 32) proclamation in *The God Delusion*: "A quasi-mystical response to nature and the universe is common among scientists and rationalists. It has no connections with supernatural belief."

REFERENCES

Bennett, David. 1985. "Parody, Postmodernism, and the Politics of Reading." *Critical Quarterly* 27(4): 27–43. http://dx.doi.org/10.1111/j.1467-8705.1985.tb00814.x.

Dawkins, Richard. 2008. *The God Delusion*. Boston: Mariner Books.

Jorgensen, Jeana. 2007. "A Wave of the Magic Wand: Fairy Godmothers in Contemporary American Media." *Marvels and Tales* 21(2): 216–27.

Oring, Elliott. 1987. "Jokes and the Discourse on Disaster." *Journal of American Folklore* 100(397): 276–86. http://dx.doi.org/10.2307/540324.

Ward, Jay, Alex Anderson, and Bill Scott. 1959–1964. *The Bullwinkle Show*. ABC.

8

Giving the "Big Ten" a Whole New Meaning
Tasteless Humor and the Response to the Penn State Sexual Abuse Scandal

Trevor J. Blank

For the glory of old State,
For her founders strong and great,
For the future that we wait,
Raise the song, raise the song.
Sing our love and loyalty,
Sing our hopes that, bright and free,
Rest, O Mother dear, with thee,
All with thee, all with thee.
When we stood at childhood's gate,
Shapeless in the hands of fate,
Thou didst mold us, dear old State,
Dear old State, dear old State.
May no act of ours bring shame
To one heart that loves thy name,
May our lives but swell thy fame,
Dear old State, dear old State.

Fred Lewis Pattee, "The Penn State Alma Mater" (1901)

Since World War II, the area surrounding State College, Pennsylvania, has been affectionately known as Happy Valley. According to local folklore, the moniker was applied when the Great Depression spared the region from its storied web of economic hardship. At the epicenter of the valley, nestled in the shadow of Mount Nittany, lies the Pennsylvania State University, or simply Penn State, the second-oldest land-grant university in

DOI: 10.7330/9781607324188.c008

the United States, founded in 1855. Indeed, the strength of the university has been attributed to the region's reputation as being seemingly "recession proof." Known for its top-notch academics, campus traditions and, by the mid-twentieth century, athletics, Penn State is a decorated institution of higher education that has amassed a fiercely loyal and diverse base of supporters and alumni.

Few would contest that the Penn State football program in particular, with its high-profile leaders, has been especially successful in making the university (and its corresponding reputation) a household name both regionally and nationally. To be sure, "Penn State" and "football" have seemingly gone hand in hand for many members of the college's surrounding community as for individuals across the country, often overshadowing in public discourse the sterling academic reputation of the university. When I moved to State College in May 2010 to pursue my doctorate, I was struck by what could accurately be called the religious fervor attached to all things related to the Penn State Nittany Lions football team.[1] At the local dog park I met a pooch named Joseph Vincent after famed head coach Joseph "Joe" Vincent Paterno.[2] Instead of idle conversations about the weather, locals chat about the Nittany Lions' win-loss record or lament the inadequacies of the team's quarterback. Navy blue and white, the team's colors, are ubiquitous in town. At Penn State football games, one half of the stadium frequently bellows, "We Are!" while the other half replies in crushing unison, "Penn State!" And yet this back-and-forth interplay of verbiage is also found in abundance outside the confines of the stadium, and beyond the rituals of game day tailgating or casual fandom. Indeed, a subtle verbal cue about one's loyalties toward Penn State can be found in the rhetorical utterance of "We Are" in face-to-face and online contexts, locally and even nationally or internationally, for that matter.[3] Supporting the team through rhetoric and symbolic gesturing is a marker of belonging to both the Penn State community and the region as a whole.

Perhaps none of this should be surprising. Folklorist Danille Christensen Lindquist (2006) has shown how college football and the deep-seated traditions and loyalties symbolically brought to the fore on game days constitute a kind of nationhood that meaningfully enhances the social significance of a particular team in a given locale (see also Bronner 2012). Still, it cannot be understated how special and pervasively positive the Penn State football program has historically been in the areas surrounding the university.

But then, seemingly in an instant, all of the goodwill and plaudits associated with Penn State dramatically changed in November 2011, when the football program's longtime assistant coach, Gerald "Jerry" Sandusky, was arrested on forty counts of child sexual abuse.

This chapter chronicles how the communal identity of Penn State and the surrounding areas was shaken by the revelations of pedophilia and neglect in the months that followed Sandusky's indictment, and how many local residents and students of the university resorted to the sharing of "sick" humor—both online and (selectively) in person—to process their complex emotional responses to the unfolding news. As a resident of State College, Pennsylvania, throughout the spectacle of the Jerry Sandusky investigation and trial, I rely on over a year of ethnographic fieldwork in collecting, organizing, and analyzing the various types of humor to demonstrate how some individuals negotiated their roles within a revered college community while struggling to define a more compassionate—or, conversely, defiant—voice in constructing an identity that could reconcile Penn State pride within a larger moral compass. In this essay, I show how individuals utilize their cultural inventories—cognitive storehouses of information on folk and popular culture—to invoke humorous analogues to test shifting social boundaries and process strenuous emotional events through vernacular discourse in face-to-face and online environments.

As the late Alan Dundes (1966, 509) once remarked: "The meanings and traditional interpretations of folkloristic materials are transmitted from individual to individual and from generation to generation just as is folklore itself." The process of storing and recalling information in the cultural inventory necessitates the simultaneous dissemination of metafolklore, which subsequently informs and contextualizes new information in relation to analogues from existing folk knowledge. In the creation of parodic humor (which constitutes most of the material in the Jerry Sandusky joke cycle), individuals also rely on this metafolklore to appropriately craft the joke's form and content to meet folk expectations; as a result, many of these jokes are self-referential and imitative, often taking shape in response to other jokes. What is more, the content and/or targets that populate this emergent humor frequently incorporate references to the people, products, and specific news events that dominate contemporary mass media and popular culture at that contextual moment in time, and thus also underscore joke tellers and audiences' keen awareness and understanding of the interplay between folk and popular culture in constructing timely and relatable parodic humor. Accordingly, this chapter will also explore how and why the cultural inventory is a concept that is inherently entwined with notions of the folkloresque.

HAPPY VALLEY NO MORE: DETAILS OF
THE CASE AND CONTEXTS

Joe Paterno spent more than sixty years as a member of the Penn State football program, including forty-five years as head coach, from 1966 to 2011. During that time, he received numerous athletic and professional accolades, famously stressed academic success among his athletes, donated substantial sums of money to university educational endeavors, and ultimately achieved the National Collegiate Athletic Association (NCAA) record for most wins by a head coach in major college football (see Bérubé 2012). Paterno was inextricably linked to the football program he led, serving as a symbol of good—he was a role model for young men seeking to improve themselves as athletes and budding intellectuals as well as a pillar of the community, a community that grew to hold football so dear in large part because of Paterno's efforts on and off the football field. In 2001, a bronze statue of Paterno was placed in front of Beaver Stadium, where the Nittany Lions play, to commemorate his achievements as a coach, educator, and humanitarian. In the areas surrounding Penn State, Joe Paterno was, and in many ways remains, a saint. A salty, steadfast competitor and statesman, Joe or Joe Pa, as many simply called him, stood as the positive symbolic embodiment of Penn State. But in fall 2011, that symbol came under attack in the wake of more detailed revelations about longtime assistant coach Jerry Sandusky's rampant sexual abuse of children, which took place for over a decade during Paterno's tenure as head coach.

Jerry Sandusky served on the Penn State football coaching staff for over thirty years. The acclaimed defensive coordinator behind "Linebacker U,"[4] he officially retired in 1999 (though he maintained an office on campus until 2011) after head coach Joe Paterno elected to remain as the team's coach instead of retiring himself and naming Sandusky as his successor.[5] Like Paterno, Sandusky also received professional accolades, including Assistant Coach of the Year in 1987 and 1999, among others (Athlon Sports 2011; see also Flounders 2011). In his time as a prominent figure within the Penn State football program and surrounding community, Sandusky also notably founded a nonprofit foster home for underprivileged youths called the Second Mile, valued at $9 million in 2010 (Ganim 2011a).

When Sandusky was arrested on staggering charges of child sexual abuse after a two-year investigation, his public persona quickly underwent redefinition as the disturbing allegations made their way to the newswire. Chief among the accusations: Sandusky had molested or raped at least ten boys, aged eight to fifteen, over a period of at least fifteen years.[6] Many of Sandusky's victims were troubled children whom he reached through his involvement in the Second Mile charity he founded. Sandusky lavished gifts on many of these boys, taking them on expensive trips and even promising some an eventual place on the Penn State football team.

There had been hints of wrongdoing earlier. In 1998, shortly before his retirement, Sandusky was under investigation for inappropriately touching an eleven-year-old boy while the two showered together on the Penn State campus; no charges were filed, though Sandusky was advised never to shower with the boy again. But perhaps the most damning story in the later indictment came from an account of an incident that took place in 2002: a graduate assistant—later identified as Mike McQueary (quarterbacks coach for the Nittany Lions from 2004 to 2011)—claimed to have witnessed Sandusky anally penetrating a young boy in the showers of a Penn State locker room. McQueary reported the incident to head coach Joe Paterno the next day; Paterno then passed on the information to athletic director Tim Curley who, along with Penn State's vice president for finance and business, Gary Schultz, later met with McQueary to confirm the facts of the report. E-mail records later revealed that Curley and Schultz spoke about the incident with university president Graham Spanier, but the three dismissed the incident as mere horseplay, despite their awareness of the 1998 allegations against Sandusky. The 2002 shower incident was never reported to any police agency or child protective services, in violation of state law. No attempt was made to identify the child in the shower. The only consequence, approved by Spanier, was that Sandusky was instructed to no longer bring children onto campus, although his own campus privileges remained intact.

Curley and Schultz later testified to a grand jury that McQueary's 2002 report did not indicate that anything of a sexual nature had taken place between Sandusky and the boy (see Cosentino 2011).[7] Unsurprisingly, this particular incident became the most frequently deliberated of the case, both locally and nationally, because the alleged actions that immediately followed McQueary's story seemed to unequivocally show that several prominent Penn State administrators were culpable in failing to protect the welfare of Sandusky's victims.[8] Paterno in particular met with great wrath from the national media for not using his own grandiose symbolic role (and its accompanying power) to help further prosecute Sandusky and protect other potential victims.[9]

Soon after the story broke in November 2011, members of the Penn State Board of Trustees fired Paterno, distanced themselves from Tim Curley and Gary Schultz,[10] and prompted the resignation of university president Graham Spanier.[11] In addition, the board appointed former FBI director Louis Freeh to conduct an independent investigation of the crimes committed by Sandusky as well as Penn State administrators' role in covering them up. The 267-page *Freeh Report*, published in July 2012,[12] damningly confirmed and elaborated upon the initial reports of institutional neglect and enablement surrounding the case. Joe Paterno, who had died just two months after his firing (prompting some to cite the scandal as an impetus for his death), was posthumously reprimanded in the *Freeh Report* for his inaction, which further sealed the fate of his legacy. The university removed the statue of Paterno,[13] and the NCAA penalized the Penn State football program with historic fines, disciplinary measures, and scholarship revocations. Moreover, all of the program's wins from 1998 to 2012 (112 games in total) were vacated, which by extension revoked Paterno's record for winningest head coach of all time.[14]

The widely publicized facts of the case, the main actors involved in the drama, and the symbolic dysfunction of Penn State as an institution powerfully resonated in vernacular discourse, both locally and nationally.[15] The pervasiveness of the scandal in media circles and everyday conversation played a major role in how individuals processed the nuances of the entire debacle. In the next section, I document how parodic humor was both a cathartic and a punishing force throughout these processes.

A LITANY OF NITTANY LIONS JOKES: ON THE CULTURAL INVENTORY AND TASTELESS HUMOR

Few things are more difficult to discuss openly than the sexual abuse of a child or the graphic details that constitute such acts of violence, degradation, and perversion. It is for these precise reasons, however, that humor flourishes in the aftermath of such horrific occurrences when they are brought to the attention of mass culture. According to Gershon Legman, the purpose of sharing obscene and grotesque humor is "to absorb and control, even to slough off, by means of jocular presentation and laughter, the great anxiety that both teller and listener feel in connection with certain culturally determined themes" (Legman 2006, 13–14).[16] Moreover, as Alan Dundes observes, folklore "provides a socially sanctioned outlet for the discussion of the forbidden and taboo" (Dundes 1979, 146). Rather than requiring one to confront the emotional weight of the despised acts or to expose oneself to the necessary vulnerability required to process them, humor affords individuals a platform for testing the social boundaries of decorum and the ability to circumvent or challenge hegemonic media forces that repeatedly seek to install a dominant narrative when widely publicized tales of horror and despair come to the fore.[17] Thus, collecting and analyzing such humor is critically important to understanding the folk response to a major disaster or scandal.

The new humor that emerges in vernacular discourse following a major disaster, death, or scandal self-consciously emulates existing joke-telling formulas, performance practices, and strategies (see Blank 2013). Sometimes this involves self-referentially recycling and modifying previous popular joke cycles, using their familiar setups and punch lines but replacing the original targets with new ones whose actions or circumstances—often analogous and symbolically equated with those of their besmirched predecessors—have come under intense scrutiny in contemporary mass media and popular culture, prompting a folk (and folkloresque) response. To be sure, the one-upmanship that goes into the creation and dissemination of the parodic folkloresque in the digital age is predicated on collective knowledge about the structure and expectations of joke-telling forms (and conforming to or violating those expectations when sharing humor). But more important, the content and targets of the parodic folkloresque represent a kind of insider knowledge, one that is informed by recognition of popular culture and news media analogues and the ability to collaboratively infuse materials influenced by ever-changing updates of ongoing media events. To successfully frame the parodic folkloresque following a calamitous event requires joke tellers' up-to-the-minute attentiveness to new developments, which serve as fodder for fresh material and subsequent metacommentary about the humor, its targets, and the still-unfolding contexts that sparked their creation.[18] It is an inherently self-aware process.

When accessed, the cultural inventory follows a folkloresque mode of integration that very much relies on allusion and pastiche to craft, as Michael Dylan Foster articulates in this volume's introduction, "a hodge-podge suturing of bits and pieces of other things to create a coherent new whole." Cultural inventories vividly convey the patterns of media consumption and dissemination of traditional knowledge in contemporary vernacular discourse, often serving as a springboard for symbolic interaction by invoking analogues from folk and popular culture, especially in the form of humor (Blank 2013). Furthermore, cultural inventories comprise images that symbolically encapsulate an idea or event; these images are drawn from individuals' interactions with mass-mediated information and visual data (see Malmsheimer 1986).

In practice, the cultural inventory is strategically invoked to enlighten and at times even rationalize the present through the directed reappropriation of nostalgia, mass media, personal experience, and metafolklore for new expressive and/or processual purposes.[19] As a site of intersection between folklore and popular culture, the cultural inventory blurs the boundaries of each; this frequently results in the amalgamation of motifs and structures, which impacts how folkloric materials are subsequently conceptualized and reappropriated in vernacular expression.[20] Altogether, the cultural inventory represents a bold constellation of shared metafolkloric knowledge pertaining to folk and popular culture that, when activated by interacting individuals and groups, provides both an impetus and source material for metacommentary.

Of course, there are some calculated risks and constraints. By tapping into popular culture to explain something or to tell a joke, individual tellers wager that their audience will also hold some knowledge of the tangential cultural references that they call upon in the course of their interaction. If the audience does not understand the reference from the teller's cultural inventory, the joke will be ineffective. Similarly, as Greg Kelley argues in chapter 9 of this volume, the comic value of a joke often hinges on an audience's awareness of the joke's prototype. One of the first jokes to be found in wide circulation online and in oral transmission following the arrest of Jerry Sandusky was a two-part riddle joke:

> Q: What do you call an old woman who is attracted to young men?
> A: A cougar.
> Q: What do you call an old *man* who is attracted to young men?
> A: A Nittany Lion. [First collected November 7, 2011]

The first part of the joke is the setup, since the joke teller assumes and hopes that the audience is familiar with the slang term *cougar*. This subtly bonds the teller and audience; they share mutual knowledge from their individual cultural inventories and are thus able to progress further into the joke. The second part of the joke plays off the slang for the punch line, but the joke's overarching effectiveness is again reliant on the audience's shared knowledge with the teller, in this case familiarity with the Penn State sex abuse scandal and the Penn State team mascot, to achieve maximum impact.

The joke's setup is certainly metafolkloric in that it assumes and projects the audience's existing knowledge of other jokes and narrative genres. Metafolklore may sometimes "comment on the formal features [of a joke] other than the content of folklore," but in doing so it draws attention to "the distinct characteristic reduplicative opening formula of jokes" in a given cycle (Dundes 1966, 510). In this case, the very structure of the joke setup immediately connects the material with a popular existing narrative tradition, the riddle joke, and establishes the text as parody. Here, the setup draws from folk knowledge about riddle joke traditions to frame the joke's style and composition in a recognizable package. The culminating humorous text is a metacommentary on competing joke texts in circulation and the underlying traditions that sustain them.[21]

By plugging shared knowledge about the Penn State sex scandal into the familiar cadences (form, content, and delivery) of existing humor traditions, tellers and audiences also forge a baseline for judging the merit of a joke's composition and punch line as a reflection of both their own expectations associated with the joke form and the presentation of the joke's target. The metafolkloric establishment of the two-part riddle joke tradition requires the teller to follow up with a leading rhetorical question and, after generating a brief suspenseful pause, deliver the answer/punch line.

In the first few days following the arrest of Jerry Sandusky, I heard this Nittany Lion/Cougar joke orally on at least five separate occasions while walking around the Penn State campus as well as from several of my students in class; I encountered it many more times as the weeks pressed on. The marriage of inescapable news coverage and the folk adaptation of humor traditions resulted in a dazzling array of original joke material that spanned the boundaries of taste while also repurposing the "greatest hits" of previous joke cycles targeting the earlier pedophile scandals surrounding the Catholic Church and pop star Michael Jackson. Joke tellers were certainly aware that they were borrowing from these repertoires; in fact, recycling the material symbolically equated Jerry Sandusky with the controversial and often despised targets that preceded him. In addition, the self-referential humor helped create a platform for critical metacommentary in a new context.

Even so, it is interesting to note how the jokes that initially appeared after Sandusky's arrest reveal shifting targets as media attention moved from the institutional woes of Penn State to the individual acts of Jerry Sandusky to the negligent behaviors of Tim Curley, Gary Schultz, Graham Spanier, and Joe Paterno.[22] While Sandusky remained the unquestionable main target throughout, the shifting tone of the jokes also reveals how intensely tellers were aware of the facts of the case as new information became available throughout the saga's continual national media coverage.

The following jokes are representative examples I collected online in the days immediately following the groundswell of media attention stemming from Sandusky's arrest on November 5, 2011:

Penn State: turning tight ends into WIDE receivers. [Collected November 9, 2011][23]

Penn State: giving the big ten a whole new meaning! [Collected November 10, 2011]

Penn State: the only place [variation: university] where you can major in minors. [Collected November 10, 2011]

It turns out that Penn State is actually [a] Jesuit school for young boys. [Collected November 10, 2011]

Is it worse to be in a shower in Penn State or State Penn? [Collected November 10, 2011]

At Sandusky's arraignment, the judge reportedly asked him, "How does 8–9 years sound?"

He replied, "Sexy." [Collected November 10, 2011][24]

During the Grand Jury investigation, Sandusky reportedly remarked, "I wish I had known that I was going to grow up to be pedophile." When asked "Why?" he responded, "Because I'd have taken pictures of myself naked when I was younger." [Collected November 10, 2011]

You may hate Jerry Sandusky, but at least he drove slowly through school zones. [Collected November 10, 2011]

It has been reported that Jerry Sandusky was often late for work . . .

Which is understandable as he liked to come in a little behind. [Collected November 10, 2011][25]

An investigative reporter discovered that in his younger days, Sandusky was fired from his first job as a lifeguard . . . Turns out the kids have to be dying before you can kiss them. [Collected November 10, 2011]

Most people probably don't know that Jerry Sandusky was also a ventriloquist:

He would put his hand up a boy's bum and tell him not to talk. [Collected November 10, 2011]

On a scale of 1–10, how old is Jerry Sandusky's boyfriend? [Collected November 10, 2011]

Jerry Sandusky walks into an elementary school just as classes are let out
for the day, when a teacher approaches him and asks, "so which child is
yours?"

Sandusky replies: "I don't care, surprise me." [Collected November 10, 2011]

Q: What's the difference between a Bride and a Groom?

A: Jerry Sandusky doesn't Bride school kids. [Collected November 10, 2011]

Q: What's Sandusky's favorite thing about 29 year olds?

A: There's twenty of them. [Collected November 11, 2011]

Under Jerry Sandusky's tenure, the Penn State football program's motto was
"Taking young boys and turning them into men." [Collected November 13,
2011]

The next two jokes, which also surfaced less than a week after Sandusky's
arrest, show explicit invocations of the cultural inventory for humorous
deployment in the form of film and celebrity references:

Sandusky is set to remake two Schwarzenegger films into one . . .

It's going to be called Kindergarten Predator. [Collected November 10,
2011][26]

One of the most sickening things about this whole ordeal is how a lot of
people apparently saw the warning signs, yet did nothing about it . . .

For example, one night Jerry Sandusky & Tim Curley were watching "Pirates
of the Caribbean" together, when Jerry asks, "Would you bone Keira
Knightley?"

Curley replied, "She's got a skinny ass and no tits . . . it'd be like shagging a
school boy." Jerry replies, "Yeah, so would I." [Collected November 10,
2011]

Note the specific naming of Tim Curley, who is mentioned alongside—at the same level as—Jerry Sandusky in the joke's structure. In the
next joke, also an early example found online, there is further implemen-
tation of the parties who did not report the 2002 shower incident and
thus enabled Sandusky to continue to do harm while the officials served
their own interests in protecting the reputation of Penn State and the
legacy of Paterno:

Jerry Sandusky, Tim Curley and Gary Shultz [*sic*] are on a plane with a bunch
of Second Mile kids, when suddenly the plane careens out of control and
is on course to crash . . . Curley yells out, "Here, there are 3 parachutes!"

"What about the kids?!?!" replies Shultz.

Curley angrily replies, "Fuck the kids!!!"

To this, Sandusky calmly asks: "Have we got enough time?" [Collected
November 10, 2011; also collected orally numerous times thereafter][27]

And, of course, Paterno himself was not spared for his seeming inaction when he learned of the 2002 showering incident from Mike McQueary:

Jerry Sandusky was only doing the little boys because he didn't want to worry
about Paterno-ty. [Collected November 10, 2011]

Apparently Joe Pa is ok with helmet to helmet[28] contact as long as it's in the
shower. [Collected November 10, 2011]

Q: Does a tree falling in a forest make a sound?

A: It makes the same sound Joe Paterno does when he finds out his assistant
coach is raping a 10-year-old boy. [Collected November 13, 2011]

Many of these jokes specifically refer to the 2002 incident, which again
underscores joke tellers' keen awareness of the story as they have encountered it in the mass media.[29] A key example is:

Q: What did Jerry Sandusky want for his birthday?

A: A new shower curtain. [Collected November 13, 2011. Without specific knowledge of the 2002 incident witnessed by McQueary, the tastelessness of the
joke is lost. With this knowledge in place, it is a grimace-inducing jolt as the
listener pieces the joke's logic together.]

Together, these joke examples embody what Sylvia Grider identifies as
"media narraforms" in that they represent "a symbiotic relationship between
the media and oral tradition: the media provide the content, and oral tradition provides the situations and format for the performance of these
contemporary, hybrid narratives" (Grider 1981, 126; see also Koven 2003).
Although electronic transmission can now be added to this summation, the
larger point remains intact: folklore and the mass media are not mutually
exclusive; in fact, they can actually be quite interdependent, especially in the
formation of narratives. The parodic jokes about Jerry Sandusky and Penn
State rely on audiences' active knowledge of the scandal's portrayal in the

mass media—recalled from their cultural inventories—in order to garner a positive reception. Of course, these jokes also rely on audiences' metafolkloric expectations for their composition and delivery. A joke teller's mastery of parodic humor also suggests critical awareness of metafolklore. Without a doubt, joke tellers must embrace a multifaceted gambit in navigating through the intricacies of style, form, content, and audience expectations.

Delving further into the swath of Penn State jokes in circulation reaffirms the traditionality of the humor, as evidenced by the liberal rebranding of preexisting joke cycles and formulas from years past. That said, joke tellers were not always safe from audience reprisal when reusing old material—even in online settings. In replying to an online thread dedicated to Sandusky jokes, one commenter wittily remarked on the lack of creativity in recycling previous formulas, posting on November 16, 2011: "Those jokes are old enough to feel safe alone with Jerry Sandusky." On another forum, a commenter quipped: "These Jerry Sandusky jokes are old . . . unlike those boys in the shower" [collected November 10, 2011].[30] These critiques of recycled jokes are metadiscursive commentaries that humorously chide the recycled jokes' lack of originality (see also Kelley's chapter 9 in this volume). They rhetorically judge content originality, continuity, and innovation. At the same time, they are also metafolkloric; the audience's dissatisfaction with the jokes reflects how the material did not live up to narrative expectations. Nevertheless, the critics display comedic aptitude and awareness of both joke forms and the Sandusky saga in their self-referential, sardonic retorts. These kinds of comments also speak to the important moderating role of folk commentary in online settings that is so central to vernacular discourse in digital environments.

The following examples represent jokes that have clear precedents in oral and electronic humor transmissions that predate the Penn State scandal:

Q: How is a Jerry Sandusky like a tortoise?

A: He gets there before the hare. [Collected November 10, 2011][31]

breaking news: Jerry Sandusky has attempted suicide by jumping into the sea . . .

Coastguards found him bobbing up and down on a small buoy! [Collected November 10, 2011]

Q: What's the difference between Jerry Sandusky and a terrorist?

A: Sandusky actually gets his virgins. [Collected November 10, 2011]

Q: When's bedtime at the Sandusky house?

A: When the big hand touches the little hand. [Collected November 10, 2011]

Q: What did the sunbather say to Sandusky?

A: Excuse me, you're in my son.

Q: What time is curfew in the Penn State athletic dorms?

A: When the big hand touches the little hand.

Q: What do Sandusky and JC Penny [*sic*] have in common?

A: They both have young boys' pants half off.

[Variation]: I hear the Sandusky mall in Ohio is running a big sale . . . "Little boys' jeans . . . Half Off."

Q: What do Sandusky and caviar have in common?

A: They both come on little white crackers.

Q: What's the difference between acne and Sandusky?

A: One waits till your [*sic*] 13 to cum on your face.

Q: How did this whole [scandal] leak out anyway?

A: One of the boys farted.[32]

The reuse of previous joke cycles to suit new contexts is a humor tradition that has been well documented by folklorists, especially following significant deaths, disasters, scandals, or shocking news events (Blank 2009, 2013; Bronner 1988, 2009; Davies 1999, 2003; Ellis 2001, 2003; see also Frank 2004; Kuipers 2005; Oring 1987; Smyth 1986). As these examples indicate, cultural inventories are necessarily accessed in the course of harkening back to earlier jokes and joke formulas as they are repurposed for new targets and their corresponding contextual relevancies. By extension, recycled jokes carry value as traditionalized forms of expression that are often intentionally used to emulate previous joke cycles and correlate them with the present. This vernacular invocation of past cultural responses to define and confront present circumstances again calls attention to the intersecting paths of mass media and folklore as a powerful locus for the cultivation of tradition.

As Michael Dylan Foster aptly notes in his introduction to this volume: "The way consumers receive a folkloresque product depends on the particular interpretive community or folk group of which they are a part."

To this end, it is noteworthy that orally transmitted jokes about the Penn State scandal, like their online brethren, did not adhere to a latency period (Ganim 2011b; see also Ellis 2001). But in contrast to the jokes I collected in online settings and their delocalized disseminators, the material I collected in face-to-face settings used greater insider or local knowledge in establishing punch lines. Orally circulating local humor took on a different shape—one that reflected a deeper level of intimacy and emic knowledge of the scandal's complexities and the region as a whole. The jokes born from this self-conscious, self-referential context rarely made their way online, predominantly because their full appreciation would be lost on those who didn't have a true sense of what it is like to be a part of the Penn State community. This is significant in that it distinguishes the regional response from the mass-mediated narrative in popular culture.

For example, the Penn State campus is home to the Berkey Creamery, the largest university creamery in the nation and the maker of beloved and delicious ice cream and dairy products.³³ The creamery is also known for occasionally devising quirky names for its flavors of ice cream, such as "Peachy Paterno," a flavor named after coach Joe Paterno that was introduced sometime after 1989.³⁴ This information is well known to locals and members of the Penn State community. Unsurprisingly, a handful of the jokes that I collected in person incorporate ice cream:

> There's a new flavor at the Penn State ice cream shop,: the Jerry Sandusky: packed fudge topped with ten-year-old nuts! [Collected November 10, 2011]³⁵

> [Variation:] The Penn State creamery discontinued the Jerry Sandusky ice cream flavor. It was banana with whipped cream and a smear of chocolate. [Collected November 20, 2011]

Local knowledge also lands in the form of regional awareness, as with the joke:

> Q: What's Jerry Sandusky's favorite [Penn State] branch campus?
> A: DuBois [pronounced locally as "do boys"] [Collected November 28, 2011]³⁶

There were several other jokes that I collected from various points on and near campus beginning in November 2011. The first example is meta-folkloric in that it uses the riddle joke format and wordplay to frame the contextual relevancy of the widely publicized scandal. However, it is also self-aware, self-referential, and metadiscursive in that it directly points out the ease of creating humor about Jerry Sandusky while actually joking about the process:

Q: What's the difference between Jerry Sandusky and a Jerry Sandusky joke?

A: Jerry Sandusky is hard for kids. A Jerry Sandusky joke isn't hard for any-body. [Collected November 14, 2011]

Most of the other examples use parody to channel existing humor foundations but rely on grotesque or disturbing details to challenge the boundaries of taste in their performance:

Q: What's the difference between Jerry Sandusky at age six and at age sixty?

A: When he was six his hair was brown and his penis was white. [Collected November 16, 2011]

I heard that Jerry Sandusky was always the first one ready to leave the team hotel the morning after road games. He had his shit packed the night before. [Collected November 16, 2011]

Q: What is the least popular Christmas gift this year?

A: Penn State children's pajamas. [Collected November 16, 2011; note the self-referential frame of the joke]

Q: How does Jerry Sandusky make a ten-year-old cry twice?

A: He wipes his bloody dick off on their T-shirt. [Collected November 19, 2011]

A great majority of these jokes were collected at fraternity gatherings on the campus of Penn State University. In face-to-face social settings, joke telling requires a kind of subtle social contract between tellers and their audience. Many of the tellers gathered groups of four to eight peers, usu-ally with one or two female counterparts in tow, and competed for attention in shouting out different jokes in small playful bursts. The tellers cackled loudly as their girlfriends winced and scolded them. The scenes were clearly performative and highly festive.

In addition to text- and narrative-based humor, there was also a consid-erable amount of visual humor in circulation online in the months follow-ing Jerry Sandusky's arrest, including animated GIFs showing a simulation of Sandusky seemingly raping ESPN sport commentator Kirk Herbstreit and numerous memes (in the form of image macros)[37] of Sandusky

Figure 8.1. The end of an era: Paterno's statue meets the same fate as Saddam Hussein's.

pictured with children or in a shower setting, juxtaposed with humorous text. Photoshopped images of Joe Paterno as a Wal-Mart greeter and as the pope (with all of the roles' symbolic baggage in tow) also popularly circulated. In addition, several different Photoshopped images of the Paterno statue being dismantled surfaced that incorporated the backdrop of the April 2003 fall of the Saddam Hussein statue in Firdos Square, Baghdad, Iraq for effectiveness (figure 8.1).[38] Here again, individuals relied upon existing knowledge from historical contexts, popular culture, and actual news events (while borrowing from existing humor traditions) to produce new folkloric creations. Indeed, memes, as they are conceptualized in vernacular discourse, are tied very closely to the cultural inventory, for referential humor loses its punch without proper contextualization, self-aware/self-referential content, and audiences' prior knowledge of existing folkloric forms, often through visual communication.[39]

It is also worth mentioning that the popular Comedy Central cartoon show *South Park* aired an episode, "The Poor Kid" (season 15, episode 14), on November 18, 2011—just over a week after Sandusky's arrest. The episode makes numerous jokes in reference to the Penn State scandal, such as: "Penn State likes to be losing at halftime, because at Penn State they like it when you're a little behind in the locker room" and "On a scale of 1–10, how old should you be to stay away from Penn State?" while also using the incongruities found in more traditional "A man walks into a bar" type jokes, like: "Joe Paterno doesn't walk into a police station" and "Two Penn State administrators walk into a butt." The episode even self-deprecatingly notes how many of the Penn State jokes aired are merely poorly recycled Catholic priest jokes, which was a complaint often lodged in online forums. My point in rehashing these examples is to underscore how this intersection of humor, social commentary, and mass-mediated discourse further embeds into metafolklore and thus appears vividly in subsequent vernacular discourse. *South Park*, with its conspicuous role as a beacon of popular culture and adult humor, served as a vessel for perpetuating folk commentary on the Penn State scandal not only by drawing attention to the facts of the case (and therefore supplementing or introducing information about it into viewers' cultural inventories) but also by creating a humorous baseline for dissecting it. It is no surprise that online dissemination of Penn State jokes (including those from *South Park*) noticeably increased after the episode's airing.

CONCLUSIONS

Historian Fred Inglis rightly observes that celebrity is "one of the adhesives which, at a time when the realms of public politics, civil society, and private domestic life are increasingly fractured and enclosed in separate enclaves, serves to pull those separate entities together and to do its bit towards maintaining social cohesion and common values" (Inglis 2010, 4). In a significant way, jokes about Jerry Sandusky and the enabling individuals who contributed to the Penn State sex scandal underscore this power. Their actions made them celebrities through nonstop coverage in the mass media while their evisceration in folk culture boldly unveiled the symbolic clout and dexterity of everyday people in times of discontent. Humor—distinguishably drawn from folklore and popular culture—served as an agent for reclaiming power from the scandal while acknowledging the emotional toll it left in its wake.

Alan Dundes famously noted that folklore "is always a reflection of the age in which it flourishes" (Dundes 1979, 155). The humor collected in the aftermath of the Jerry Sandusky saga is no exception. Beyond the social justifications for sharing shocking, grotesque, and racy jokes and visual humor about the Penn State sexual scandal, other motivations persist. Even though the material is rather graphic and tasteless on the whole, the humor in circulation is also most certainly a response to the collective attempts by campus administration, media outlets, and even competing peers to assert the authority of their opinions and values about appropriate decorum amid a rapidly changing and emotionally charged situation. The success of this kind of humor depends on shared, self-referential knowledge that is skill-fully deployed in new contexts.

The folkloresque dwells in cultural inventories. In a world where the dissemination of information can be achieved with the click of a button, popular culture has become an increasingly dynamic component of vernacular expression in the wake of death, disaster, and scandal. As I have previously noted, "When a tragedy penetrates national news coverage . . . regional folklore does not remain regional" (Blank 2013, 33). The media's coverage of the Penn State sex scandal played a significant role in perpetuating an environment of social unrest locally while simultaneously bolstering national conversations on institutional hegemony and child abuse. In the process, the scandal's ubiquity in mass media circles and popular culture led to the proliferation of extensive joke repertoires at the same time as it reinforced the narrative conventions associated with humor. Significantly, a great deal of that humor-based folklore advantageously invoked materials from popular culture to maximize its appeal and recognition in the course of its deployment. To make sense of nonsense and to apply or invent humor in response to an ongoing news event, joke purveyors and audiences must rely upon their knowledge of folklore, popular culture, and other forms of creative expression to better frame or process the event and its contexts during the times that are most emotionally stressful. It is here, in the cultural inventory, where the valuable intersection of folklore and popular culture becomes most evident.

The cultural inventory represents the shared body of knowledge that encompasses folk and popular culture; individuals reference the information therein to analogize and contextualize the present through vernacular expression and discourse. It is a vehicle that converts the daily barrage of mass-mediated stimuli into meaningful (and manageable) snippets, available for easy storage and recall. But most essentially, the cultural inventory breeds metafolklore, which fundamentally shapes perceptions, values, and expectations associated with all components of folk and popular culture, and self-referentially influences how they are engaged. In the words of folklorist José Limón (1983, 203): "Implicit in the mastery of metafolklore is an equivalent mastery of its folkloric object." Parodic jokes about the Sandusky saga reflect popular knowledge about the case and function as a metacommentary on the scandal, how it has been reported, and the corpus of humor that has framed the story. More important, these parodic jokes also reveal individuals' awareness and mastery of joke-telling forms and their narrative expectations, a process that also entails making conscious judgments of what does and does not work as critical humor in the course of fitting new information into existing joke formulas.

Acknowledgments

I am indebted to Jeff Tolbert for his thoughtful comments and critiques of earlier drafts of this chapter. The essay has undoubtedly benefited from his keen editorial eye.

NOTES

1. Mind you, I grew up in Maryland as a diehard fan of the Washington Redskins football team; learning the team's victory cheer, "Hail to the Redskins," was part of the elementary school curriculum, and wearing the team's colors, burgundy and gold, was a cherished custom on Sundays (and still is in my household). Yet I can unequivocally attest that even the level of devotion expressed by such rabid Redskins supporters as myself and my fellow fans paled in comparison to the uniform loyalty demonstrated by the residents I encountered while living in Happy Valley.

2. I distinctly recall the dog's owner telling me that "the Paterno is silent" in explaining his dog's distinct name. This interaction took place before the Penn State sex abuse scandal; otherwise, I would have suspected the existence of a self-deprecating joke in such a comment, given the controversy as to whether or not Paterno did enough to protect the abuse victims.

3. During his travels to Hong Kong in October 2013, folklorist Simon Bronner—a Penn State professor—wore a Penn State hat during a campus stroll one day, only to be greeted by a passerby with a proud shout of "We Are!"

4. Linebacker U is a nickname for Penn State that arose in recognition of the fact that the football program has historically developed numerous exceptional linebackers, many of whom played defense under the tutelage of Jerry Sandusky (see Flounders 2011). Despite Sandusky's role in shaping the moniker, the nickname has been proudly retained since the scandal. It would be fair to suggest that the name Linebacker U does not automatically register as something associated with Sandusky for most students at Penn State since it has been around for so long.

5. See Cosentino 2011 for even more expansive and detailed information on Sandusky's life at Penn State as a coach, "philanthropist," and child sexual predator.

6. These were the charges on which Sandusky was convicted, though it has been argued that he abused more than these ten victims (see Perion 2012).

7. This raises the question of what they did say the incident had been about. In any event, as a result of these testimonies, both Tim Curley and Gary Schultz were later accused of perjury.

8. Graham Spanier, Tim Curley, and Gary Schultz were ultimately charged in November 2012 with obstruction of justice and conspiracy. The complete grand jury presentment detailing the charges and case background can be accessed via http://www.scribd.com/doc/111801208/Spanier-Schultz-Curley-Presentment-11-1-12 (November 1, 2012). See Dawson (2013) for a brief summary of the presentment. As of July 2015, all three individuals were still awaiting trial in Dauphin County Court, Harrisburg, Pennsylvania (Garrett 2014; see also http://www.centredaily.com/2015/07/17/4838779_judge-grants-penn-state-administrators.html?rh=1).

9. Although Paterno faced significant criticism in the media, many Penn State students and local residents defiantly stood by their beloved coach. Candlelight vigils and unofficial student rallies were held outside of Paterno's home (which was on a very average street in a

neighborhood within walking distance of campus—the address was well known in the community as the house stood next to a small public park). When rumors began to circulate in 2011 that Paterno's statue was to be removed—long before those rumors came to fruition in July 2012—folks lined up to take pictures with the statue, and many left notes, gifts, and candles in support of Paterno, even after his death in January 2012. Online, a real photo of the Paterno statue being *installed* was misconstrued as photographic evidence that the statue was being lifted away. This photo caused a minor panic among locals, who raced to get one last look at the statue before it was gone. In short, the statue was a particularly contentious site for locals seeking to defend Paterno and Penn State's honor; for many outsiders, the statue was a symbol of the corruption exposed by the scandal. Shortly before the statue came down, a plane flew over Beaver Stadium with a banner bearing the ominous threat: "take the statue down or we will."

10. A fact little known, at least initially, to those unaffiliated with Penn State University was that a brand-new, $11 million childcare center had just opened on campus six weeks before Sandusky's arrest: the Gary Schultz Child Care Center at Hort Woods. The university moved quickly to place a piece of large plywood over the center's name and worked to rechristen it in the months to follow, but this sad happenstance was clearly another huge blow to the institution's credibility.

11. The university also made the controversial decision to fully fund these individuals' legal defense.

12. The entire *Freeh Report* can be downloaded online via http://media.pennlive.com/midstate_impact/other/REPORT_FINAL_071212.pdf.

13. As one might expect, there were (and still are) a considerable number of rumors pertaining to the status and/or location of the Paterno statue. In October 2013, I learned that students shared the belief that the Paterno statue is destined to be reinstated at some point (they occasionally even cite supposed remarks by university officials as evidence), but many contend that the statue's location is unknown even to Penn State officials. Indeed, university president Rodney Erickson stated as much, possibly fueling the folk speculation (Combs 2013; see also Carroll 2013).

14. For a complete overview of the specific sanctions (and their repercussions) imposed on Penn State, see Ganim 2012.

15. Naturally, many local residents were very sensitive about the scandal's reflection on the community and the individuals who comprise it. I can recall walking through the tailgate—a large, public gathering spot located outside of an actual sports stadium in which crowds engage in various forms of fun and revelry in tandem with the ongoing sporting event—of the 2011 Penn State–Nebraska game and witnessing a near brawl between Penn State fans and a few drunken Cornhusker fans who jeered, "We Are . . . rapists!" to the home crowd.

16. Legman goes on to explain that "the rationalizing purpose of the humorous insanity is to excuse or explain *the inexplicable irrationalities of the sane*, which are obviously felt by the folk-tellers to be more serious, somehow, and more disturbing—more necessary to be *laughed off*, in the popular and very exact phrase—than mere insanity" (Legman 2006 [1968], 21; emphasis in original).

17. Elliott Oring makes this abundantly clear in noting that humor "is singularly suited to circumvent modernist inhibitions of sentiment . . . as a form of intellectual play, humor demands an ability to deal with the things and events of this world—even the most emotionally charged things and events—as ideas to be manipulated within the structure of a joke. Consequently, *a level of detachment is a prerequisite for the production and appreciation of humor*" (Oring 2003, 78; emphasis added).

18. A good example of this practice can be observed from pro golfer Tiger Woods's widely publicized sex scandal in November 2009. When reports of Woods's car accident in his own driveway surfaced, the first jokes to circulate played off that particular angle. A few days later, when it was revealed that Woods crashed after being hit and chased with a golf club by his wife—who was apparently enraged by allegations of his rampant adultery—the jokes immediately shifted to incorporate Woods being physically attacked, mentioning his wife by name and, of course, the adultery accusations. For a more in-depth examination of the Woods saga as it relates to the cultural inventory and parodic folkloresque, see Blank 2013, 70–82.

19. For example, an individual entering a strange and unfamiliar locale might nervously exclaim, "We're not in Kansas anymore" to symbolically connect to and identify with the general unease experienced by Dorothy in *The Wizard of Oz* (1939). As if to illustrate my point, the folk-moderated website for Internet slang, Urban Dictionary, even has an entry for "We're Not in Kansas Anymore" (http://tinyurl.com/UDnotinkansas, accessed December 2, 2008), which describes a similar sentiment.

20. For instance, knowledge about films or scenes from a popular television show can equally be accessed and adaptively redeployed as metafolklore in order to heighten expression in a new context. The lyrics of a popular song or poem can be repurposed to impart life lessons, give solace, or take on some other, deeper meaning in a new light. Individual creation seemingly imitates collective folk tradition, effectively drawing from the nostalgia of recipients, mass media, and politics (see Bendix 1988, 9). Conceptually, these practices are also reminiscent of the work of Michel de Certeau (1984) and Henry Jenkins (1992) on "textual poaching," which at minimum has an ancillary connection to notions of the folkloresque.

21. The "antilegend" is another type of humorous narrative that relies on metafolklore to enable parody. These legend stories employ the performative and structural expectations associated with the genre but, surprisingly, end with a humorous, antithetical twist that parodies legend forms and intentionally mocks the audience's gullibility (Vlach 1971). Parodies of the legend genre are metafolkloric in that they play off expected delivery meters to problematize the ritual of belief associated with these kinds of narrative (see Limón 1983). Moreover, the jokes resourcefully use existing knowledge of legend conventions to deceptively package a humorous metacommentary about those very same conventions. See also Dégh and Vázsonyi 1976.

22. See Davies 2011 for a great in-depth discussion of jokes and targets in humor.

23. The play on words making use of "tight end" and "wide receiver" appeared in numerous jokes about the incident. Among the variations I collected in the initial month of Sandusky's arrest: "Sandusky turned tight ends into wide receivers" (collected November 10, 2011); on Penn State football: "We start you at tight end, then make you a wide receiver" (collected November 10, 2011); and, in the riddle joke format, "Q: What was Jerry Sandusky's defensive philosophy at Penn State? A: Get penetration and always cover the tight end" (collected November 13, 2011). Alan Dundes explicitly notes how the "tight end" position inherently carries an erotic nuance in the game of football (Dundes 1978, 82; see also *Time* 1978). Clearly, joke tellers take advantage of this nuance to advance their own displays of verbal prowess.

24. This particular joke remained in oral repertoires for some time after its initial dissemination.

25. Variation, in riddle format: "Q: What does Sandusky like more than winning? A: Coming from behind" (collected via e-mail, November 16, 2011).

26. This is, of course, a fusion of the Schwarzenegger films *Kindergarten Cop* (1990) and *Predator* (1987).

27. One variation of the joke went as follows: "One time Jerry Sandusky was on a plane full of kids from his Second Mile charity. The pilot said the plane was going to crash. Sandusky said 'we have to save the children.' Someone else said 'fuck the children.' Sandusky replied 'do you think we have the time?'" (collected November 20, 2011).

28. For the uninitiated, the head of the penis is sometimes euphemistically referred to as a helmet. I am also reminded of Gershon Legman's provocative assertion that the "penis is almost invariably understood in folklore to be primarily a weapon and not an instrument of pleasure" (Legman 2006, 268). It would appear that joke tellers have taken note.

29. Another example surfaced when individuals learned that Jerry Sandusky had penned an autobiography titled *Touched: The Jerry Sandusky Story*, in 2000. The title's sick irony served as a launching pad for many a joke.

30. These interactions were just a few of the many times I was reminded of the Internet's incredible power to transform interested lay individuals into overnight experts on the minute and complex details of a given saga.

31. Like many of the Sandusky jokes discussed in this list, I encountered this riddle joke online while collecting Michael Jackson death jokes (Blank 2009). I also found numerous traces of this particular joke circulating on the Internet even before Jackson's passing. Most commonly, "pedophile" (or, more predominantly in its British spelling, "paedophile") was used in place of where Jackson and now Sandusky's names are found in the joke's meter. These instances further validate the presence of repetition and variation, which is central to identifying the dissemination patterns of folklore (an occasionally cumbersome task in online settings).

32. Curiously, I recorded a similar joke, told by a fourteen-year-old male, about two homosexual lovers who get into an argument when one of them accidentally farts out semen in their shower after intercourse. See Blank 2010, 67–68.

33. The Berkey Creamery maintains a website that includes nutrition information and product details, including a list of its available flavors at http://creamery.psu.edu (accessed November 10, 2013).

34. The flavor remains on the menu despite the scandal, although the creamery announced in July 2012 that all proceeds from selling the product will go to an organization that works with issues of child sexual abuse (Santoliquito 2013).

35. This is reminiscent of Michael Jackson jokes that also included commercial items, such as the one about McDonald's new burger, the "McMichael" (among numerous name variations): fifty-year-old meat between ten-year-old buns (Blank 2009). As Jackson was a national figure, a national food chain was incorporated. As Sandusky was a regional character (relatively speaking), a regional food icon was employed.

36. I collected (incidentally, also on a Penn State campus) a variation of this joke following the death of Michael Jackson.

37. Image macros are digital picture files typically featuring a figure or analogue from popular culture or an Internet meme that superimpose one or two lines of bold, white-colored text (most commonly using the "Impact" font style) that carry a humorous message.

38. This particular image (and others employing variations on its theme) widely circulated in numerous discussion boards online shortly after the Penn State child abuse scandal broke in November 2011; an archived version of the image can be found at http://www.tonyrocks.com/wp-content/JoeKnows.jpg (last accessed November 23, 2014). It is important to note that a substantial portion of the humor-laced conversations and creative Photoshopping sprees that populated these compact but robust threads has since become difficult for outsiders to access, or no longer exists at all.

39. For more on memes and image macros, see Blank 2012; Börzsei 2013; Brubaker 2008; and Shifman 2007, 2013. For more on Photoshopping humor in times of social distress, see Achter 2008; Blank 2013, 38–56; Frank 2004; Gournelos and Greene 2011; and Kuipers 2005.

REFERENCES

Achter, Paul. 2008. "Comedy in Unfunny Times: News Parody and Carnival After 9/11." *Critical Studies in Media Communication* 25(3): 274–303. http://dx.doi.org/10.1080/15295030802192038.

Athlon Sports. (Original work published 1987) 2011. "Jerry Sandusky: From Rising Star to Most-Hated Man in America." *Athlon Sports*, November 10. http://athlonsports.com/college-football/jerry-sandusky-rising-star-most-hated-man-america.

Bendix, Regina. 1988. "Folklorism: The Challenge of a Concept." *International Folklore Review* 6:5–15.

Bérubé, Michael. 2012. "Why I Resigned the Paterno Chair." *Chronicle Review*, October 15. http://chronicle.com/article/Why-I-Resigned-the-Paterno/134944/.

Blank, Trevor J. 2009. "Moonwalking in the Digital Graveyard: Diversions in Oral and Electronic Humor Regarding the Death of Michael Jackson." *Midwestern Folklore* 35(2): 71–90.

Blank, Trevor J. 2010. "Cheeky Behavior: The Meaning and Function of 'Fartlore' in Childhood and Adolescence." *Children's Folklore Review* 32:61–85.

Blank, Trevor J., ed. 2012. *Folk Culture in the Digital Age: The Emergent Dynamics of Human Interaction.* Logan: Utah State University Press.

Blank, Trevor J. 2013. *The Last Laugh: Folk Humor, Celebrity Culture, and Mass-Mediated Disasters in the Digital Age.* Folklore Studies in a Multicultural World Series. Madison: University of Wisconsin Press.

Börzsei, Linda. 2013. "Makes a Meme Instead: A Concise History of Internet Memes." *New Media Magazine* 7. http://works.bepress.com/linda_borzsei/2/.

Bronner, Simon J. 1988. "Political Suicide: The Budd Dwyer Joke Cycle and the Humor of Disaster." *Midwestern Folklore* 14:81–90.

Bronner, Simon J. 2009. "Digitizing and Virtualizing Folklore." In *Folklore and the Internet: Vernacular Expression in a Digital World*, edited by Trevor J. Blank, 21–66. Logan: Utah State University Press.

Bronner, Simon J. 2012. *Campus Traditions: Folklore from the Old-time College to the Mega-University.* Jackson: University Press of Mississippi. http://dx.doi.org/10.14325/mississippi/9781617036163.001.0001.

Brubaker, Jed R. 2008. "wants moar: Visual Media's Use of Text in LOLcats and Silent Film." *Gnovis Journal* 8(2): 117–24. http://www.gnovisjournal.org/files/wants-moar.pdf.

Carroll, Matt. 2013. "Location of Paterno Statue Remains a Mystery." *CentreDaily.com*, January 22. http://www.centredaily.com/welcome_page?shf=/2013/01/22/3473198_location-of-joe-paterno-statue.html.

Combs, Cody. 2013. "Searching for Paterno's Statue." *WeAreCentralPA.com*, November 7. http://www.wearecentralpa.com/news/searching-for-paternos-statue.

Cosentino, Dom. 2011. "A Guide to the Penn State Sex Scandal." *Gawker*, November 6. http://deadspin.com/5856777/a-guide-to-the-sexual-child-abuse-charges-against-jerry-sandusky-and-to-penn-states-alleged-willful-ignorance.

Davies, Christie. 1999. "Jokes on the Death of Diana." In *The Mourning for Diana*, edited by Tony Walter, 253–68. Oxford: Berg.

Davies, Christie. 2003. "Jokes That Follow Mass-Mediated Disasters in a Global Electronic Age." In *Of Corpse: Death and Humor in Folklore and Popular Culture*, edited by Peter Narváez, 15–34. Logan: Utah State University Press.

Davies, Christie. 2011. *Jokes and Targets*. Bloomington: Indiana University Press.

Dawson, Mike. 2013. "Former Penn State Officials Spanier, Curley, Schultz Face Preliminary Hearing Monday." *Centre Daily Times*, July 28.

de Certeau, Michel. 1984. *The Practice of Everyday Life*. Translated by Steven Rendall. Berkeley: University of California Press.

Dégh, Linda, and Andrew Vázsonyi. 1976. "Legend and Belief." In *Folklore Genres*, edited by Dan Ben-Amos, 93–123. Austin: University of Texas Press.

Dundes, Alan. 1966. "Metafolklore and Oral Literary Criticism." *Monist* 50(4): 505–16. http://dx.doi.org/10.5840/monist196650436.

Dundes, Alan. 1978. "Into the Endzone for a Touchdown: A Psychoanalytic Consideration of American Football." *Western Folklore* 37(2): 75–88. http://dx.doi.org/10.2307/1499315.

Dundes, Alan. 1979. "The Dead Baby Joke Cycle." *Western Folklore* 38(3): 145–57. http://dx.doi.org/10.2307/1499238.

Ellis, Bill. 2001. "A Model for Collecting and Interpreting World Trade Center Disaster Jokes." *New Directions in Folklore* 5.

Ellis, Bill. 2003. "Making a Big Apple Crumble: The Role of Humor in Constructing a Global Response to Disaster." In *Of Corpse: Death and Humor in Folklore and Popular Culture*, edited by Peter Narváez, 35–82. Logan: Utah State University Press. Earlier version published in *New Directions in Folklore* 6 (2002). http://www.centredaily.com/welcome_page?shf=/2013/07/28/3708022_former-penn-state-officials-spanier.html..

Flounders, Bob. 2011. "Jerry Sandusky Was Penn State's Coordinator for Decades." *Patriot News* (Harrisburg, PA), March 31. http://www.pennlive.com/midstate/index.ssf/2011/03/jerry_sandusky_was_penn_state.html.

Frank, Russell. 2004. "When the Going Gets Tough, the Tough Go Photoshopping: September 11 and the Newslore of Vengeance and Victimization." *New Media & Society* 6(5): 633–58. http://dx.doi.org/10.1177/1461444804047004.

Ganim, Sara. 2011a. "Jerry Sandusky Started the Second Mile to Aid Children: Name Was Inspired by PSU Players and Sermon." *Patriot-News* (Harrisburg, PA), March 31. http://www.pennlive.com/midstate/index.ssf/2011/03/jerry_sandusky_started_the_sec.html.

Ganim, Sara. 2011b. "Sister of Jerry Sandusky Victim Talks about the Pain of Life at Penn State Where Students Are Joking about Being 'Sanduskied.'" *Patriot-News* (Harrisburg, PA), November 9. http://www.pennlive.com/midstate/index.ssf/2011/11/sister_of_sandusky_victim_talk.html.

Ganim, Sara. 2012. "Penn State Sanctions: What They Mean for Fans, Players, Coaches and Your Tax Dollars." *Patriot-News* (Harrisburg, PA), July 23. http://www.pennlive.com/midstate/index.ssf/2012/07/penn_state_sanctions_what_they.html.

Garrett, Michael Martin. 2014. "Three Years Later, Impact of Sandusky Scandal Still Being Felt." *State College News*, November 5. http://www.statecollege.com/news/local-news/three-years-later-impact-of-sandusky-scandal-still-being-felt,1461565/.

Gournelos, Ted, and Vivica Greene, eds. 2011. *A Decade of Dark Humor: How Comedy, Irony, and Satire Shaped Post–9/11 America*. Jackson: University Press of Mississippi. http://dx.doi.org/10.14325/mississippi/9781617030062.001.0001.

Grider, Sylvia. 1981. "The Media Narraform: Symbiosis of Mass Media and Oral Tradition." *Arv* 37:125–31.

Inglis, Fred. 2010. *A Short History of Celebrity*. Princeton: Princeton University Press. http://dx.doi.org/10.1515/9781400834396.

Jenkins, Henry. 1992. *Textual Poachers: Television Fans and Participatory Culture*. New York: Routledge.

Koven, Mikel J. 2003. "Folklore Studies and Popular Film and Television: A Necessary Critical Survey." *Journal of American Folklore* 116(460): 176–95. http://dx.doi.org/10.1353/jaf.2003.0027.

Kuipers, Giselinde. 2005. "'Where Was King Kong When We Needed Him?' Public Discourse, Digital Disaster Jokes, and the Functions of Laughter After 9/11." *Journal of American Culture* 28(1): 70–84. http://dx.doi.org/10.1111/j.1542-734X.2005.00155.x.

Legman, Gershon. (Original work published 1968) 2006. *The Rationale of the Dirty Joke: An Analysis of Sexual Humor.* New York: Simon and Schuster Paperbacks.

Limón, José E. 1983. "Legendry, Metafolklore, and Performance: A Mexican-American Example." *Western Folklore* 42(3): 191–208. http://dx.doi.org/10.2307/1499417.

Lindquist, Danille Christensen. 2006. "'Locating' the Nation: Football Game Day and American Dreams in Central Ohio." *Journal of American Folklore* 119(474): 444–88. http://dx.doi.org/10.1353/jaf.2006.0046.

Malmsheimer, Lonna M. 1986. "Three Mile Island: Fact, Frame, and Fiction." *American Quarterly* 38(1): 35–52. http://dx.doi.org/10.2307/2712592.

Oring, Elliott. 1987. "Jokes and the Discourse on Disaster." *Journal of American Folklore* 100(397): 276–86. http://dx.doi.org/10.2307/540324.

Oring, Elliott. 2003. *Engaging Humor.* Champaign: University of Illinois Press.

Perion, Patrick. 2012. "Child Abuse Expert: How Many More Sandusky Victims Are There?" *CBS Chicago,* June 27. http://chicago.cbslocal.com/2012/06/27/child-abuse-expert-how-many-more-sandusky-victims-are-there/.

Santoliquito, Gabriella. 2013. "Creamery Donates Peachy Paterno Revenue to Charity." *Daily Collegian,* August 1. http://www.collegian.psu.edu/news/campus/article_27fd7de2-fa46-11e2-a3bb-0019bb30f31a.html.

Shifman, Limor. 2007. "Humor in the Age of Digital Reproduction: Continuity and Change in Internet-Based Comic Texts." *International Journal of Communication* 1:187–209.

Shifman, Limor. 2013. *Memes in Digital Culture.* Cambridge, MA: MIT Press.

Smyth, Willie. 1986. "Challenger Jokes and the Humor of Disaster." *Western Folklore* 45(4): 243–60. http://dx.doi.org/10.2307/1499820.

Time. 1978. "Behavior: Football as Erotic Ritual." November 13. http://content.time.com/time/magazine/article/0,9171,946181,00.html.

Vlach, John M. 1971. "One Black Eye and Other Horrors: A Case for the Humorous Anti-Legend." *Indiana Folklore* 4:95–140.

9

"The Joke's on Us"
An Analysis of Metahumor

Greg Kelley

A rabbi walks into a bar with a frog on his shoulder.
The bartender says, "Hey, where did you get that?"
The frog says, "Brooklyn. They got hundreds of 'em."

IN THE WORLD OF JOKES, WHERE THE FANTASTIC and absurd are common, we can readily accept that a rabbi might indeed walk into a bar with a frog on his shoulder. The humor comes from the unexpected development of the frog talking. Here we see the effect of comic incongruity, which depends on unpredictability. The structural essence of incongruity in jokes is a tension between two oppositional scripts. The listener is (mis)guided into following the path of one of the two scripts but suddenly, in the punch line, the other takes its place. As humor theorists Attardo and Raskin observed, a punch line "triggers the switch from the one script to the other by making the hearer backtrack and realize that a different interpretation was possible from the very beginning" (Attardo and Raskin 1991, 308). In the frog joke, there is an "appropriate incongruity" of interrelated domains, to use Oring's (1992, 1–15) terminology: the opening sentence depicts the rabbi as the active agent entering the bar, and we naturally assume that the bartender's "you" is addressing him. The punch line reveals otherwise, and it is the derailment of our assumptions and expectations that elicits the laugh.

In formal terms, this is quite a conventional joke, characterized by a brief narrative opening in a familiar joke setting and a punch line that turns on the comic effect of thwarted expectations. It serves as a point of reference for another joke, comparable in its setting and cast of characters, that accomplishes something quite different in its punch line:

DOI: 10.7330/9781607324188.c009

A priest, a rabbi, and a minister walk into a bar. The bartender looks up and says, "Hey, what is this—some kind of joke?"

It is indeed some kind of joke, but we don't expect that observation to come from an imagined character within the text. As an idiom in everyday parlance, the question "What is this, some kind of joke?" is an expression of incredulity, and the referent has nothing to do with verbal jokes per se, but with actual lived situations. It appears plausibly that way as part of the fictive frame: we might well imagine a real-life bartender saying something similar were a real-life priest, rabbi, and minister to walk together into his bar. But the idiom has a multivalent sense and that's why it works well here. As a comic device the meaning is only denotative, and the bartender's *this* refers to the fiction in which he as a character exists. So he is literally—self-consciously—aware of himself and the others as participants in the action. The notable difference here is the fact that the joke itself comprises the unexpected secondary script upon which the humor hangs.

This kind of reflexivity in jokes is ponderable—certainly compelling in analytical terms—and suggestive of a larger body of metajokes, that is to say—simply, to begin with—jokes about jokes. It is their self-awareness as a communicative form and their circulation across folk and popular culture that locate metajokes in the realm of the folkloresque. Furthermore, since metajokes by definition are "treatments" of other jokes, when promulgated through conduits of commercial media they provide pop cultural commentary on folk ideas, notions of genre, and audience expectation.

I am reminded of a few topical jokes about (relatively) recent events that all received extensive media coverage and prompted much discussion. In the aftermath of the shocking mass suicide at the Jonestown compound in Guyana, I was earnestly asked by a friend why there were so few jokes about it. As I pondered the possible reasons, he answered dryly, "Because the punch lines were too long." Later, in 1997, there was a frenzy of gallows humor following Princess Diana's tragic death in Paris. Commenting on that fact, one colleague asked me rhetorically, "Don't all these Princess Diana jokes just drive you up the wall?" And when the Asian tsunami of 2004 was still a top story across news conduits, another colleague, aware of my interest in humor cycles, advised me to be on the lookout for tsunami jokes because surely they would be coming in waves.

In all of these instances, I recall that the tellers integrated the jokes into the surrounding (nonjoking) conversation, catching me and other listeners off guard. As folk forms, these kinds of jokes may be related to antilegends.[1] The benchmark is that one mode of discourse is disguised as another. What seemed at first to be discussions with friends *about* jokes were in fact jokes themselves, with discernible punch lines and the conventional joking device of puns related to particular details of the respective joke topics. Although they weren't initially perceived as such at the moment of their performance, these generically hybrid jokes have a "meta" quality in that they take on jokes as their subject.

Most of the metajokes that I've collected for this study work differently, however: from their beginnings they are framed as what we might consider typical narrative jokes, but then as they unfold they become notably atypical by their self-awareness. Incongruity is often an operative device in these jokes, but the violated expectation is not a function of some unanticipated twist in the narrative script (as in the frog joke); rather, the surprise comic moment occurs when the joke veers unpredictably to metanarrative by announcing its own status as joke, parsing its own characters, or pointing up the formulaic conventions of humor itself. Although metajoking is fashionable and appears frequently in all manner of contemporary popular media, it has been undertheorized by humor scholars, and I am hoping here to address that lack in some measure.

Comedian Bobcat Goldthwait's stand-up act included a bit in which he would proclaim loudly from the stage, "My wife is so fat," prompting the audience to respond, "How fat is she?" To this he would reply disdainfully, "She's just fat, okay, I can't make a joke about everything!" Of course, the entire exchange, which is clearly designed to elicit laughter, is a managed joke from the outset, but the audience is purposely misguided as the joke skews its anticipated paradigm, or template. In this case, the template had been firmly established by Johnny Carson on *The Tonight Show*. A tradition developed in the show's early years, when it was broadcast from the Rockefeller Center in New York (1962–1972): Carson would comment during his monologue, "It was so [hot/cold/windy]. . ." and members of the audience would customarily call back, "How [hot/cold/windy] was it?"—setting up Carson's riposte to complete the joke. As in, "It's so cold here in New York that the flashers are just describing themselves" (quoted in Kashner 2014). The recurring call-and-response bit became even more regular once the show moved to Burbank, California, in 1972. As a sort of tribute, the model was further reinforced, usually with bawdy undertones, by Gene Rayburn on *The Match Game* series. So, by the time Goldthwait took the stage as a stand-up comedian, this joke formula was well known in American popular culture, and the humor in his routine stemmed from the familiar made strange or unpredictable.

Through that lens, we might view other metajokes appearing in folk culture. Joke templates—that is, standard joke "types" with recurring characters, settings, and circumstances—are sometimes subverted for reflexive comic effect. Initially, we can consider one of the most tenacious joke templates, the chicken crossing the road. The form is so familiar that the riddling question "Why did the chicken cross the road?" began to elicit variable responses besides the original "To get to the other side" (e.g., "To get away from Colonel Sanders" or "To show the possum [or armadillo] that it could be done"). Notably, many of these alternate versions could stand alone and make comic sense to someone with no prior knowledge of the existing template. Other variations are more squarely metadiscursive because they trade on the audience's recognition of the form, like this one collected from an eleven-year-old boy in 2001: "Why did the dinosaur cross the road? Because chickens hadn't been invented yet." This joke registers only if the audience is familiar with the template, for the dinosaur anachronistically replacing the chicken—a sort of prehistoric ur-form—is the key to the humor. Or, similarly, this one, which puns on a double meaning: "Why did the turkey cross the road? Because he wasn't chicken." One variation has an essentialist appeal: "Why did the chicken cross the road? To have his motives questioned for years to come." In a single stroke, this metajoke abstracts the entire enterprise of the chicken-crossing-the-road template at the same time that it structurally embodies the form it is ostensibly describing. Here, as with the dinosaur and turkey jokes, the comic value depends on an awareness of the prototype. These all might be considered joke parodies, intertextually resonating with a well-worn joking form. In a sense, every parody is metacommentary on another known text. That is not to say that all joke cycles—clusters of jokes around particular trending topics—operate necessarily as metajokes. However fashionable or tenacious they may be, popular joke cycles (or any jokes, for that matter) are metadiscursive only when they: (1) parody a known joking *form* (as with parodic joke templates), (2) take on jokes as their subject (metahumor), (3) are self-referential, or (4) are shorthand allusions to jokes (that is, joke metonyms).

TWISTED TEMPLATES

Some metajokes function on a two-part mechanism. The first is narrative orientation, which introduces the characters and the setting. At this point, the metajoke looks very much like other conventional narrative jokes. But then instead of proceeding into its next typical narrative stage—what Labov and Waletsky (1967) call the complicating action—the metajoke retreats essentially into typological summary. For instance: "Three blokes go into a pub. One of them is a little bit stupid, and the whole scene unfolds with a tedious inevitability" (Bailey 2004). This gibe comes from British comedian Bill Bailey, who has established himself as something of a specialist in metajoking. A recent interview in the *Guardian* introduced Bailey as one who "hates jokes—always has done. When somebody tells him one, he says, he feels as if he's being mugged—the buildup, the promise that he'll find this one funny, the forced reaction." His career effectively launched in 1994 when he received a call to fill in for another comedian who had canceled at the Joker Comedy Club in Essex. Recalling the fateful gig, Bailey says,

> The Joker is quite raucous: they like their comedy and they let you know one way or the other. Then some bloke said, "Oi, mate, tell us a joke!" I thought, "Oh my God, I can't think of any jokes at all." So I went, "OK, three blokes went into a pub," and straight away there was attention because this was something the audience could respond to . . . I'm thinking, "I'm so in the shit here." So I said, "I say three—it was probably more like four or five," and that got a couple of laughs. Then I said, "Well, I say five—it was 10. OK, 10 blokes go in a pub," and I say, "OK, there were quite a few more than that—20–30 blokes," and then it was 100, 200, a village, a small town, an area of Holland, northern Europe, and it went on and on, extrapolating this thing from three to most sentient blokes. "OK, the entire male population of the world goes into a pub and the first bloke goes up to the bar, and says, I'll get these." And I said, "What an idiot!" And it got a huge laugh, and I thought: that just came out of nowhere. (Hattenstone 2013)

Bailey stylized the joke (which voiced his long-held aversion to traditional one-liners) and made it a regular part of his act, later incorporating it into his 1995 comedy tour Cosmic Jam. An absurdly exaggerated extension of a conventional joke template, it opened the door for a particular brand of humor that would become his signature, what he regards as the "nonjoke." As a comedian who travels on international tours, sells out stadium venues, and whose jokes appear all over the Internet (often without attribution), Bailey has been instrumental in propagating and publicizing metajokes of this form. In the first episode of his BBC stand-up/sketch comedy series *Is It Bill Bailey?* he told this condensed joke: "Three blokes go into a pub. Something happens. The outcome was hilarious!"[2] It compares to a similarly abridged joke from folk tradition that supplies an even more abbreviated summary: "A priest, a rabbi, and a minister get into a rowboat. Hilarity ensues." Bailey's manipulation of these familiar joke templates exemplifies a common marker of the folkloresque—pop culture's frequent co-optation of folkloric form (as opposed to particular content).

Sometimes the generic summary creeps even into the joke's narrative orientation, like this: "Three people of different nationalities walk into a bar. Two of them say something smart, and the third one makes a mockery of his fellow countrymen by acting stupid."[3] Jokes of this sort lampoon the prescribed expectations of common joke templates—and if they strike us as funny, we are essentially laughing at our own joking conventions. One example is a classic riddle-joke template rendered almost clinically as a typological digest: "How many members of a certain demographic group does it take to screw in a light bulb? A finite number—one to screw in the light bulb and the remainder to act in a manner stereotypical of said group."[4] This is metadiscursive caricature, really—the joke template becomes the joke itself. Folklorists might regard this as an instance of type becoming variant.

These typological parodies make comic sense only when they are derived from well-trafficked forms. Not surprisingly, they appear often in the shtick of late-night television, which relies heavily on established comedic conventions and always chases the next cleverly winking reference for a knowing audience. Megan Kelly of *Fox News* invited a media firestorm in mid-December 2013 when she made the emphatic claim that Santa Claus is white, sparking vociferous commentary across cable media and the blogosphere, and dominating the news cycle for a full forty-eight hours. As a playful response, CNN's Don Lemon hosted a discussion panel of four different multicultural Santas (a white Santa, black Santa, Latino Santa, and Filipino Santa)—prompting Stephen Colbert to weigh in: "One white, one black, one Latino, and one Filipino Santa? That reminds me of a great joke I can only tell to a white Santa" (*The Colbert Report*, 2013). Colbert's send-up manipulates the template of a familiar type of multiethnic slur; the humor relies solely on audience awareness of the type, but it is only an *allusion* to a (nonexistent) joke that never actually gets told. Still, his jocular remark elicits the largest laugh of the segment.

Other commonly parodied types include the lightbulb joke, the bar joke—and the limerick. Gershon Legman's *The Limerick*, which remains the most comprehensive study of the subject, credits the genre as being "the only fixed poetic form original to the English language" and boldly claims that the limerick is "the *only* kind of newly-composed poetry in English, or song, which has the slightest chance whatever of survival" (Legman 1969, lxxii). Legman's (in)famous bluster notwithstanding, we can agree that the limerick, with its strict rules of rhyme and metrics, is perhaps the most formularized mode of folk poetry, and as such it lends itself to the same kind of metajoking typology we've already seen:

There once was an X from place B,
That satisfied predicate P,
He or she did thing A,
In an adjective way,
Resulting in circumstance C.[5]

Showing and telling simultaneously, this limerick generically typifies the form it describes. Similarly, the topic of faulty scansion is expressed in a separate metrically "de-formed" limerick:

There was a young man of Japan
Whose limericks never would scan.
When someone asked why,
He replied with a sigh,
"It's because I always try to get as many words
Into the last line as I possibly can." (Attardo 2014)

In addition to reflexively toying with their own typological form like these limericks, metajokes may at the same time interrogate the boundaries of what is considered to be fair game topically, as Bailey demonstrates: "Three blind mice walk into a bar, but they are unaware of their surroundings, so to derive humor from them would be exploitative" (Bailey 2004). Perhaps this satirizes hypersensitivity around handicapped jokes—or political correctness in general. In any case, structurally this is like Goldthwait's joke: it begins with a familiar trope that creates certain performative expectations, and the humor comes when those expectations are denied; what we get instead is the postured claim that, in the interest of propriety, the joke cannot be completed. The politics of humor is more aggressive in the following joke: "How many feminists does it take to screw in a lightbulb? That's not funny!" The abrupt reply is a non sequitur—certainly not a viable answer to the posed question. It is, instead, the imported voice of censure. So, on one level, the joke impugns the very topic it raises—and on another level it is patently male chauvinistic, reinforcing a stereotype of militant feminists incapable of laughing at themselves.

Sometimes the stereotype is a function of place. For instance, New Yorkers, fairly or not, are often typecast as impatient and belligerent—a perception institutionalized by the fact that *Travel +Leisure* magazine routinely ranks New York near the top of its annual "Rudest Cities in America" list. Of course, folklore has long reified that negative opinion: "How many New

Yorkers does it take to screw in a lightbulb? None of your fuckin' business!" (which seems to be a variation on the classic tourist's wisecrack to a New Yorker: "Can you tell me what time it is or should I just go fuck myself?"). Other lightbulb jokes target groups because of their national identity, as with the common stereotype of Germans being authoritarian and militaristic, behavioral markers that read as equivalents of Nazism: "How many Germans does it take to change a light bulb? Ve are asking ze qvestions here!" (Davies 2011, 217).[6] Analysts, too, can find themselves in the dark, leaving us to ask, "How many Freudians does it take to change a lightbulb?" The answer is "Two. One to hold the lightbulb and one to hold the penis—I mean mother—I mean ladder." The verbal gaffes here seem at first disintegrative to the joke, but they fit thematically given the common caricature of doctrinaire Freudians, who are thought to link every morphemic misstep to some deeper phallic or maternal fixation. Like most lightbulb jokes, these all tease out the stereotypes of selected target groups. But they do so in nuanced ways. The highlighted stereotypes are not described or demonstrated in some action of the bulb changer (that would be typical); rather, the stereotypes infiltrate the verbal texture of the jokes themselves in the form of humorless censure or ungainly Freudian slips.

So hackneyed is the lightbulb joke template that parodies of it need not even mention changing a lightbulb, so long as the riddling construction "How many *x* does it take to *y*?" remains intact (where *x* stands for some targeted social group and *y* an identified task for members of that group to perform); that alone is sufficient to conjure up the conventional form. For example, "How many geeks does it take to ruin a joke? You mean nerd, not geek. And not joke, but riddle. Proceed." This joke, like the others, introduces an ancillary voice whose proscription against the posed question demonstrably answers the question. Thus, metajokes achieve a particular kind of comic traction by the ways in which they foster, and then promptly dislocate, our expectations about familiar, and somewhat predictable, joke structures. The violated expectation is largely a contrivance of destabilizing the anticipated generic "architecture" of the template.

SELF-REFERENTIAL JOKES

Self-reference is not new to human expression. *Hamlet* gives us a play within a play, one Escher hand draws another, Groucho is unwilling to join a club that would have him as a member, *Seinfeld* characters promote a sitcom called *Jerry*—and so on. There are countless examples. With the emergence of reflexivity in the social sciences, scholars became especially attuned to cultural performances and ethnographies that "[show] ourselves to ourselves" (Myerhoff 2007, 32). In that climate metajokes have particular resonance. Like Escher's circuit of drawing hands, these jokes show us what jokes do. The reflexivity is especially exaggerated when joke characters become self-aware, recognizing themselves as types: "A priest, a rabbi, and a minister are sitting together on a plane. The rabbi looks at the other two and asks, 'Say, did you hear the one about us?'" Cognizant that he inhabits "the one about us," the rabbi heralds another anticipated joke performance, and we might guess where things could go from there. If the rabbi were to relate *this* very joke, which itself frames the beginning of another telling, it conceivably could stand as the inaugural link in a perpetual chain of jokes within jokes, a comic self-referential *mise en abyme*. Other examples carry us further yet into the metadiscursive, with characters who are not only self-aware or self-referential but also self-determining. Like Flann O'Brien's *At Swim, Two Birds*, in which the characters seize control of the novel, these jokes unfold by the prerogative of the characters.

> A newlywed couple, a blind man, a used-car dealer, a proctologist, and a hooker, along with a nun, a man who just received a gorilla brain transplant, two Hassidic Jews, a stuttering hotel clerk, and a chicken are riding in a compact car. Suddenly, they hear a siren and a state trooper motions the vehicle to pull over. "License and registration," says the cop. "You've exceeded the legal character limit in this joke."

The notion that there exists some codified, enforceable set of joke regulations is playfully appropriate, for jokes *do* persistently violate what we might call statutes of expectation—and this one does so in a grandly overstated manner: the outrageous array of characters populating the joke could leave humor aficionados salivating at the possibilities (besides just the comical image of them all stuffed into one small car).

Joke characters may behave unpredictably, and indeed punch lines often rely on that, but we still expect them to inhere within the fictive frame of the joke. When they do not, the anticipated path of the joke deviates into a particular genre of comic metadiscourse. For example, among the ubiquitous traveling salesmen in jokes, who find themselves fortuitously stranded at the houses of farmers with daughters, there are a few who step outside of, and rewrite, the conventional scripts of their own jokes: "A traveling salesman knocks on a farmer's door at night and says, 'Sorry to bother you, but my car has broken down. Can I stay the night?' The farmer replies, 'Sure, but you'll have to share a bed with my son.' The salesman says, 'Your son? Never mind. I must be in the wrong joke.'" Perhaps homophobic, or at least obstinately heteronormative, this salesman effectively ends the joke himself because the circumstances don't fit his own sexual proclivities. Alternately, a variant with the same standardized setup ends this way: "[The farmer says to the salesman,] 'Sure, I'll give you a bed for the night . . . But I gotta tell you that I have no daughter for you to sleep with like you always hear about in those jokes.' After thinking for a minute or two, the salesman says, 'How far to the next house?'" Meaning, effectively, how far to the next traveling salesman joke, where his sexual fantasy with a farmer's daughter might be realized. It's an intriguing thought—fictional characters drifting along in the universe of jokes searching for their most appropriate role, and empowered to recast familiar texts along the way. It is an enactment of postmodernism: authorship itself is deposed.

JOKE METONYMS

As we have seen, some metajokes derive their humor from unexpected turns in narrative stance (from active narration to mediating summary), improbable shifts in voicing, and exaggerated reflexivity. There is another sort of metajoking, however—not jokes about jokes but rather joke metonyms, which are shorthand substitutions, typically just the decontextualized punch lines of larger narrative jokes. These are reminiscent of a truncated form that Bill Ellis (1989, 40) termed a legend metonym, which reduces narrative to the level of simple allusion and, he claims, "recalls the whole story simultaneously present in the minds of the group's members, without interrupting the present topic of conversation to replay it." We might compare, as well, proverb metonyms, which operate similarly. The abbreviated phrases "gift horse," "spilled milk," or "silk purse," for example, would trigger unmistakable recollections of their fuller proverbial forms.

Conversely, joke metonyms maintain a comic potential even when the "host" texts are unknown to the listener. That is to say, extracted punch lines can be inherently funny in their own right. There are websites dedicated to the "punch line only" format, and I remember playing this as a sort of party game when I was a teenager. Someone would recite just the punch line from his or her favorite offensive joke, invariably eliciting laughter from the other participants. Rarely are the punch lines obscene in and of themselves, but in a moment they conjure up flashes of elaborate *potential* plots with prurient details:

> "There's no way that kangaroo is left-handed."
> "Dalai Lama, Dolly Parton—there's a difference?"

"Now wash your hands and make me a pastrami sandwich."

"Hey, lady, how do you think I rang the doorbell?"

"Gee, that's nice music, mister, but I think your monkey's on fire."

Oblique allusions to unknown texts, disembodied punch lines like these remain comically viable because they essentially invite listeners to create retroactively their own accompanying jokes.

The pop culture equivalent is a widely used television and film comedic device known as the "orphaned punch line." The action cuts to a new scene to show a character telling a joke *in medias res*; the audience hears only the isolated joke punch line, detached from any narrative setup, and the reactions of other characters vary from "rip-roaring hilarity, monocle-popping disgust [to] a deathly quiet."[7] The orphaned punch lines are most often extracted from salacious jokes, allowing the filmmakers to insinuate a level of obscenity that would never be permitted overtly. For example, an allusion to a traveling salesman and farmer's daughter joke appears in a Laurel and Hardy film titled, appropriately enough, *Come Clean* (1931). Having asked his friend to distract their wives with a "funny story," Hardy returns to an apartment to find Laurel mid-sentence: ". . . then the farmer came in and he shot the traveling salesman," at which point Hardy's wife says, "How dare you?!" and attempts to slap Laurel across the face (missing, and slapping Hardy instead).[8]

In *Men in Black* a new scene begins with Tommy Lee Jones's character K telling a joke to Will Smith: "But, honey, this one's eating my popcorn!" It's the punch line to the old chestnut of a joke about the man who sneaks a chicken into a movie theater by stuffing the bird down his pants. The same orphaned punch line appears in *The Sting*, delivered in the background by an unnamed burlesque house comedian. Screenwriters sometimes invent the setups/punch lines outright, and when they do, they often introduce exceedingly peculiar narrative details just for fun, leaving the audience to ponder what joke could possibly accommodate such absurdity. That is probably the case with the orphaned punch line that appears in *Some Like It Hot*. Tony Curtis and Jack Lemmon, cross-dressed and traveling with a women's jazz band to hide from the mob, find themselves on a train with their band mates. Early in the trip, the trombonist begins an apparently off-color joke (about a girl tuba player stranded on a desert island with a one-legged jockey), but is stopped short by the band manager, who warns, "Now cut it out, girls, none of that rough talk." The action takes us away from that narration, until a full twenty minutes later in the film when we see the same character in a new scene delivering just the punch line "So the

one-legged jockey says, 'Don't worry about me, baby, I ride sidesaddle!'"
(to uproarious laughter from the other characters). The sitcom *Night Court*
had a running gag with an orphaned punch line plucked from a familiar
joke about a lascivious nun: "Twenty dollars, same as in town!" There were
occasional variations like "So Anna Karenina says, 'Twenty rubles, same as
in St. Petersburg.'"

So popular were orphaned punch lines that they began to spring up in
all types of mainstream entertainment, far afield from just film and TV sit-
coms. David Letterman's recurring top ten list segment on *Late Night* once
included the category "top ten punch lines to Scottish dirty jokes":

10. It took me a fortnight to get out of the thistles.
 9. I didn't know you could also get wool from them!
 8. It's not a bagpipe, but don't stop playing.
 7. What made you think I was talking about golf?
 6. I've heard of comin' through the rye—but this is ridiculous!
 5. Of course she's served millions—she's a McDonald.
 4. Oh, so *you're* Wade Boggs.
 3. Care to shake hands with the Loch Ness monster?
 2. Who's burning argyles?
 1. She's in the distillery making Johnnie Walker Red.

Likely, the entries on the list were all invented, written just for the show
(I have been unable to identify from folk or popular sources the host jokes
for any of these punch lines). However, in an interview with *Empire* magazine, comedian Leslie Nielsen admitted that although he had forgotten the
setup to his favorite joke, he well remembered the punch line (a variation
of number eight from Letterman's list): "It's not a bagpipe, lassie, but keep
blowin'!"[9] Whether or not he truly had forgotten the joke's setup (or if the
joke ever existed in the first place), Nielsen, a master of deadpan delivery,
clearly played the punch line for all its *intrinsic* comedic value.

A 2010 television commercial for Miller Lite beer began with a
young man at a bar telling a joke to his apparent girlfriend, delivering the
(invented) orphaned punch line, "So I get to his house, and he has thirteen monkeys!" Her cued laughter is presumably an indication of their
amicable relationship. Dave Barry's *Claw Your Way to the Top*, a send-up of
job market and business success books, advises job candidates to begin
letters of application this way: "So then the priest says to the rabbi, 'But
how did you get the snake to wear lipstick?'" The suggestion is that any
employer receiving such a letter would be unable to resist calling the appli-
cant in for an interview just to find out how the joke begins (Barry 1986,
18). One *Far Side* cartoon by Gary Larson shows an anthropomorphized

fork standing on a stage behind a microphone delivering stand-up comedy to an audience of other forks. The caption reads, ". . . And so the bartender says, 'Hey! That's not a soup spoon!' But seriously, forks . . ."[10] This is just a small sampling from among hundreds of instances of orphaned punch lines across popular media. These joke snippets all figure into the larger creative vision of their auteurs, but they also capture, in abridged fashion, mediated renditions of the folk processes of joke telling. Of course, television and film screenwriters, advertisers, humorists, and cartoonists have all witnessed authentic joke telling in natural contexts; these artistically manipulated detached punch lines metonymically reference those real-life folk performances. And like the adapted joke templates, these direct allusions/subversions to joking patterns make conscious use of the audience's indexical relationship to recognizable folk forms. This captures something of the nature of the folkloresque in a pop cultural context: entertainers are invoking joke format and types but also metadiscursively playing with the sense of authenticity and familiarity that such formats and types project.

These metonyms invite another question: could a joke be reduced further yet, to a unit that is even more distilled than just its punch line? It might not surprise us that this question has been addressed in another metajoke:

> A new prisoner is at his first lunch. One of the other prisoners stands up and yells out, "73" and everyone laughs—they're banging trays on the table and laughing their heads off. Another prisoner stands up and yells, "139" and everyone laughs—even harder than before. So the new prisoner asks a guy next to him what's going on. "Oh, that? Well, we've been here so long that we just memorized a big book of jokes. We figure we save time by calling out the numbers of the jokes."
>
> So the new guy decides he'll give it a try. He stands up and calls out, "41." No one laughs—nothing. So he tries it again, louder: "41." Nothing. Then he asks the other prisoner, "What did I do wrong?" And the prisoner says, "Well, some people can tell jokes and some can't."[11]

In other versions, the new prisoner is told that no one laughs because his joke is in poor taste or that his timing is off. Whereas disembodied punch lines give the sense of narrative contexts, if only imagined ones, in this scenario, where the jokes (within the joke) are simplified to catalogue numbers, all performative elements are stripped away. This one may be a particular curiosity to contemporary humor theorists, who are inclined to pore over the social, situational, and textural complexities of joke performance. That a joke could be rendered funny, distasteful, or poorly timed under such circumstances is the implausibility that makes us laugh. Moreover, the joke may resonate especially with folklorists, who could hear it as a commentary on their discipline, or at least on a certain kind of folklorist. After all, folklore is the field that indexed and assigned type numbers to popular tales (e.g., AT 510, AT 300), and designated ballads by their numbered order in the Francis James Child compendium (i.e., Child 12, Child 84). Indeed, there was a moment in the history of folklore study when these index tags were bandied about as if they were narrative texts themselves.

CONCLUSION

Years ago, my brother asked me, "What's wrong with lawyer jokes?" Before I could respond to what I thought was a foray into a theoretical discussion of humor, he shot back: "Lawyers don't think they're funny and no one else knows they're jokes." I laughed. And upon reflection, I think it was this exchange that sparked my initial interest in metajoking. What I didn't know at the time was that my brother's short riddle-form joke was an adaptation—distilled and made palatable for rapid transmission in oral folk culture—of a humorous anecdote told by former U.S. Supreme Court chief justice William Rehnquist. Speaking to an audience of lawyers and nonlawyers at the dedication of a new building at the University of Virginia Law School in 1997, the chief justice explained: "In the past, when I've talked to audiences like this, I've often started off with a lawyer joke, a complete caricature of a lawyer who's been nasty, greedy and unethical. But I've stopped that practice. I gradually realized that the lawyers in the audience didn't think the jokes were funny and the non-lawyers didn't know they were jokes" (quoted in Galanter 2005, 3). Of course, Rehnquist's widely publicized commentary on the nature of lawyer jokes, since the 1980s one of the most active joke cycles in America (Galanter 2005; Davies 2011, 184–212), is itself a lawyer joke—a metajoke—and it points up precisely what we have seen in other examples: the dialogic relationship between one expressive form of folklore, mass culture, and popular media.

E. B. White once quipped that "humor can be dissected, as a frog can, but the thing dies in the process and the innards are discouraging to any but the pure scientific mind" (White and White 1941, xvii). I hope that I haven't killed the metaphorical humor frog here; but metajokes, in a sense, dissect themselves. If we accept, as Greg Urban (2001, 4) posits, that metaculture necessarily engenders interpretation of and promotes the culture upon which it is based, then the study of metajokes will be seen as a useful exercise in interrogating the generic boundaries of jokes. And since commercial media and popular culture are operative conduits in the widespread propagation of metajokes, we are observing a process of the folkloresque—the folk and the popular feeding, and feeding on, each other.

Acknowledgments

I am grateful to Elliott Oring, Moira Marsh, and Charles Clay Doyle, who all provided helpful comments as I prepared this essay.

NOTES

1. The term *antilegend* was coined by John Vlach in 1971 to designate presumed horror stories, usually narrated by children, that reveal themselves in the end to be jokes.

2. Episode 1 (1998), 1:36.

3. Eriksgata2, "anti-joke chicken," n.d., http://www.quickmeme.com/meme/2p4s/ (accessed December 15, 2014).

4. Mr.Tea, *The Escapist*, April 18, 2010, http://www.escapistmagazine.com/forums /read/18.189302-Anti-Joke-time?page=1.

5. "The Limerick," Snowclones Database, March 17, 2008, http://snowclones.org /2008/03/17/the-limerick/.

6. For his full discussion of jokes directed at the stereotype of German militarism, see Davies 1990, 202ff.

7. http://tvtropes.org/pmwiki/pmwiki.php/Main/OrphanedPunchline.

8. The Motion Picture Productions Code of 1930 included "traveling salesmen and farmer's daughter jokes" on its list of "profanity." This scene from *Come Clean* remained uncut, however, as the code was merely advisory and not much heeded until it became enforced censorship law in 1934. See David Hayes, "Laurel & Hardy vs the Censors," http://laurelhardy.dhwritings.com/Censorship.html (accessed December 15, 2014).

9. "Leslie Nielsen," *The Empire*, n.d., http://www.empireonline.com/interviews/inter view.asp?IID=1127 (accessed December 15, 2014).

10. July 1, 1994.

11. Other variants of the joke, with their own subtexts, have monks telling jokes at a monastery, old folks at a convalescent home, or locals at an Irish pub while a curious outsider is visiting for the first time (thanks to Charles Clay Doyle and Tim Tangherlini, respectively, for pointing out these last two).

REFERENCES

Attardo, Salvatore, ed. 2014. "Limericks." In *Encyclopedia of Humor Studies*, March 18. Los Angeles: Sage.

Attardo, Salvatore, and Victor Raskin. 1991. "Script Theory Revis(it)ed: Joke Similarity and Joke Representation Model." *Humor: International Journal of Humor Research* 4(3–4): 293–347.

Bailey, Bill. 2004. *Bill Bailey Live—Part Troll*. DVD, Universal Pictures, UK.

Barry, Dave. 1986. *Claw Your Way to the Top: How to Become the Head of a Major Corporation in Roughly a Week*. Emmaus, PA: Rodale.

The Colbert Report. 2013. Episode 1283. December 12.

Davies, Christie. 1990. *Ethnic Humor around the World.* Bloomington: Indiana University Press.

Davies, Christie. 2011. *Jokes and Targets.* Bloomington: Indiana University Press.

Ellis, Bill. 1989. "When Is a Legend? An Essay in Legend Morphology." In *The Questing Beast: Perspectives in Contemporary Legend IV*, edited by Gillian Bennett and Paul Smith, 31–53. Sheffield: Sheffield Academic Press.

Galanter, Marc. 2005. *Lowering the Bar: Lawyer Jokes and Legal Culture.* Madison: University of Wisconsin Press.

Hattenstone, Simon. 2013. "Bill Bailey: Bill's Excellent Adventure." *Guardian*, April 19. http://www.theguardian.com/culture/2013/apr/19/bill-bailey-interview -qualmpeddler.

Kashner, Sam. 2014. "*Theeeeere's* Johnny!" *Vanity Fair*, January 27. http://www.vanityfair .com/hollywood/2014/02/johnny-carson-the-tonight-show.

Labov, William, and Joshua Waletsky. 1967. "Narrative Analysis: Oral Versions of Personal Experience." In *Essays on the Visual and Verbal Arts*, edited by June Helm, 12–44. Seattle: University of Washington Press.

Legman, Gershon. (Original work published 1964) 1969. *The Limerick.* New York: Bell.

Myerhoff, Barbara G. 2007. *Stories as Equipment for Living.* Ann Arbor: University of Michigan Press.

Oring, Elliott. 1992. *Jokes and Their Relations.* Lexington: University of Kentucky Press.

Urban, Greg. 2001. *Metaculture: How Culture Moves through the World.* Minneapolis: University of Minnesota Press.

Vlach, John. 1971. "One Black Eye and Other Horrors: A Case for the Humorous Anti-Legend." *Indiana Folklore* 4: 95–140.

White, E. B., and Katharine S. White, eds. 1941. *A Sub-treasury of American Humor.* New York: Coward-McCann.

10

The Fairy-telling Craft of *Princess Tutu*
Metacommentary and the Folkloresque

Bill Ellis

A COMMON FORM OF POPULAR CULTURE TAKES a folktale (i.e., "Snow White") and uses its motifs as a platform for a contemporary adaptation that reveals or imposes new meanings on old plots. Less common are works that call attention to "fairy-telling," the underlying generative structure that produces a narrative that audiences recognize as traditional in form. Such a work is the Japanese anime series *Princess Tutu* (Satō 2002–2003), in which a young girl is given the magical task of protecting a troubled classmate, who is in fact the heroic fairy-tale prince Mytho. In the process, however, she and other characters slowly recognize that they are being used as puppets in the hands of a sinister storyteller, who is monitoring and directing their actions from another dimension. They rebel against their stereotypical roles, but to change their fates they must first become competent fairy-tellers in their own rights.

The series shows how they learn and master the praxis of telling—or rather enacting—an alternative fairy tale that follows the rules of the genre and liberates them from the manipulative storyteller. *Princess Tutu* uses elements from many fairy tales, but it is not a direct adaptation of any existing folk narrative. Thus it represents a folkloresque mode of discourse, using metacommentary as a narrative device. This mode encourages audiences to look past the curtain of motifs and observe the generative grammar that guides the plot's structure.

JAPANESE FAIRY-TALE TRADITIONS

Japan, like most world cultures, has maintained an indigenous tradition of magical folktales that are distinguished from other forms of narrative by a

DOI: 10.7330/9781607324188.c010

characteristic set of formulas and motifs. One clear example is the traditional opening formula, "Mukashi mukashi," literally "Long ago, long ago,"
an exact parallel to the Anglo-American "Once upon a time." The preva-
lence of this formula gives rise to the most common Japanese term for such
stories, *mukashi banashi*, or "long-ago tales" (Eubanks 2008, 514). A closing
formula of some kind is also usually present (Yanagita 2008, 67–68). Many
mukashi banashi are more like legends in Western tradition, as they deal
with the origins of place-names and the activities of distinctively Japanese
supernatural creatures such as *oni* (similar to ogres) and *kappa* (similar to
the Germanic Nix, or water sprite). Still, a rich heritage of household tales
parallels the international *Märchen* tradition by focusing on the adventures
of an ordinary person (male or female) in a magical realm.[1]

Yet Japanese folktales depart from the Western model in a number
of significant ways. One is the greater prominence and independence of
female characters, who are often the protagonists or whose actions determine the fate of the male protagonist. Another is the tendency to separate male and female protagonists at the end, rather than unite them in
the "happy ever after" conclusion familiar in the West. Both traits contrast
with Japan's cultural definition of female social roles; although the "essential equality of the sexes" was guaranteed by the country's new constitution
in 1945, Michiko N. Wilson (2013, 224) notes that patriarchal expectations
continue to govern most marriage bonds. This turns the wife's role into
what feminist critics have termed an "unequal treaty" (*fubyōdō jōyaku*) that
insists on the authority of the male and the limitation of female activities
to a small number of supporting roles. Other commentators have observed
artists' tendency to present women—innocently or satirically—as man-
nequins or dolls, highlighting their status as elaborate automatons whose
individual human nature has been subordinated to their status as socially
manufactured commodities for males.[2]

Noriko Reider (2010) thus argues that Japanese tales' emphasis on
women is explicitly political, a carnivalesque response to a hegemonic culture that otherwise denies most women freedom to express their needs and
desires. She finds that those featuring the *yamauba*, or mountain ogress, most
directly challenged male authority with an indigenous matriarchal sensibility. If the only options open to women within human society forced them
to be subservient to males, Reider argues, then the only way for them to
liberate themselves was to become inhuman. Feminist author Ōba Minako
discerns a similar political perspective in yamauba tales, using allusions to
them in her otherwise naturalistic accounts of Japanese life. Like Reider,
Ōba suggests that women trapped like dolls in unloving relationships could

reconcile themselves to becoming monsters, if only in the privacy of their minds (Wilson 2013).

On the other hand, Jungian psychoanalyst Kawai Hayao argues that the female characters in tales constituted archetypes that manifested in the egos of both genders. "The Japanese mind," he proposed, was essentially feminine in nature,[3] and while Western cultures gave tales a patriarchal emphasis, Japanese narrative tradition gave greater respect to female consciousness (Kawai 1996, 189). This view does not dispute the strong patriarchal nature of Japan's *social* structure but sees tales as having psychological significances that were understood as equally relevant to the life situations of both genders. "Patriarchal consciousness tends to aim at perfection," he concludes. "It cuts off the evil with a sharp sword, while female consciousness tries to accept whatever comes and aims at completeness" (187). Discussing the dreamlike plots of Japanese anime, Susan Napier (2005, 149) agrees that the "magical girls" (*mahō shōjo*) who play a major role in this art form are not just feminist prototypes but appeal strongly to both genders. For females, their location in a liminal realm between childhood and adult society give them amorphous identities capable of exploring both worlds and both gender identities with greater license. For this reason, males, who are themselves often caught in workplace situations as restrictive as patriarchal marriage contracts, participate vicariously in magical girls' abilities to transform their identities and enact "unfettered change and excitement" in society. Thus the adventures of a prepubescent female character who struggles against the mechanistic duties she is assigned by society and learns to use her own powers to determine her own destiny could be seen as politically subversive in the contemporary feminist landscape and also as psychologically liberating by *both* males and females.

One of the most widespread folktale types in Japanese tradition casts the marriage relationship in terms of a beast/human relationship. In Western systems of classification, these include variants of tale-type 400, "The Animal Bride." But one need not see the Japanese tales simply as local adaptations of a tale type. Charlotte Eubanks (2013) suggests that these narratives, particularly as they are seen and used by Japanese feminist writers, are best understood emically as "interspecies sex tales." In one common type, a woman is seduced by an unfamiliar man. Curious about his identity, she spies on him and discovers that he is a snake or some other animal. A complementary type features a female beast, usually a bird, who transforms herself into the form of a human female to become romantically involved with a human male. She places an interdiction on her partner, and when he violates it (as he always does), she returns to her inhuman form. Eubanks argues that the appropriation of such tales by Japanese female writers suggests that they are read in a political sense, allowing readers to engage with issues such as gender inequality and the male exploitation of their maternal nature (215).

However, Kawai observes that Western analogues of these tales, where sexual exploitation was equally part of the patriarchal landscape, take quite different paths from the Japanese versions. European tales feature a young girl who is *unwillingly* transformed into beastly form. She *reveals* her true nature to a male hero, who *carries out* her instructions, defeats the villain, and returns her to her true form, whereupon they are *married*. In Japanese versions, by contrast, the female truly is a beast by nature who *willingly* transforms herself to entice a human male to be her mate. She *conceals* her true nature from her husband, but he invariably *ignores* a taboo she gives him and when he does so, she returns to her true form and the two are *parted forever*. From Kawai's Jungian perspective, the Western tale ends patriarchally with a marriage bond, while the Japanese tale concludes matriarchally with the female liberating herself from her mate (Kawai 1996, 109). Such an ending, as with the close of many well-known Japanese fairy tales, often seems unsatisfying to a Western audience enculturated to watch for a happy ending, at least seen from a male perspective. Kawai observes that Western scholars (male ones, at the time he was writing) found it difficult to recognize the conclusion to many Japanese tales without the hint of the closing verbal formula (121).

The ending of the beastly bride tales seems especially inconclusive, particularly as Western versions end with the female disenchanted and in the arms of her savior. But Kawai counters that "the story ends happily—at least for Japanese it seems a happy ending." The human and the bird-turned-human have, in this analyst's reading, enjoyed a marvelous but temporary relationship, and in the end they choose to coexist in their separate worlds, where "there is no sense of controlling each other" (Kawai 1996, 120–21). Paraphrasing Kawai's overall approach in folkloristic terms, the reason is that such narrative patterns fit an emic Japanese model. In Western tales (as some Marxist interpretations propose), the purpose of fairy-tale adventures is to provide a culturally validated means of achieving economic or sexual goals, while Japanese narrators and their audiences use tales to explore the way things are and how they ought to be. So it makes sense that many such stories (and anime narratives, too) conclude undramatically, with protagonists returned to a mundane world. They are, however, enriched by the memories of an extraordinary experience that suggests the possibilities of transforming the social world in liberating ways that benefit both sexes.

In 1917, one of the first Japanese experiments with Western-style film animation presented a short version of the popular fairy tale "Urashima Tarō."[4] Other early Japanese animated shorts followed, and anime, that country's distinctive form of visual storytelling, became a major industry in the 1960s.[5] Japanese narrative tradition has always included a strong visual arts component, with scrolls, books, and wall hangings created to accompany oral performances. So it is not surprising that anime, drawing on this tradition, quickly matured as an art form, attracted a wide international audience in the 1980s, and developed a strong North American fan base in the late 1990s. It continues to command a substantial niche market here, with an increasing number of series being made available in English subtitled or dubbed versions within months or days of their initial broadcasts in Japan. Dani Cavallaro (2011) has argued that the seemingly novel form of popular culture is in fact permeated with elements that are drawn from the fairy-tale tradition, both indigenous and international.

In fact, the Japanese have shown particular interest in Western folktales. Tōei Animation, one of the landmark studios in the development of anime, adapted the French fairy tale "Puss in Boots" into a feature animated film in 1969, which was popular enough to spin off two sequels and an early video game. Mushi Production, another pioneer anime studio, followed in 1971 with a year-long adaptation of the literary fairy tales of Hans Christian Andersen, beginning in January with "The Ugly Duckling" and concluding in December with "The Little Match Girl." Other adaptations of familiar Western tales followed, both as feature films and TV series, notably Nippon Animation's *Grimm Masterpiece Theatre* (1987–88), which presented forty-one tales, including "Snow White" and "Cinderella."[6] Such renderings made Western tales familiar enough that they soon became widely "quoted" in anime series whose plots are otherwise based on indigenous narrative models. Sometimes these "quotations" come in the form of a book being read out loud (e.g., "Sleeping Beauty" in *Sailor Moon* and "Little Red Riding Hood" in *Jin-Roh: The Wolf Brigade* [1998]). In other cases, the occasion is a "class play," with characters in the larger anime plot acting out parts in a Western fairy tale (e.g., "Sleeping Beauty" in *Cardcaptor Sakura* [1998–2000] and "Little Red Riding Hood" in *Kamikaze Kaitou Jeanne* [1999]).

As I have argued (Ellis 2008, 2012), these "quotations" sharpen the tension between Western and Japanese narrative expectations, creating an opportunity for complex metacommentary. The Western tales are chosen because they superficially mirror the narrative situation in the larger plot. However, such performances are always rescripted because of how the "actors" interpret their roles. And the performances are interrupted, typically when characters break the "fourth wall" of their play within the play and act in ways that have important consequences in the larger narrative in which the fairy tale is embedded. The contrast between the action-oriented Western narratives and the internal drama emphasized by Japanese narratives often becomes explicit at such moments.[7]

ANIME AS FAIRY-TELLING

Princess Tutu[8] originated with a story idea by the animator Itō Ikuko, who had a lifelong fondness for ballet music, developed with the help of director Satō Junichi, who had worked with Itō during production of the *Sailor Moon* anime in 1994–96. After some eight years of preliminary discussion, it was produced by the animation studio Hal Film Maker and broadcast on the Japanese network NHK from August 16, 2002, to May 23, 2003.[9] Its plot first seems similar to the pattern of fairy-tale "quotation" seen above. The protagonist, Ahiru, is a young girl who is training to become a ballet dancer. In a way familiar to anime audiences, she becomes a magical girl (mahō shōjo) with the ability to transform into Princess Tutu, an alter ego given enhanced physical and magical powers in order to carry out a supernatural quest. Along the way, the series references the plots of famous ballets based on fairy tales, notably Tchaikovsky's *Sleeping Beauty*, *Swan Lake* and, in a particularly explicit way, *The Nutcracker*, whose libretto is based on the literary fairy-tale by E.T.A. Hoffmann. This story is musically quoted at the climax of the opening animation, which precedes every episode, where the transformed Tutu begins to dance to the familiar tune of "The Waltz of the Flowers." Her mentor and antagonist Drosselmeyer, too, is drawn from the ballet's scenario, where he also functions as a backstage puppet master. In addition, other fairy tales, such as "Hansel and Gretel," are referenced along the way.

Although Hans Christian Andersen's literary tale "The Ugly Duckling" is never explicitly mentioned in the plot, it is the source of frequent visual "allusions." In the opening animation we see an awkward little duckling struggle to lift itself into the air with its wings, then gradually morph into a beautiful swan. So we are implicitly primed to experience a tale in which Ahiru enacts the role of Andersen's gawky duckling, first being marginalized in society for her "odd duck" nature, then eventually maturing into a graceful and self-confident adult.

However, the concept of the fairy tale informs the direction of the plot in ways more far-reaching than mere quotation or allusion. In fact, the entire series is framed as a reflexive view of how a narrator creates a fairy tale. "Mukashi mukashi," an invisible narrator begins each episode, following with a scrap of story that introduces the challenge of that particular installment. The opening introduction defines the problem that motivates the entire series:

> *Mukashi mukashi.*
> *Once there was a man who died.*
> *Writing and telling stories had been his life,*
> *but death he could not defy.*
> *His last story told of a brave and handsome prince*
> *who sought to vanquish a crafty raven.*
> *But now their conflict will have no end.*

The story itself opens with an ambiguous dreamlike scene: a little duck watches with fascination while a young man dressed as a prince dances on the surface of the lake where she is resting. Haunted by his lonely eyes, the duckling longs to turn into a human and become his partner. Then she is frightened by an apparition, which we later learn is the ghost of the storyteller Drosselmeyer. The scene at once shifts to a room in a boarding school dormitory, where a young girl awakens in terror from a bad dream.

We quickly learn that she is a ballet student named Ahiru, a Japanese word that means "duck" (and is not a common name for humans).[10] She has a childish crush on a handsome upperclassman, a common theme in female-oriented anime. But Ahiru sees that while her idol is an accomplished dancer, he suffers from a strange illness. His name is Mytho, also *not* a common Japanese word or name. Whenever she says that she would "give her life" to heal him, the eyes of the grotesque apparition in her bad dream quickly pass across the screen. And that night she has an encounter with the dead-but-not-dead storyteller, who seeks a person to help him complete his unfinished fairy tale. Her sickly idol is indeed the tale's prince, he tells her, but his heart is shattered: the pieces of his heart, each representing one of his feelings, are scattered around the town. "Tell me a story," the sinister intruder requests.

When Ahiru agrees, she gains the power to perform a *henshin*, or "metamorphosis," into a magical form, Princess Tutu. And while she is in this form, she gains both the confidence and the physical skills she needs to locate the lost pieces of Mytho's heart. This is a conscious use of a well-known motif from mahō shōjo anime (itself borrowed from the henshins performed by Western fairy-tale heroines like Cinderella). The anime highlights this borrowing by recycling the exact same animation footage each time the transformation occurs.[11] When she is in her magical form, she wears the ballet costume of Odette, the White Swan in Tchaikovsky's *Swan Lake,* complete with its distinctive feathered headpiece.[12]

But in return for gaining the power to become a mahō shōjo, she is afflicted by a curse. When flustered, she is prone to stuttering, making an involuntary sound something like the quack of a duck. Now when she does this, she transforms into a real little duck. And so, as the story continues, it becomes unclear which of the three roles she enacts really *is* her true identity. Is she Princess Tutu, the beautiful swan maiden, or is she the gawkish ugly duckling of a girl who is struggling to gain control of her body and her social life? Or is she quite literally the little duck who appears in the opening scenes?

As Drosselmeyer's new "story" begins to develop, Ahiru/Tutu begins gathering the scattered shards of Mytho's heart, itself a common narrative format in Japanese manga and anime plots.[13] But the first emotions he recovers are negative ones—disappointment, loneliness, sadness, fear—thus increasing his sufferings rather than healing him. And as he regains his feelings, his dancing partner and girlfriend Rue also recovers her memory of her place in the tale. She, too, is a princess determined to wed the hero, but an evil one, the raven's daughter, Princess Kraehe. Ahiru/Tutu comes to understand that her intervention in the story has in fact made matters worse rather than better, but now she is unable to back out of her destined role of moving the developing story onward.

And so the progress of the mahō shōjo anime model, which focuses on gathering the shards and healing Prince Mytho's shattered personality, comes into full conflict with the European tale model, which wants to move toward a climactic showdown with a villain. Even that thread becomes tangled when Kraehe tries to secure victory by poisoning one of the heart shards, morphing the prince into beastly form—half human and half raven—and horrifying even the villainess. The result is a messy stalemate: neither plot can be brought to conclusion, except in a direction at odds with every one of the characters' wishes. And so in the end the characters, individually and collectively, rebel against their roles and take over the task of bringing the tale to a satisfying conclusion. They cannot physically fight the omnipresent storyteller Drosselmeyer, but they can and do subvert the generative model that he uses to produce the tale.

QUEERING THE JAPANESE FAIRY TALE

Postmodern critics analyzing animation and fairy tales have called this act of subversion "queering." The term arose in academic discourse to show

how artists challenge traditional definitions of gender identity, particularly straight versus gay. However, as the approach developed, it came to recognize additional modes of "queerness," viewing it as a strategy that challenges economic, political, and aesthetic conventions of all sorts. Sexual liberation continues to play an important part in most queer studies discussions, but its scope now includes the individual and social transformations needed to carry it out.

Judith Halberstam (2011), for example, has argued that the most popular animated films made by the Pixar Studio in fact include coded agendas inviting viewers to rebel against the social narratives planned for them by a patriarchal/materialistic culture. Animation, the critic contends, is the ideal medium in which to do this. The visibly fantastic visual world that animation generates makes the bodies of the characters fluid in ways that are impossible for humans or animals. This environment, then, is the ideal place to tell stories that radically deform social conventions as well as express revolt against the forces that would otherwise artificially constrain our lives.

Kay Turner and Pauline Greenhill make a similar argument about the magical realm described in European fairy tales. Like Halberstam, they emphasize the ways in which such tales challenge sexual identity, but "queerness" has a much larger social significance, dealing with the ways in which individuals are marginalized or find it difficult to fit into society (Turner and Greenhill 2012, 4). Queer theory also challenges any majoritarian social definition in order to suggest alternative ways of viewing human relationships with the capacity to transform society (14). In her rhetorical analysis of the Grimms' "Allerleirauh,"[14] Margaret R. Yocum makes a point that directly relates to the protagonist's situation in *Princess Tutu*. The heroine, in Yocum's reading, "journeys back and forth among bodily locations: between human and animal, as well as among man, woman, thing, or a bodily state that combines all of the above" (Yocum 2012, 92–93). Ahiru/Tutu likewise is from the beginning an ambiguous being: is she animal or human or a kind of fairylike supernatural being?

Her journeys back and forth make up much of the suspense of the plot, particularly when she discovers that she can manipulate this ambiguity, shifting between her little girl and duckling identities to spy on the other characters or gain entry to places where she would otherwise be excluded. As in Yocum's reading of "Allerleirauh," the protagonist learns that "delineations of gender and sex are themselves disguises, [that is,] social constructions" (Yocum 2012, 115), and as Ahiru/Tutu accepts these multiple selves as equally "herself," she simultaneously subverts them to allow herself unique access to alternative landscapes inside the emerging story. Charlotte

Eubanks agrees that Japanese interspecies sex tales fulfill the same encoded narrative function. They are not making claims about whether beasts could literally assume human form; rather, they use the anomalous "to reveal the consistent, persistent, but generally unseen or invisible workings of a gendered and sexually violent world" (Eubanks 2013, 215).

Of course, the entire world of the anime plot, like that of many fairy tales, is radically queered. Humanized animals (like *Tutu*'s "Puss-in-Boots"–inspired ballet teacher Mr. Cat) enter and leave the story freely. The central role of "interspecies sex" in queered narratives is noted by both Halberstam and Yocum. The first critic sees cross-species characters as a coded narrative device that challenges cultural definitions of "humanness" and allows storytellers and their audiences to explore new forms of social relationships outside of prevailing norms (Halberstam 2011, 32–33). Yocum, in a parallel way, notes that one question emerges in nearly all the international variants of "Allerleirauh": "But who are you really?" There are simple answers—the heroine is who she is inside of the disguise she voluntarily puts on. And there are more complex ones, Yocum suggests, which can be answered by the protagonist only once she has tasted many different selves, some human, some beastly, with the help of her disguises. "Perhaps delight in those multiple bodies with their ambiguous gender lingers," Yocum muses (Yocum 2012, 101–2).

Certainly, the fairy tale becomes Ahiru/Tutu's story—indeed, *her* mythos, as the name of the ailing prince suggests. She functions as the story's catalyst, and she is the first one who becomes self-aware of her multiple selves. But her reflexivity, along with her acceptance of all three of her identities—duckling, awkward little girl, and ballet goddess—leads the others to become aware of the restrictive identities they have been given in Drosselmeyer's plot and challenge them to develop subversive alter egos.

The protagonist's evil counterpart, the disdainful Rue/Kraehe, initially relishes the villainous role she has been given to play, but once she has infected her prince, she finds her fairy-tale function more and more distasteful. As a beastly lover, it seems, she could fascinate and dominate a human mate. But as Mytho adopts an inhuman identity, Kraehe's advantage disappears, and their future union becomes a stereotypically "unequal treaty" in which the raven prince will of course rule over the raven princess. Meanwhile, Fakir, the emotionless sidekick who is prepared to die in battle defending his prince, becomes fascinated by the duckling turned human, and as his humane side develops, Ahiru/Tutu finds her affections switching from Prince Mytho to his supporter Fakir. So, as the plot develops, the characters are pulled in all directions. All must choose the role they will play or, like Ahiru/Tutu, accept the incurable ambiguity of their identities. And "queerness," whatever else it has come to mean in scholarship, denotes liminality, a willful and transgressive blurring of boundaries.

PRINCESS TUTU AS METACOMMENTARY

The anime thus is folkloresque in a number of ways. It appropriates character types and motifs from folklore and uses them to create an original plot that is represented as an emergent folk narrative. Such a motion has been suggested in recent times through adaptations, novels, movies, and television series. These have been the topic of serious research (e.g., Bacchilega 1997, 2013), and adaptations of both native and Western tales have become a popular genre among belletristic writers in Japan (Sebastian-Jones 2013). In the introduction to this volume, Michael Dylan Foster notes that self-aware use of folk material makes a work folkloresque, often in the form of parody, though in the spirit of homage rather than mockery. *Metacommentary* would be as accurate a term, Foster suggests, and this seems a more potent key to the folkloresque qualities of *Princess Tutu*. While many of the motifs and plot situations used in the anime are recognizably borrowed from Western fairy tales (sometimes by way of literary adaptations such as Tchaikovsky's ballets), the narrative does not privilege any existing model. It is what Foster terms an *integration* of folkloric content, a *bricolage* of motifs and formulas from available traditional and folk-influenced literary sources. Collectively, these bits and pieces create the illusion of an "authentic" fairy tale being made up on the spot using the generative grammar of the Western fairy-tale tradition. Stretching our usual language, we could say that *Princess Tutu* is not about fairy tales at all but about *fairy-telling*, the ongoing tradition of generating new versions of old tales and inventing entirely new tales out of bits and pieces of existing ones.

In the anime this is represented by the conflict between Drosselmeyer, who claims to be the omnipotent puppet master controlling the direction of the story, and the characters, who refuse to give up their free will. If *Tutu* were an adaptation of an existing tale, this eerie antagonist might well be impossible to defeat: even parodic "fractured" fairy tales obey the superstructure of a narrative shared by the teller and audience, even if some of its functions are altered for comic or satirical effect. But the mad storyteller, in fact, is constantly surprised by how his "puppets" use their fairy-tale roles in unexpected ways, and in the end he is unable to resist the course of the alternative plot that they construct. This makes him less of a villain than a metacritic of the tale who constantly calls attention to its plot elements as superorganic social artifacts rather than inflexible laws of the universe he supposedly controls. He is no less committed to steering his tale in the direction of a "beautiful tragedy" and defying the wishes of his characters. But the metacommentary he gives on the course of his story shows Ahiru/Tutu and her companions (and, of course, the audience) that the narrative *can* and *should* be "queered." That is, it needs to be reframed, using the underlying fairy-tale grammar, to make a statement that subverts the social definitions that this type of tale traditionally affirms.

In a critical episode (episode 23, "Marionettes"), Drosselmeyer draws Ahiru/Tutu into his world, presented as the inside of a giant clock filled with cogs and wheels, and tries to convince her that she is nothing more than a marionette, enacting a predestined role in the story exactly as a ballet dancer follows the choreography designed for her movements. The ballet emphasis of the series, we now see, is a metaphor for the way in which the structure of this art form, like many other forms of social interaction (including gendering and marriage) is culturally predetermined. As in Ōba's adaptation of the yamauba tale, many females find themselves bound by the conventions of *tatemae,* a Japanese term referring to behavior expected and required by society (Wilson 2013, 225). A good wife, in this sense, cares for her husband and children much as a ballerina performs her choreography, tracing the steps predetermined for her like a well-programmed android.

Nevertheless, when Drosselmeyer *asks* her to *choose* a certain way of fulfilling her next function, Ahiru/Tutu realizes that her role in the tale cannot be predetermined. If it were, she would simply carry out this move without emotion or awareness of her larger place in the plot. And indeed, Japanese culture holds the convention of tatemae in tension with the ideal of *hon'ne,* or expressing what is truly on one's mind as a free-thinking individual. As Wilson (2013, 225) states, the smooth interplay of both expectations forms a rhetoric for public behavior, much as the distinctive style of a ballerina is as important to a successful performance as her physical ability to perform the choreographed steps. "My feelings belong to *me,*" Ahiru/Tutu exclaims, "just like anybody's feelings. They are precious—and so I am no marionette!" Her resistance allows her to escape from Drosselmeyer's power, and simultaneously Fakir, who has now become her loyal companion in the battle against the tale's hegemony, finds himself liberated from the limitations of the character he has been playing. "She changed me!" he exclaims, and at once he begins to draft the conclusion of the tale himself. "She's not to be underestimated," the baffled Drosselmeyer comments.[15]

Applying this insight to the craft of fairy-telling, we could say that some element of "queering" is integral to the creation of any successful narrative in this tradition. If they were no more than parallel creations of a superorganic generative model, all adhering to an ideal form of a given tale type, then that trend would itself lead to the demise of that form of folk narrative. As John Quincy Wolf (1967) observed many years ago about ballads, the singers who simply memorize texts verbatim and replicate them in unchanged form do little to conserve the tradition. By contrast, the most celebrated ballad singers understand the aesthetics of ballads as a creative force, and rework the songs they learn into fresh and effective variants. They, rather than the unimaginative conservators of antique texts, are the ones who ensure the future of the ballad as a living art form. So, as with the Japanese perception of social rhetoric, there is a tension between a tatemae tool kit of motifs that audiences expect to see used, and a hon'ne impulse to use these elements in unexpected ways to express the precious emotions shared by storytellers and audiences. From this point of view, *Princess Tutu* is folkloresque not only in its use of plot elements borrowed from the past but also in the sense that it makes us more conscious of an authentically folk process, the ongoing interplay of dynamic and conservative elements that must exist in any living tradition.

We can see this interplay in the details of the competing plots of the anime. A scholar familiar with Vladimir Propp's (1968) *Morphology of the Folktale* can see the implicit deep structure of Drosselmeyer's "The Prince and the Raven": a hero (Prince Mytho), a villain (the raven), an interdiction (the forbidden art that Drosselmeyer uses to confine the raven), a lack (the need to restore the prince's heart), and a donor (Princess Tutu). The tale moves toward a showdown with a villain or, as folklorists would say, the functions of Struggle, Victory, Liquidation of Lack, and ultimately Marriage. This implicit structure allows the audience to recognize Drosselmeyer's unfinished narrative as an "authentic" fairy tale, even though it has never been told to its finish and turns out to be untellable.

The competing tale, which blocks the motion toward this climactic battle, comprises many elements drawn from the native versions of "The Animal Bride," as seen partly through the medium of the popular culture genres of manga and anime. But in its folkloresque way this thread only vaguely follows the pattern of the Japanese fairy tales. As in Miyazaki Hayao's film *Spirited Away*, the plot is infused with a folktale-like familiarity that gives it a feeling of integrity. But when we compare *Tutu* to the plots of existing Japanese fairy tales, we find only vague parallels. Ahiru/Tutu, who longs to "dance" with the prince, could be compared to the bird-beasts who choose to become human to engage in interspecies sex. But this narrative direction is blocked when Drosselmeyer places an interdiction on Ahiru/Tutu: if she confesses her love to Mytho, she will vanish. This thread, then, is doubled by the appearance of the evil Princess Kraehe, who likewise is a beast in female form bent on enjoying the prince's love. But the success of her first move turns Mytho into a grotesque human/raven hybrid that inspires her disgust. So this narrative direction too is blocked. The series does not directly adapt either culture's narrative tradition but integrates elements from both into a tale that has never been told before and also proves untellable.

This is a tale in which Ahiru/Tutu comes to terms with the contradictory roles imposed on her externally by society and becomes a competent fairy-teller. In the end, she decides who she is, accepts her identity as a duckling and, in so doing, she helps the others choose their identities as well. At the moment Tutu escapes from Drosselmeyer's clockwork prison, Kraehe suddenly "remembers" that she is not a raven's daughter at all but a human bewitched into beastly form. She liberates herself from her inhuman side not through the prince's heroism but through her own willpower; then, in a moment of hon'ne, she declares her love for Mytho and disenchants him as well. That choice in effect retrospectively changes the underlying taletype expectations of the story line, opening a new path toward its resolution. The final battle for control of the fairy tale is hotly contested, but the characters inside the tale prevail, and the device that Drosselmeyer uses to manipulate events in their world is destroyed.

True to the Western "Swan Princess," Mytho and Rue, both now fully human, fly off to a happy ever after wedding. But the anime does not follow them; instead we are left contemplating the fate of Ahiru/Tutu, who, true to the Japanese analogues, has sacrificed her shape-shifting power to bring the story to a finish and now accepts her true identity as a duckling.[16] We see her last swimming and diving in the lake where the narrative began, as Fakir sits on a pier, peacefully fishing and fairy-telling his next story with his quill pen. It is an odd and, to a Western mind, inconclusive ending, for we expect that Ahiru, like Mytho and Rue, will be "disenchanted" at the story's climax, become fully human, wed Fakir, and live happily after.[17] But it is not to be: the two continue to enjoy each other's company, but as bird and human, not as lovers. For an audience that appreciates the way in which queered fairy tales challenge traditional gender identities, it is a fine ending.

CONCLUSION: WHO WINS?

Drosselmeyer is at first crushed by his defeat. "My beautiful tragedy is ruined!" he laments, adding, "I never dreamed a character inside the story would change the story." Then he stops, looks directly at the audience, and exclaims, "Wait! What if I'm a character in someone's story too?" Of course he is: all the characters and situations in this complex anime were scripted, storyboarded, and animated by a team of studio artists. But breaking the fourth wall in this way challenges the audience's response to the story's conclusion, adding yet another layer to its self-referential nature. It sharply undercuts the power of the happy ending by suggesting that the rebellion the tale's characters mount against the fairy-tale frame was just a commercial trick played on the audience by unseen puppet masters. So it is not surprising that *Princess Tutu*'s master storyteller is in fact pleased by the idea that he might be the puppetlike creation of an even more powerful puppet master. But rather than responding with passive homage to his creators' tatemae, he instead makes his final departure with a paradoxical affirmation of hon'ne: "Oh, well, even if I am, I'll just do what I want, that's all."

Seen from the folkloresque perspective, this pushes the story's implications to a new and profoundly illuminating conclusion. To what extent does our ability to construct stories govern our perception of the world in which we live? Religious studies scholar Jeffrey J. Kripal (2010) argues that the human mind generates identity and understands the world in terms of narratives: stories that are, in turn, governed by tatemae, the "commonsense" cultural expectations that give culture stability. If "mind" is, as some neuroscientists argue, no more than the chemical workings of an essentially unconscious biocomputer that has been programmed by one's physical and social environments, then it works in a way similar to Drosselmeyer's storywriting clockwork, which is supposed to determine everything that happens in *Princess Tutu*.

The anime too is a fiction generated by a team of storytellers manipulating puppets from behind the scenes. Perhaps this suggests an infinite regress, as these creators, their audience, and the economic system that brings them together through the production and broadcast of the series are likewise governed by an even more powerful puppet master, hardwired into our brains by impersonal sociolinguistic processes. Folklorists like Jack Zipes (2008) would argue that fairy tales function as "memes," self-replicating packages of information that have evolved in order to program human minds to accept certain forms of behavior (e.g., gendering and marriage) as culturally normative.[18] From either point of view, Drosselmeyer wins, and the uplifting happy ending is no more than a function of the unthinking clockwork of the fairy-tale generative grammar wedded to the forces of capitalism.

But Kripal, like the rebellious characters in the anime, rejects this pessimistic assessment. Surveying the conclusions both of medical science and the history of religion, he concludes, "Mind is not the brain, but Mind is indeed filtered through the brain, with all its mindboggling evolutionary, neurological, cultural, linguistic, emotional, and historical complexities. We are *both*" (Kripal 2010, 256). From this point of view, the human brain is constantly constructing a heuristic set of narratives with which to understand experience. A side of the human mind has the power to challenge and at times transcend the filtering process of biology and sociology. This is most apparent when individuals respond to some experience that they perceive as anomalous, paranormal, or religious. Illuminated by such experiences, these persons "wake up" from the narratives through which they have been enculturated and recognize that there are other stories available to them, perhaps better ones.

When we do this, Kripal argues, then we "decide to step out of the script or story we find ourselves caught in," just like the central characters of *Princess Tutu*, and become creative authors of our lives. And so, Kripal concludes, we can "take back the book of our lives from those who wrote us long ago . . . and begin writing ourselves anew" (Kripal 2010, 269–70). This of course means becoming self-aware of the stories we know and constantly enact, and of the unseen workings of all the social rules we take for granted. More than that: it involves the much more difficult task of understanding the cultural grammar that governs fairy-telling and the gender conventions it makes visible, and gaining the skills to create new myths, ones that we can genuinely call our own.

NOTES

1. Yanagita Kunio, the founder of Japanese folkloristics, generated a detailed catalogue of orally collected folktales (Mayer 1986), and his follower, Seki (1966), organized these into a system influenced by the Aarne/Thompson *Tale Type Index*. See also Ikeda 1971.

2. See Murai Mayako for a survey of this tendency, as deconstructed by the contemporary artist Yanagi Miwa (Murai 2013). Many of the same social stereotypes have been adopted by the Japanese artistic movement termed Superflat, founded by Murakami Takashi in the early 2000s. As Castano (2013) shows, this movement likewise tends to use self-consciously *kawaii* commodified feminine images in disturbing ways. A major subgenre of Japanese anime features female characters who are partially or wholly transformed into androids and whose essential "humanity" thus becomes problematic. See Napier 2005, 103–16.

3. In advancing this theory, he relied on concepts developed by Jung's student Erich Neumann (1955), author of *The Great Mother: An Analysis of the Archetype*.

4. As reported by Reuters, "Japan Finds Films by Early 'Anime' Pioneers," March 27, 2008, http://www.reuters.com/article/2008/03/27/us-japan-anime-pioneers-idUST23069 120080327.

5. For a comprehensive survey of the major genres of anime and their themes, see Napier 2005.

6. This series enjoyed widespread syndication to Western markets as well, and was aired in North America as *Grimm's Fairy Tale Classics* on Nickelodeon from 1989 to 1995.

7. An especially good example of this contrast is embedded in the manga series *Fruits Basket*, by Takaya Natsuki (1999–2006). The characters agree to put on a performance of "Cinderella" for their high school, but they find the roles they are to play completely incompatible with their personalities. Accordingly, the play is rescripted as "Sorta Cinderella," in which the protagonist chooses not to court the handsome prince but instead achieves personal independence by founding a chain of fast-food restaurants. Nevertheless, the performance is marked by frame breaking which, recorded on a digital camcorder and slipped to another character, provokes the events that eventually lead to the resolution of the manga's complex, Dickensian plot. Manga, the Japanese form of graphic novels, is a form of storytelling closely related to anime: most successful mangas are quickly adapted to anime form and vice versa.

8. Material from this work is quoted or paraphrased from the "Complete Collection" DVD set published by ADV Films in 2007. This company disbanded in 2009, but AEsir Holdings picked up the license and now publishes the DVD set. A useful fan-generated Wiki on the series is available online: http://princesstutu.wikia.com/wiki/Princess_Tutu_Wiki (accessed November 5, 2014).

9. As planned, it was to run in twenty-six episodes, or two seasons, as thirteen episodes typically make one season, or a quarter of a fifty-two-week broadcast year. However, during the second season (episodes 14–26) only half an episode was run each week, so the series actually ran thirty-eight weeks, or nearly three seasons.

10. Strictly speaking, *ahiru* refers to a "domestic duck" since a different word, *kamo*, is used for wild ducks. "Minikui ahiru no ko," however, is the Japanese translation of the title of Hans Christian Andersen's famous tale "The Ugly Duckling," so the character's given name may be yet another subtle allusion to this tale.

11. This animation strategy was originally a way of saving time and expense by animating a complicated scene once and reusing the footage over and over. As *Princess Tutu* was produced using computer-generated imagery, this recycling was not technically necessary. However, the henshin banks for *Sailor Moon* (on which *Tutu*'s director and character designer worked) had become a popular, much-loved cliché of the mahō shōjo genre, so the studio retained it in homage to its predecessors.

12. Similarly, her antagonist, the evil Princess Kraehe, wears the Black Swan ballet costume of Odile, the sorcerer's daughter who enthralls Prince Siegfried and dooms his love for the White Swan Odette. For a global survey of the "Swan Maiden" tale, on which the libretto for Tchaikovsky's *Swan Lake* is based, see Leavy 1995. However, the libretto for the ballet was already folkloresque, as no extant folktale or literary predecessor to the ballet's libretto has ever been found that contains more than a general parallel to the story line. In addition, the plot of the ballet is fluid. The original 1877 production had a happy ending, with the hero overcoming the villain and disenchanting Odette. But when the ballet was revived after Tchaikovsky's death, the producers had the lovers both commit suicide when they realize their love cannot be consummated. This tragic ending, rather than the one Tchaikovsky intended, is now the usual one. Drosselmeyer wins.

13. For instance, *Inuyasha* (Takahashi, 1996–2008 [manga]; Ikeda and Aoki, 2000–2010 [anime]) is based on a young girl's effort to collect the shards of a powerful sacred jewel. In a similar vein, *Cardcaptor Sakura* (CLAMP, 1996–2000 [manga]; Asaka 1998–2000 [anime]) involves a young girl's quest for a set of magical cards that have accidentally been released from a magic book. In both series, the need to find all the fragments of a lost whole and

achieve completeness generates the story arc that holds together the individual adventures of both narratives.

14. This tale was adapted as episode 35 of Nippon's *Grimm Masterpiece Theatre*. The anime version, faithful to the original tale, thus would have been readily available as a source to the creators of *Princess Tutu*.

15. Indeed, not by the anime's creators either. The "Path to Tutu" special feature, included as an extra on DVD #5 in the published set, records the sense among the animators that "even after the story began being broadcast, [the plot it followed] changed little by little, just as if it were a living thing."

16. This is how we see her last; but it is significant that at her moment of triumph she briefly turns into a beautiful swan. This visual detail, appearing and disappearing so quickly as to be nearly subliminal, is one final allusion to Andersen's folkloresque tale "The Ugly Duckling."

17. When Itō Ikuko, the creator of the anime's concept, gave an interview at the anime convention Ushicon (Austin, Texas) in 2006, fans pointedly asked her if she had plans for a sequel in which Ahiru returned to human form and reunited with Fakir. An attendee reported that she "was somewhat vague on this answer," neither rejecting nor affirming the sequel idea. Instead, she encouraged fans to imagine for themselves what might happen next. Tell your own story, she seemed to be saying. See Wandering Mage Chichiri, "Ikuko Itoh at Ushicon: Q & A, and Other Fun," blog post in *Princess Tutu Community*, hosted by LiveJournal, http://princesstutu.livejournal.com/57459.html (accessed November 5, 2014). It is interesting that the *Tutu* story has inspired a large number of *dōjinshi*, or mangas created by fans of the anime who use the characters and motifs to spin out alternative story lines.

18. Schrempp (2009) gives a vigorous critique of Zipes's use of memetics, observing that while it purports to apply a scientific approach to traditional materials, in fact its assumption that memes are selfish and self-promoting at the expense of human behavior indicates that it is as subjective as the humanistic modes of analysis it attempts to replace. See also Ellis 2001, 75–92 for an earlier critique of Dawkins's effort to describe contemporary legends as "mind viruses." Dawkins, interestingly, maintained that humans did have the ability to discern memes and consciously rebel against their social influence, but his critic Daniel Dennett perceptively observed that this was a contradiction in terms: if memes truly were viruslike in their abilities to exploit minds, then one would indeed not be able to recognize them as memes, much less evaluate and choose which ones to accept and which to reject (quoted in Ellis 2001, 84). So if memetics were a valid theory, Drosselmeyer wins and Dawkins loses.

REFERENCES

Bacchilega, Cristina. 1997. *Postmodern Fairy Tales: Gender and Narrative Strategies*. Philadelphia: University of Pennsylvania Press. http://dx.doi.org/10.9783/9780812200638.

Bacchilega, Cristina. 2013. *Fairy Tales Transformed? Twenty-First-Century Adaptations and the Politics of Wonder*. Detroit: Wayne State University Press.

Castano, Claudine. 2013. "Into the Witch's Barrier: Superflat Influences on *Puella Magi Madoka Magica*." PowerPoint presentation at AnimeNEXT, Somerset, NJ, June 8, 2013.

Cavallaro, Dani. 2011. *The Fairy Tale and Anime: Traditional Themes, Images and Symbols at Play on Screen*. Jefferson, NC: McFarland.

Ellis, Bill. 2001. *Aliens, Ghosts, and Cults: Legends We Live*. Jackson: University of Mississippi Press.

Ellis, Bill. 2008. "Sleeping Beauty Awakens Herself: Folklore and Gender Inversion in *Card-captor Sakura.*" In *The Japanification of Children's Popular Culture: From "Godzilla" to "Spirited Away,"* edited by Mark I. West, 249–66. Lanham, MD: Scarecrow.

Ellis, Bill. 2012. "Fairy Tales as Metacommentary in Manga and Anime." In *Marvelous Transformations: An Anthology of Fairy Tales and Contemporary Critical Perspectives,* edited by Christine A. Jones and Jennifer Schacker, 503–8. Peterborough, ON: Broadview.

Eubanks, Charlotte. 2008. "Japanese Tales." In *The Greenwood Encyclopedia of Folktales and Fairy Tales,* edited by Donald Haase, 513–18. Westport, CT: Greenwood.

Eubanks, Charlotte. 2013. "Envisioning the Invisible: Sex, Species, and Anomaly in Contemporary Japanese Women's Fiction." *Marvels and Tales* 27(2): 205–17.

Halberstam, Judith. 2011. *The Queer Art of Failure.* Durham: Duke University Press. http://dx.doi.org/10.1215/9780822394358.

Ikeda, Hiroko. 1971. *A Type and Motif Index of Japanese Folk-Literature.* Folklore Fellows Communications no. 209. Taipei: Orient Cultural Service.

Kawai, Hayao. 1996. *The Japanese Psyche: Major Motifs in the Fairy Tales of Japan.* 2nd ed. Translated by Hayao Kawai and Sachiko Reese. Woodstock, CT: Spring.

Kripal, Jeffrey J. 2010. *Authors of the Impossible: The Paranormal and the Sacred.* Chicago: University of Chicago Press. http://dx.doi.org/10.7208/chicago/9780226453897.001.0001.

Leavy, Barbara Fass. 1995. *In Search of the Swan Maiden: A Narrative on Folklore and Gender.* New York: New York University Press.

Mayer, Fanny Hagin. 1986. *The Yanagita Kunio Guide to the Japanese Folk Tale.* Bloomington: Indiana University Press.

Murai, Mayako. 2013. "The Princess, the Witch, and the Fireside: Yanagi Miwa's Uncanny Restaging of Fairy Tales." *Marvels and Tales* 27(2): 234–53.

Napier, Susan J. 2005. *Anime from Akira to Princess Mononoke: Experiencing Contemporary Japanese Animation.* New York: Palgrave.

Neumann, Erich. 1955. *The Great Mother: An Analysis of the Archetype.* Translated by Ralph Manheim. Princeton: Princeton University Press.

Propp, Vladimir. (Original work published 1920) 1968. *Morphology of the Folktale.* 2nd ed. Translated by Laurence Scott. Edited by Louis Wagner and Alan Dundes. Austin: University of Texas Press.

Reider, Noriko T. 2010. *Japanese Demon Lore: Oni from Ancient Times to the Present.* Logan: Utah State University Press.

Satō, Junichi. 2002–2003. *Princess Tutu.* DVD. ADV Films.

Schrempp, Gregory. 2009. "Taking the Dawkins Challenge; or, The Dark Side of the Meme." *Journal of Folklore Research* 46(1): 91–100. http://dx.doi.org/10.2979/JFR.2009.46.1.91.

Sebastian-Jones, Marc. 2013. "Preface to the Special Issue on the Fairy Tale in Japan." *Marvels and Tales* 27(2): 172–78.

Seki, Keigo. 1966. *Types of Japanese Folktales.* Nagoya: Society for Asian Folklore; http://nirc.nanzan-u.ac.jp/nfile/912.

Turner, Kay, and Pauline Greenhill. 2012. "Once upon a Queer Time." In *Transgressive Tales: Queering the Grimms,* edited by Kay Turner and Pauline Greenhill, 1–24. Detroit: Wayne State University Press.

Wilson, Michiko N. 2013. "Ōba Minako the Raconteur: Refashioning a Yamauba Tale." *Marvels and Tales* 27(2): 218–33.

Wolf, John Quincy. 1967. "Folksingers and the Re-creation of Folksong." *Western Folklore* 26(2): 101–11. http://dx.doi.org/10.2307/1498933 http://web.lyon.edu/wolfcollection/re-creation.htm.

Yanagita, Kunio. (Original work published 1910) 2008. *The Legends of Tono.* Translated by Ronald A. Morse. New York: Rowman and Littlefield.

Yocum, Margaret R. 2012. "But Who Are You Really? Ambiguous Bodies and Ambiguous Pronouns in 'Allerleirauh.'" In *Transgressive Tales: Queering the Grimms*, edited by Kay Turner and Pauline Greenhill, 91–118. Detroit: Wayne State University Press.
Zipes, Jack. 2008. "What Makes a Repulsive Frog So Appealing: Memetics and Fairy Tales." *Journal of Folklore Research* 45(2): 109–43. http://dx.doi.org/10.2979/JFR.2008.45 .2.109.

11

Science and the Monsterological Imagination
Folkloristic Musings on David Toomey's Weird Life

Gregory Schrempp

"Monster" is an anthropocentric concept: the being of monsters inheres precisely in their *aberration from us* or from our sense of the normal. Etymologically, a *monstrum* (Latin) was an omen defined by a departure from the ordinary and, as all aberrations contain the trace of their departure point, monsters confirm that point as the center from which the monstrous is elaborated. The imagining of monsters is thus necessarily constrained: if we were capable of imagining an alien being that was entirely free of us—a "totally other"—it would not be monstrous.

Like the ordinary and the monstrous, science and mythology form a perennially entangled epistemological pair, one term defined by aberration from the other—except that alternative formulations would disagree about which of the two marks the starting point and which the aberration. The nineteenth-century notion of myth as a "proto-science" fully embodies this antinomy. On one hand, myth is the baseline from which science departed (in the oft-cited words of Karl Popper, "Science must begin with myths"); while on the other hand, the very notion of "proto-" suggests that science is the true starting point—which, however, makes its appearance only after mythology's false start. In science writing one encounters a fascinating, complex rhetoric revolving around the dichotomy of myth and science, a rhetoric full of intriguing turns. The attitude toward mythology displayed in science writing is generally hostile and polemical, but not always. For example, Lynn Margulis, in her *Microcosmos: Four Billion Years of Microbial Evolution*, makes the following comment relevant to monsterology:

DOI: 10.7330/9781607324188.c011

241

> Human religion and mythology have always been full of fantastic combi-
> nations of creatures—the mermaids, sphinxes, centaurs, devils, vampires,
> werewolves, and seraphs that combine animal parts to make imaginary
> beings. Truth being stranger than fiction, biology has refined the intuitively
> pleasing idea with its discovery of the overwhelming statistical probability
> of the reality of combined beings. We and all beings made of nucleated
> cells are probably composites, mergers of once different creatures. The
> human brain cells that conceived these creatures are themselves chimeras.
> (Margulis 1986, 120)

Margulis's passage forms one variant of an earnest strategy often
adopted by popular science writers to draw readers from pseudo- to allegedly real science, specifically, the claim that those who hunger for escape
from the quotidian will find that human imagination (as expressed in fantasy and in mythology, for example) lags behind nature itself in the production of the wondrous. Whatever experiences the scientific attitude rules
out, weirdness is not among them. In his recent fascinating book *Weird Life:
The Search for Life That Is Very, Very Different from Our Own*, David Toomey
refers to Margaret Robinson's compendious *Fictitious Beasts*, remarking: "To
a biologist, what is striking about this imaginary bestiary, especially in comparison with the bestiary that nature actually has produced, is its paucity"
(Toomey 2013, viii).

One of the most persistent claims to be met in the rhetoric of popular
science is that the difference between mythology and science lies in the fact
that archaic mythologies happily portray the cosmos anthropocentrically
while modern science is committed to heroically transcending our anthropocentric conceits. I have recently argued (Schrempp 2012) in detail that,
for at least some purposes—notably, in the creation by popular science
writers of visions concerning the human place in the cosmos—science still
aspires to become mythology: the claimed surmounting of anthropocen-
trism by popular science writers amounts to, instead, their development of
more subtle versions of it. My argument can be extended into the realm of
nominally scientific investigation that Toomey documents as the search for
weird life; for purposes of this essay I rechristen his project *scientific monsterology*, summarizing my claim that the search bears a substantial relation to
the forms of pre- or nonscientific (hereafter, folkloric) monsterology that
folklorists encounter throughout the world. Scientifically imagined, weird
life rightly belongs to the monsterological and the folkloresque.

Would Toomey agree with this placement? While his book is mostly
blank with respect to this question, there are a few hints. Most notably, *Weird
Life* contains a section of photographic plates bearing images of some of

the more exotic and less well-known forms of earthly life that biologists have discovered unexpectedly within recent years as well as photographs of distant planets that might contain life, and artists' renderings of undiscovered life-forms that scientists have imagined as possible within the universe. But notably, the first image that appears in Toomey's series is a drawing of the legendary griffin: part eagle, part lion, specifically, John Tenniel's griffin from Lewis Carroll's *Alice's Adventures in Wonderland*. What can the unexplained inclusion by Toomey, a scholar from the humanities writing about science, of this "prescientific" monster imply if not a connection between the new scientific and the old folkloric monsterology?

One of the most frequently discussed themes in *Weird Life* is the role of the late Carl Sagan in spearheading the search for extraterrestrial life (e.g., see Toomey 2013, 76–79, 91); and in Sagan's larger corpus one senses, in a way that he might wish to deny, the closeness of the two monsterologies. I have written previously (Schrempp 1998) concerning the folkloristic relevance of Sagan's (1997) famous work *The Demon-Haunted World: Science as a Candle in the Dark*, and here I would like to explore one further point about it, specifically regarding the science that Sagan offers as a replacement for pseudo-science. *Demon* is fundamentally a denunciation of the gullibility toward pseudo-science that, Sagan fears, is about to plunge the contemporary world into (or back into) superstitious darkness. For example, the chapter "Obsessed with Reality"—appearing, perhaps strategically, as chapter 13—takes off from a litany of widely held beliefs that begins with astrology, the Bermuda Triangle, and Bigfoot. Many of these beliefs are, or resemble, themes that one encounters in urban legends. One of Sagan's favorite targets is stories of UFOs and alien abductions; regarding these he cites (Sagan 1997, 130) folklorist Thomas E. Bullard, who approaches them as a form of modern legend. Given the sharpness of Sagan's diatribes against such stories and/or beliefs, one might expect that he would end up championing only the most sober science, a science chary of speculation and closely tied to the experimentally verifiable.

Not so! Instead, Sagan's passions flow toward forms of scientific investigation that are imaginative, highly speculative, lie on the periphery of fundable research, and carry a popular if not sensationalist appeal. Most important, what Sagan is searching for—cosmically distant, alien beings that we might communicate or interact with—strongly and directly overlaps the content of the folklore or pseudo-science of UFOs and alien abductions that he dismisses. Sagan develops a strident rhetorical opposition between the folkloric and the scientific—the one allegedly rooted in gullibility and superstition, the other claiming critical rigor and empirical observation—but the poles arise out of, and converge into, a shared fascination with speculative cosmic possibilities. Sagan gives us not a distant opposite to folklore but a close, flirtatious opposite, one with as much similarity as difference, whose closeness is camouflaged by rhetoric.

If one wants a single term to capture the complicated reciprocal relationship between mythology and science that infuses popular science writing, *parody* is a worthy contender; and it is one of the linchpin terms that inspires the idea of the folkloresque. Parody implies imitation coupled with critique; and both elements infuse the way that science is related to mythology in popular science writing. Again, the process is reciprocal: science criticizes mythology; but at least in its popularized versions, science creates (without admitting it) new myths that carry a double critique. On one hand, the new scientific myths criticize prescientific mythologies, and on the other, they criticize contemporary science for losing its moral commitment and relevance to human life and to the interests of the broader public. In this convoluted context, scientific monsterology offers something like a parody of folkloric monsterology.[1] As suggested above, the science of weird life is never very far from the pseudo-science of weird life. Moreover, in the hands of its more theatrical exponents, popular science as a genre often stops just short of self-parody. In *Demon*, Sagan positions science as a rational alternative to the view that nature is haunted by demons; yet the trope through which he develops his argument is that of demons of irrationality gathering to devour us. Even though from a scientific view *millennia* are entirely anthropocentric fabrications, Sagan plays the millennium (near at hand when *Demon* was published) as a moment when we are particularly vulnerable to demons: "The candle flame gutters. Its little pool of light trembles. Darkness gathers. The demons begin to stir" (Sagan 1997, 27). The book's cover is Halloween orange and black. In short, Sagan, to dramatize his critique, teasingly imitates the sort of fear-mongering, rooted in wrongheaded folk belief, that he sets up as emblem of our downfall. This particular folkloresque gesture is rather blatant, but the spirit of the gesture in more subtle ways runs through much popular science persuasion.

The issue of the relation between *popular science* and its cousin genre *science fiction* deserves comment at this point. One way that the relation between these two genres of literature inspired by science can be conceptualized is through comparison of the relative role of two components that belong to both. One component is a plot: that is, humans engaged in some pursuit with which the reader identifies, be it an adventure, quest, or battle. The other is the delineation of a scientific ambience—indeed, a cosmos—in which the plot is set and which makes possible the actions and events depicted in the plot. The energy of the popular science writer is directed toward the delineation of the cosmos as it is revealed by science for an audience that wants to understand something about science and its discoveries; this exposition is emplotted only loosely, typically with some version of a narrative of human progress (which, for Sagan, also carries the imperative that humans should colonize space). By contrast, the energy of science fiction is directed into the construction of a plot about human passions and personalities engaged in some specific *agon*, aimed at an audience that is looking for a good story. Here the delineation of the cosmos serves merely to enable the story; science is tapped to open up new plot possibilities—such as time travel or the teleportation of matter, and of course many alien life-forms—by referencing new understandings of the nature of matter that flow from modern science. The actual science presented in science fiction is often fairly cavalier; one merely has to invoke a quantum wave collapser (or whatever) to achieve the sort of paranormal possibilities formerly provided through magic, sorcerers, and demons.[2]

In the authors of these genres themselves, one sometimes encounters a sort of dialogue about the relation of popular science and science fiction. For example, in *The Physics of "Star Trek,"* Lawrence Krauss (1996) examines the happenings in this science fiction series from the more sober, scientifically accountable attitude of the popular science writer. The most interesting reciprocal move—that is, from popular science to science fiction—is provided by Sagan himself when he moves from the spirit of SETI as proclaimed in *Demon* and *Pale Blue Dot* (Sagan 1994) to his science fiction novel *Contact* (Sagan 1985), which is his variation on a favorite plot of science fiction in both literature and film, namely, humans' first extraterrestrial contact. A quirk of *Contact* relevant to the methodology of scientifically searching for weird life is that the plot is based on humans building a device for moving through a wormhole from plans supplied by superior alien intelligence: humans do not understand the theory of the machine and can only follow the instructions. That there may be intelligence that understands the physical reality of the cosmos much better than we seems to be regarded earnestly by Sagan; if this is so, one can be forgiven for wondering about our readiness, in such a primitive state of cosmic understanding, to scientifically engage the topic of weird life.

Toomey's book is a roundup of the ways scientists are thinking about, searching for, finding or failing to find, and proposing that we continue to search for forms of life in the cosmos that are different, mildly or radically, from those with which we are already familiar. How constrained, or how scientifically rigorous, is this new imagining of the monstrous? Not very, I am tempted to say; yet this quick answer is not adequate. It is more accurate to say that the search for weird life opens an intellectual space in which it is extremely difficult to pinpoint what counts as rigor, and in which too little imagination can be as unscientific as too much. Contemporary science is coping with a set of principles that interferes deeply with any claim that the search for extraterrestrial life can proceed with algorithmic precision. The complicating factors are too many.

First, there is contingency. There seems to be broad acceptance in the scientific community, evident in the scientific endeavors Toomey describes, that the way the cosmos evolved is not the only way it could have. Given the same ingredients, things might have gone differently at many points; and even minute differences, ramifying as a "butterfly effect" through cosmic time, could give rise to cosmic situations of vastly different character. "Whether the fundamental features of life we know are necessary to all life, is far from clear. But it may be that some, or many, or most of those features are the products of happenstance, and that life on Earth might as easily have taken a different path, the result being organisms whose fundamental features would be utterly different from those we know" (Toomey 2013, xv; see also 33, 130, 179).

The acceptance of contingency in cosmic evolution opens a floodgate of speculation about possible alternative courses in that evolution. Entangled with contingency is the principle of "emergence," a concept that folklore and other humanistic disciplines have borrowed from scientific discourse. The concept of emergence points to the fact that combinations of elements can give rise to possibilities that we are unable to predict from the properties of the elements themselves. Like contingency, this principle is obviously a brain buster, raising havoc with the idea of predicting in advance what might be out there (see Toomey 2013, 92ff).

The principles of contingency and emergence give rise to a sort of hierarchy of radicalness in attempting to imagine alternative courses of cosmic evolution, and the hierarchy grows more elaborate the further one goes back in cosmic time. For example, one can imagine as yet undiscovered organisms belonging to the carbon-based life already familiar to us; more radically, carbon in combination unfamiliar to us; still more radically, non-carbon-based life (silicon is the leading contender [see Toomey 2013, 93ff]); and, further still, even the possibility of life in two rather than three dimensions. Water is thought of as a *sine qua non* of life and an indicator of its possibility, but "astrobiologists can conceive of a variety of liquids that might serve as mediums for life, each with characteristics that life might use to its advantage" (Toomey 2013, 85). All of this is further complicated by the possibility, broached by so-called multiverse theory, that ours is not the only type of universe that could exist. It is not just that there might be other universes but that those universes might be governed by different physical constants than those that govern ours.

The project of scientifically imagining alternative life cannot avoid negative reasoning and its associated dilemmas. Partly this takes the form of mentally eliminating imagined entities that would bump up against the laws of nature and thus must be removed from consideration so as not to squander time and resources. The problem here is that mentally ruling something out requires imagining all the different ways in which the same life functions might be accomplished: a certain kind of organ could not function in such conditions for such and such reasons, but might an alternative design work instead?[3] The project of imagining alternative designs, in turn, leads to this discouraging thought: thus far at least, nature has run ahead of human intellect in discovering "engineering solutions"—for example, the structural advantages of fractal or hexagonal ("honeycomb") designs, which were realized in nature well before being taken up in formal mathematical analysis. In trying to exercise scientific rigor by ruling out life structures based on insurmountable engineering problems, how could we eliminate the possibility that nature, running ahead of us, has found an engineering solution to limitations on the possibility of life that, in our present state of knowledge, appear as intractable? Besides ruling out through logic, there is ruling out through observation. But here the project is haunted by another bugaboo of negative reasoning, summarized in the dictum that the absence of evidence is not evidence of absence (Toomey 2013, 42).

Toomey recognizes that the scientific search for weird life is haunted by the aura and legacy of metaphysics. In the absence of a clear demarcation between the two intellectual pursuits, Karl Popper's "falsifiability" arises as a possible criterion: that which is beyond the operation of falsification is not science but metaphysics. But this dividing line, however clear in theory, is difficult to think through in the search for weird life. Hypothesized forms of weird life are not necessarily unfalsifiable, but any falsification would seem to lie in an unimaginably distant future. A hypothesized form of weird life is not disconfirmed until one has searched everywhere, and if one wants to be thorough this means everywhere not only in this universe but in all possible universes.

Since the possibility has not been ruled out that the number of universes is infinite, that job might be quite large, and we are faced with new versions of paradoxes, with us at least since the pre-Socratic philosopher Zeno, that flow from the idea of infinity. Even then, if the hypothesis has been phrased as an assertion about the possibility of a form of life, and if cosmic evolution is contingent (that is, not everything that can happen has happened), then the absence everywhere of the hypothesized form of life proves only that it *does not* exist, not that it *could not* or *will not* at some point. In such speculations one senses a ripeness for the resurfacing of old metaphysical quandaries, such as the theological debates that swirled around the classical/medieval notion of "plenitude": can nature be presumed to have tried everything, or are there untried possibilities?[4] The readiness with which the search for weird life slips into metaphysical speculation threatens its claim to be science, for one of the constitutive claims of modern science is that it has left metaphysics behind, forswearing the hopeless muddles that the mind can create for itself when reason becomes detached from empirical observation—muddles that many scientists consider as having for centuries stymied and stifled the progress of knowledge.[5]

Most provocatively, Toomey emphasizes that the ongoing discovery of new life-forms and the attempt to imagine the possibilities of life are taking place in a context that lacks consensus about how life should even be defined, and in which new discoveries can suggest redefinitions; in chapter 3, "Defining Life," he offers a roundup of the contending definitions of "life" and of their respective tribulations. The bottom line is that we lack an agreed-upon definition of the phenomenon we are looking for.

Finally, the recent empirical discovery of unexpected life-forms adds palpability to the imagining of weird life, throwing the gauntlet to those who would prefer that the search parameters be tied more closely to the tried and true. "No one expected life in water much above its boiling point. But scientists found bacteria living in volcanic hydrothermal vents on the ocean floor, one species merrily reproducing at a scalding 235° F. No one thought life could survive in water at temperatures much below its freezing point. But in Antarctic ice floes, scientists found channels of slushy brine in which single-celled algae were harvesting energy from the sunlight filtered through ice and assimilating nutrients from the water below" (Toomey 2013, xiii).[6]

The aura of possibility created by the discovery of such surprising forms of life is backed by another strand in contemporary science writing. Specifically, while many popular science writers, including Sagan, as noted above, chide the public for being intellectually lax, something of a countervailing theme is sounded by writers telling us about quantum foundation of reality: here we learn that everyday logic leaves us too confined, and that to grasp the idea that something is both particle and wave we have to be ready to transcend the parochial rationality that binds everyday thinking! To be scientific, we have to open our sense of the possible, not close it down.

The main insight to which these principles lead is a realization of just how little researchers are able to pin down—or, put conversely, just how large a range of possibility is still left open—when *scientifically* investigating the possibility of weird life. It is at base a groping venture that shares considerable turf with the sort of thinking on display in traditional mythologies. Consider, for example, Hesiod's (1953) *Theogony*, a Homeric age poem that attempts to synthesize stories about gods within a genealogical framework. Of particular note here are the single-eyed Cyclopes and the 50-headed, 100-armed Hekatonkheires, monsters born from *Gaia* after she and Ouranos begat the Titans. Parallels between Hesiod's monsterology and the one described by Toomey are several.

The first and most basic of these parallels is genealogy as a cosmic frame. Hesiod's mythic poem is a giant cosmic genealogy, one that gives evidence of considerable mental turmoil as to how the different cosmic elements are interrelated. On close inspection Hesiod's giant cosmic genealogy turns out to be two genealogies, one originating from *Gaia* and another, "alien" genealogy, depicting the descendants of *Chaos*, a region lying beyond the humanizable *Kosmos*. Genealogy figures in an equally fundamental cosmic way in the scientific search for weird life as presented by Toomey. Toomey points out that biologists typically assume that all earthly life descends from a "single common ancestor" (Toomey 2013, xv); and at its most precise definition, "weird" means life that does not belong to this genealogy. *One cosmic genealogy or more?* This is a fundamental question shared by mythology (Hesiod's, of course, but others' as well) and the science of weird life. The genealogical focus spills over into a challenge to parochial assumptions about the boundary between the animate and the inanimate. Mythologies typically are generous in ascribing life to entities of the cosmos that we often consider inanimate; and, if a little less generously, the scientific search for weird life has brought into focus a rich border region between the animate and the inanimate that challenges everyday Western rationality.

Hesiod's cosmogony joins the scientific search for weird life in its pronounced sense of cosmic contingency mixed with necessity. The Olympians just barely defeat the Titans (and then only because they are helped by the aforementioned monsters); but then Hesiod also exudes a sense of fatalism, as though it must all happen as it does. Parallel attitudes intermix in the scientific search for weird life as well: along with the sense of contingency in cosmic evolution is a sense of determinacy, which takes the form of the assumption that if the *ingredients* of life are present in any part of the cosmos, then life can be expected to, and *really should*, occur there. And just as for the mythological Olympians, one of the motives impelling the search for weird life more generally, for Sagan, at least, is the possibility of forming mutually beneficial cosmic alliances.

In both Hesiod and the science of weird life we encounter a sense of wonder at the sheer exuberance and "weirdness" of life, whose potency and potential increase as one goes back in cosmic time. Hesiod's monsters, striking as they are, are but one moment in the great arc. Some of the most splendid sections in Hesiod's poem are built around an extravagant litany of imaginary creatures of the sea (see especially section 4), which in Homeric times was a mystery looming as large as distant planets now do for us. Similarly, one cannot fail to think of the vast range of possibilities that are being considered in the scientific search for weird life, and of the tendency to interlink the possibility of life with the possibility of water, or some equivalent life-engendering liquid, through the cosmos.[7]

Finally, both the mythological and scientific imagining of life proceed from the known to the unknown. In neither mythology nor science does the imagination of life move in total freedom; rather, in both it is tamed with a sense of realism rooted in the known. Hesiod's monsters are modifications of known life. Instead of two eyes, maybe one will do. Arms are useful; how about 100? Could the imagining of possible life, whether in mythology or science, proceed otherwise? Indeed, Toomey's closing thoughts sound this theme. Reviewing some of the more exotic of the scientifically imagined forms of life he has rounded up, he says:

> Many scientists who have hypothesized weird organisms made a case for their feasibility by noting parallels with familiar life. The layering of desert varnish (that candidate for weird life) is like the layering of stromatolites. Sagan and Saltpeter's hypothesized Jovian ecology of hydrogen-breathing dirigibles is borrowed from the known ecology of microfauna in sunlit waters of Earth. And Dyson and Hoyle's ideas of living interstellar clouds of dust grains and complex molecules organized by electromagnetic forces are modeled on neurotransmitters in animal brains. To make cases for the viability of these parallels, they have had to revisit the familiar. (Toomey 2013, 220–21)

My calling attention to such parallels should not be taken as an accession to the humanistically fashionable but inadequate view that science is *just one more mythology*. What I am saying, rather, is that when deployed in a project as open, nebulous, speculative, and methodologically groping as the search for weird life, science starts to feel more like "proto-science"—which, of course, is one of the condescending terms that theorists of human progress typically invoke in order to dismiss mythology in the face of science. The broadly accepted notion, noted earlier, that science begins in myth suggests a constitutively folkloresque relationship; aware of its derivativeness (see Foster's introduction to this volume), science, especially when operating speculatively, turns into parody, simultaneously imitating and, with a veneer of rigor, castigating its intellectual source. But in the methodological groping characteristic of the search for weird life, which ends up as the greater object of parody: myth or scientific rigor?

In the end, what is the relationship of scientific to folkloric monsterology? There seem to be two main possible axes of difference: the first has to do with factors that constrain the monsterological imagination, the second with factors that inspire it. Importantly, on neither of these axes is the difference between folkloric and scientific monsterology absolute.

The first axis, again, has to do with constraints on the imagination. The new scientific monsterology insists that all speculation be confined to what is scientifically possible, as set by scientifically defined laws of nature. Certainly there are in this venture many technical specifics that are lacking in traditional, folkloric monsterology, but the distinction is far from absolute. For, despite their departure from the ordinary, folkloric monsters such as the griffin typically reflect characteristics that constrain ordinary life, for example, the necessity for organs of sensation, nourishment, and motility. In other words, even though unschooled in the technicalities of modern science and engineering, the creators of folkloric monsters typically are not unmindful of the material character and limitations of matter and life.

Besides the issue of constraint, there is the second issue, specifically: what factors positively inspire the shape, form, and content of the monsters that are imagined, whether as uncanny presences in folkloric monsterology or as "hypotheses" in scientific monsterology? Folklore scholars often assume that the principles that inspire folkloric monster design are matters of the individual or cultural unconscious: deep anxieties, desires, and ontological assumptions. Such elusive principles are favored objects of scholarly probing and analysis, a process that typically proceeds by relating aspects of monsters to cultural themes or taboos that are manifested in other aspects of the society in which the monsters occur. But it is not clear that such factors are absent from the mental activities of scientists hypothesizing about weird life.

Indeed, since there is no formula that automatically converts scientific observations into explanatory hypotheses, there has always been, in philosophical attempts to portray the nature of scientific analysis, a kind of explanatory gap as to how hypotheses actually arise. Karl Popper's influential claim that the essential epistemic act of science lies in falsification has only dramatized the gap: if science consists of falsification, whence arise the hypotheses to be falsified (or not)? Given our nebulous understanding of how scientific hypotheses arise, it should be regarded as possible (and at least as not yet falsified) that the processes through which monsterological hypotheses occur to scientists overlap with the processes through which folkloric monsters arise. In sum, both in terms of negative constraint and positive inspiration, the differences between folkloric and scientific monsterology are matters of degree and not of kind. Of necessity, both start from ourselves and our world, and try out variations on them; and in neither case does imagination proceed disinterestedly.

Although at least some of the principles that constrain scientific monsterology, specifically the laws of nature, have been publicly formalized to a greater degree than the constraints that operate in the realms of folkloric monsterology, it would probably be a mistake to see scientific monsterology as more constrained *overall* than folkloric monsterology. As suggested above, the constraints imposed by the laws of nature, when filtered through the complicating factors (contingency, emergence, negative reasoning, and so on), still leave *a whole lot* to the imagination. The laws of nature operate almost more as prompts or challenges to the imagination than as constraints upon it. The engineering attitude central to some scientists and familiar to most is enlivened by a challenge that might be phrased: here are the cosmic conditions and ingredients you have to work with; see what you can come up with! It is not clear which is more accurate: that the scientific search for weird life clamps down on the unbridled, unconstrained human love of monsters; or that the constraints posed by science, filtered through the many complexities discussed above and coupled with the proliferation of newly discovered forms of life and of cosmic contexts, spark the folkloresque imagination to new monsterological heights!

The most important way that the search for weird life is similar to nonscientific monsterology, and what ultimately makes it a form of monsterology, is the fact that the search for weird life is anthropocentric: it is a search for entities in the cosmos that amount to aberrations from us, things that are like us only weirdly different. Behind the science of the scientific search for weird life is some deeper psychological and/or sociological force that impels the search for new objects of desire and cathexis. There is no reason to think that the ultimate psychological force impelling the search for weird life is any different than the omnipresent desire, mixed with fear, of humans to reencounter themselves or their world in the distance—the same force that gives rise to traditional monsters, Garfield the cat, and the belief that the planet Mars has a human face.[8] Under the guise of weird "life," a term that we are not able to define, we search for ourselves—somewhere out there.

NOTES

1. Parody can certainly operate in the opposite direction as well; the fanciful creatures offered by science fiction often are generated in parody of scientific accomplishments, missteps, and aspirations.

2. That the science is cavalier does not mean that it is not engaged in seriously by the reader. The sense of "fiction" in science fiction may apply less to the science and more to the plot and characters, which are "made up" in the manner of any novel or short story.

3. On the methodological intricacies introduced by consideration of alternative designs, see also David Hand's (2014, 215–17) recent *The Improbability Principle*, especially his critique of cosmic fine-tuning arguments.

4. On plenitude and related metaphysical tangles, see the classic statement by Arthur Lovejoy (1960), *The Great Chain of Being*.

5. The exemplary statement would be philosopher Immanuel Kant (1965), who dedicated the second (and, unfortunately, less often read) half of his *Critique of Pure Reason* to characterizing the knots that human reason ties itself in when it becomes detached from empirical experience; his recommendation was the dismantling of metaphysics as a philosophical pursuit.

6. The late science popularizer Stephen Jay Gould was particularly drawn to the celebration of the capacity of life to surpass borders hitherto assumed to limit its possibility; he explores the theme in different ways in his pair of books *Full House* (1997) and *Wonderful Life* (1989).

7. On the importance of the sea and its microbial extremophiles in debates about the origin of life and the possibility of life elsewhere in the universe, see also Stefan Helmreich's (2009) *Alien Ocean: Anthropological Voyages in Microbial Seas*.

8. See chapter 3 of Sagan's (1997) *Demon*, "The Man in the Moon and the Face on Mars." See also Roland Barthes's (2013, 38–40) excellent vignette "Martians."

REFERENCES

Barthes, Roland. 2013. *Mythologies*. New York: Hill and Wang.

Gould, Stephen Jay. 1989. *Wonderful Life*. New York: Norton.

Gould, Stephen Jay. 1997. *Full House*. New York: Three Rivers.

Hand, David. 2014. *The Improbability Principle*. New York: Scientific American.

Helmreich, Stefan. 2009. *Alien Ocean: Anthropological Voyages in Microbial Seas*. Berkeley: University of California Press.

Hesiod. 1953. *Theogony*. Indianapolis: Bobbs-Merrill.

Kant, Immanuel. 1965. *The Critique of Pure Reason*. New York: St. Martin's.

Krauss, Lawrence. 1996. *The Physics of "Star Trek."* New York: HarperCollins.

Lovejoy, Arthur. 1960. *The Great Chain of Being*. New York: Harper and Row.

Margulis, Lynn. 1986. *Microcosmos: Four Billion Years of Microbial Evolution*. New York: Summit Books.

Sagan, Carl. 1985. *Contact*. New York: Simon and Schuster.

Sagan, Carl. 1994. *Pale Blue Dot*. New York: Random House.

Sagan, Carl. 1997. *The Demon-Haunted World: Science as a Candle in the Dark*. New York: Ballantine Books.

Schrempp, Gregory. 1998. "The Demon-Haunted World: Folklore and Fear of Regression at the End of the Millennium." *Journal of American Folklore* 111(441): 247–56. http://dx.doi.org/10.2307/541310.

Schrempp, Gregory. 2012. *The Ancient Mythology of Modern Science: A Mythologist Looks (Seriously) at Popular Science Writing*. Montreal: McGill-Queens University Press.

Toomey, David. 2013. *Weird Life: The Search for Life That Is Very, Very Different from Our Own*. New York: Norton.

About the Authors

TREVOR J. BLANK is assistant professor of communication at the State University of New York at Potsdam, where he teaches courses in folklore, mass media, and digital culture. He is the author of *The Last Laugh: Folk Humor, Celebrity Culture, and Mass-Mediated Disasters in the Digital Age* (2013); coauthor of *Maryland Legends: Folklore from the Old Line State* (2014); editor of the volumes *Folklore and the Internet: Vernacular Expression in a Digital World* (2009) and *Folk Culture in the Digital Age: The Emergent Dynamics of Human Interaction* (2012); and coeditor of *Tradition in the Twenty-First Century: Locating the Role of the Past in the Present* (2013). Currently, he serves as editor of the journal *Children's Folklore Review*.

CHAD BUTERBAUGH is a doctoral candidate in the Folklore Institute at Indiana University. His research investigates the professional performance of Irish folk narratives. He has published articles in *Storytelling, Self, Society: An Interdisciplinary Journal of Storytelling Studies*; *Béascna: Journal of Folklore and Ethnology*; and *Folklore Forum*. He has presented at numerous conferences on folkloristics, Irish studies, and popular culture studies.

BILL ELLIS is professor emeritus of English and American studies at Penn State University. He is a fellow of the American Folklore Society and has served as president of the AFS's Children's Folklore Section and of the International Society of Contemporary Legend Research. He has given presentations to the AFS and to ISCLR discussing the use of folklore in animated movies and series as well as to audiences of anime enthusiasts at AnimeNext, an annual fan convention. He resides in Berlin, Maryland, where he serves as a moderator for Anime-Beta, a virtual community of animation art collectors.

TIMOTHY H. EVANS is associate professor in the Department of Folk Studies and Anthropology, Western Kentucky University, where he directs the MA track in public folklore and teaches in the undergraduate popular culture major. He holds a PhD in folklore and American studies from Indiana University. His interests include public folklore, material culture, popular culture, folklore and literature, science fiction and fantasy. His publications include *King of the Western Saddle: The Sheridan Saddle and the Art of Don King* (1998) and numerous articles in academic journals on topics including science fiction/fantasy writers William Morris, H. P. Lovecraft, and Philip K. Dick.

MICHAEL DYLAN FOSTER is an associate professor of folklore at Indiana University. He is the author of *Pandemonium and Parade: Japanese Monsters and the*

Culture of Yōkai (2009) and *The Book of Yōkai: Mysterious Creatures of Japanese Folklore* (2015) as well as numerous articles on folklore, literature, and media in Japan. He is currently editor of the *Journal of Folklore Research*.

CARLEA HOLL-JENSEN holds an MA in folklore from Indiana University, Bloomington, and an MFA in fiction from the University of Maryland, College Park, where she is a lecturer in academic and creative writing. Her work has appeared in the scholarly journal *Textual Cultures* and in literary journals such as *Pindeldyboz, Shimmer, Lady Churchill's Rosebud Wristlet,* and *Underwater New York.*

GREG KELLEY holds a PhD in folklore from Indiana University. Former president of the Hoosier Folklore Society and editor of the journals *Folklore Forum* and *Midwestern Folklore,* he has also served as coordinating publisher for Trickster Press, where he was associate editor of several books. He has taught a wide range of courses, and presented and published broadly on folklore, folklore and literary relations, popular culture, humor, and the media. Currently, he teaches in media studies at the University of Guelph-Humber, where he has been honored with multiple teaching awards.

PAUL MANNING (PhD, University of Chicago, 2001) is an associate professor of anthropology at Trent University, Ontario, where he teaches courses in linguistic and cultural anthropology and media studies. He is currently editor of the *Semiotic Review.* He has done fieldwork in Wales and postsocialist Georgia and has authored three recent books derived from his Georgian research: *Strangers in a Strange Land: Occidentalist Publics and Orientalist Geographies in Nineteenth-Century Georgian Imaginaries* (2012), *The Semiotics of Drink and Drinking* (2012), and *Love Stories: Private Love and Public Romance in Georgia* (2015).

DANIEL PERETTI studied English and communications at Grand Valley State University before moving on to complete a PhD in folklore at Indiana University. His research interests include mythology, material culture, narrative, and festivals.

GREGORY SCHREMPP is professor of folklore at Indiana University. Trained in folklore studies, anthropology, and intellectual history, he teaches courses in mythology, narrative genres, comparative cosmology, comparative epistemology, and the intellectual history of the human sciences. He has an ongoing interest in the relation of mythology, philosophy, and science. His books include *Magical Arrows: The Maori, the Greeks, and the Folklore of the Universe* (1992), *The Ancient Mythology of Modern Science: A Mythologist Looks (Seriously) at Popular Science Writing* (2012), *Science, Bread, and Circuses: Folkloristic Essays on Science for the Masses* (2014), and (with Bill Hansen) *Myth: A New Symposium* (2002).

JEFFREY A. TOLBERT is a PhD candidate in folklore at Indiana University. His research focuses on supernatural belief, and his dissertation examines belief and the landscape in contemporary Ireland. His broader research interests include folklore and popular culture, especially video games, and emergent traditions in new media, such as the Slender Man Internet phenomenon.

Index

Page numbers in italic indicate illustrations.

www.ingramcontent.com/pod-product-compliance
Lightning Source LLC
Chambersburg PA
CBHW032122020426
42334CB00016B/1042